McCALL'S EMBROIDERY BOOK

BY THE EDITORS OF McCALL'S
Needlework & Crafts PUBLICATIONS

Simon and Schuster / The McCall Pattern Company / New York

Published by Simon and Schuster
A Gulf+Western Company
Rockefeller Center, 630 Fifth Avenue
New York, New York 10020
and
The McCall Pattern Company
230 Park Avenue
New York, New York 10017

Designed by Irving Perkins
Manufactured in the United States of America
By Rand McNally & Company

1   2   3   4   5   6   7   8   9   10

Library of Congress Cataloging in Publication Data
Main entry under title:

McCall's embroidery book.

1. Embroidery.   I. McCall's needlework & crafts.
TT770.M28   746.4'4   76-28223
ISBN 0-671-22342-9

Contents

III. CLOTHING AND ACCESSORIES   241

IV. GENERAL DIRECTIONS   279

Foreword

If you ask "What is embroidery?" what will be the answer? A monogrammed handkerchief, daintily edged with lace. A marvelous shawl emblazoned with bold, vibrant flowers. A child's sampler, softened by the years. A machine-embroidered place mat. An apron bordered with rows of crisp cross-stitch. The replies will be as many and as varied as the people you ask! And therein lies the answer—*embroidery is versatile*.

One of the greatest advantages of the art is that it can be as simple or as intricate as the needleworker cares to make it. Many of the basic stitches are the heritage of assorted cultures and are centuries old. To these have been added variations and new techniques that have enriched the art with today's sense of color and design.

The embroideries in this book have been selected for their beauty and versatility. It is our hope that they will also serve as inspiration for new and innovative ways with stitchery. But whether you choose to make a line-for-line copy, adapt it with slight changes, or create an entirely new piece, we know that you will discover that embroidery offers a wonderful opportunity to add to the beauty in the world around you.

The Editors of McCall's Needlework & Crafts
Publications

1 Pictures and Wall Hangings

Samplers

WALL-SIZED SAMPLER

The beautiful sampler on page 13 is worked on burlap and repeats the same alphabets, motifs, and morality verse that were embroidered on the original (shown on page 12). The young needleworker from the 1700s had originally stitched her year of birth, but later removed the last two numbers to keep her age a secret! The antique letter formations were incorporated into the new version—hence, the reversed P for a Q and the missing J's and U's (omitted because they were not likely to be needed). The center panel is counted-thread embroidery, using tapestry yarn; the border is worked over a tissue pattern.

SIZE: 62″ x 41″, framed.

EQUIPMENT: Paper for patterns. Large sheets of tissue paper. Pencil. Scissors. Tapestry needles. White sewing thread. Sewing needle. Small straight pins. Tape measure.

MATERIALS: Green burlap 52″ wide, 2 yards. Tapestry yarn in 8-yard skeins: 10 skeins pink, 12 skeins medium coral, 7 skeins dark coral, 3 skeins red, 19 skeins yellow, 9 skeins gold, 7 skeins rust-brown, 9 skeins pale blue, 9 skeins medium blue, 5 skeins orange, 4 skeins black, 14 skeins white, 34 skeins yellow-green. Fiberboard 62″ x 41″. Large straight pins. Masking tape.

DIRECTIONS: Before doing embroidered borders, work all the lettering in center panel, following Large Chart on pages 16 and 17. See page 284 for how to cross-stitch. All crosses are worked over two horizontal and two vertical threads of burlap. Crosses are indicated on charts by symbols that represent different colors (see Color Key). Each square of chart represents two horizontal and two vertical threads of burlap. Other stitches are worked as shown on chart.

To do the star-stitch squares that make up the letters at top of chart, work each stitch from center space out over two threads of burlap, making eight stitches to complete each square. The other stitches are straight vertical stitches worked over four or more threads of burlap. Use single strands of yarn in tapestry needle throughout.

To start, measure in from top left corner of burlap 10″, then measure 10″ down; this is top left corner of Large Chart. Following chart, work row of pink cross-stitch border across and down both sides for some distance; continue cross-stitch border as work progresses. Starting two threads down and four threads in from top left corner of border, work star-stitch letter in pink yarn, following chart. Make first three letters pink, next three medium coral, next three dark coral, last letter red. Skip two horizontal threads of burlap and work row of cross-stitch in pale blue. Skip one thread of burlap and make next row of letters: first three medium blue, next three pale blue, next three yellow-green, last two yellow.

Work the cross-stitch bands following chart. On row of pointed motifs, first make outline of stars across in rust-brown. Then make straight stitches within outline: first three motifs yellow, next three yellow-green, next three pink, next three medium coral, next two dark coral, next three yellow-green, last three yellow.

On next row make letters with straight stitches, each over four threads of burlap. Make first two letters medium coral, next two white, next two yellow-green, next two pale blue, last two yellow. Make cross-stitch row across. On next row of straight-stitch letters, make first two pale blue, next letter pink, next letter medium coral, next two yellow, next letter gold, last three orange. Work cross-stitch motif row across. On next row of straight-stitch letters, make first three pale blue, last two white.

Following chart and Color Key, work remainder of chart in cross-stitch to bottom row of pointed motifs. Work cross-stitch outlines first. Fill in straight vertical stitches, making first two motifs medium coral, next motif dark coral, next two motifs medium coral, next motif white, next medium blue, next medium coral, next medium

blue, next white, next two medium coral, next motif dark coral, last two medium coral.

Using letters already worked as a guide, plan name, date, and place to give sampler your personal signature.

Following Tree Chart, work tree panel below row of pointed motifs. Start at bottom center of panel and work tree chart out to right. Work complete half chart; then work chart in reverse to left to finish tree design. Make all trees and flowers in cross-stitch, all mounds along bottom in a combination of cross-stitch and straight vertical stitches. Where indicated on chart, work a tiny bird in half crosses over one thread of burlap, following chart for Tiny Birds.

Work basket at top center of cross-stitch panel on Large Chart; then work Tree Chart baskets at each side at bottom of panel (bottom of basket lines up with last stitch of border on Large Chart).

Embroidered Border: The remainder of sampler is

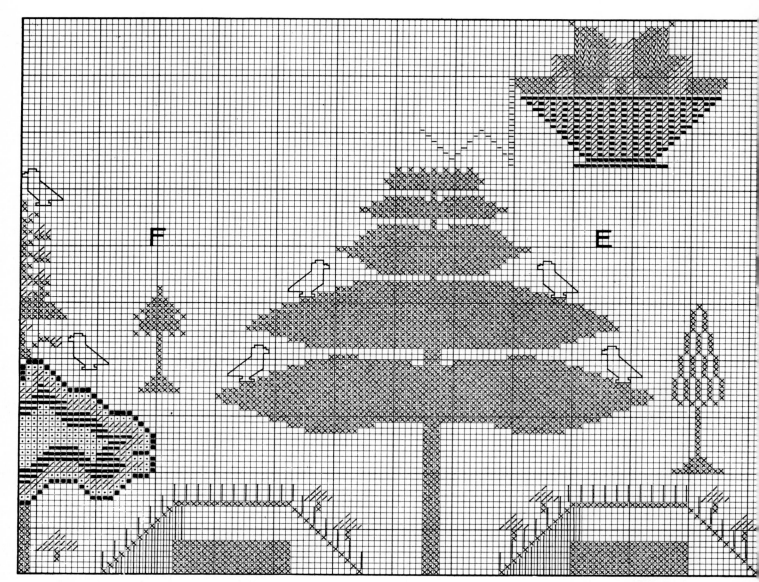

TREE CHART

worked in various embroidery stitches. See stitch details on page 282. Enlarge patterns on page 15 on paper ruled in 1″ squares. Trace patterns on tissue paper.

Starting at top of panel above right side of basket, pin Pattern A, matching short dash lines to edges of basket. With long white thread in sewing needle, make running stitches through tissue and burlap on all lines of pattern. Carefully pull away tissue, leaving running stitches as embroidery guide. Pin Pattern B around right top corner of panel and down side. Match dot-dash lines of Pattern C to B and pin C in place down side of panel to bottom basket. Make running stitches on all lines of patterns as before and pull away tissue.

Trace all patterns again. Turn each pattern over and retrace on back for left side of panel. Place patterns on left side and outline as before with white thread.

Continued on page 18

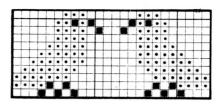

TINY BIRDS

CROSS-STITCH COLOR KEY

⊟ Pink		⊠ Yellow-green
⊠ Medium coral		⊡ White
⊠ Dark coral		▬ Rust-brown
		■ Black

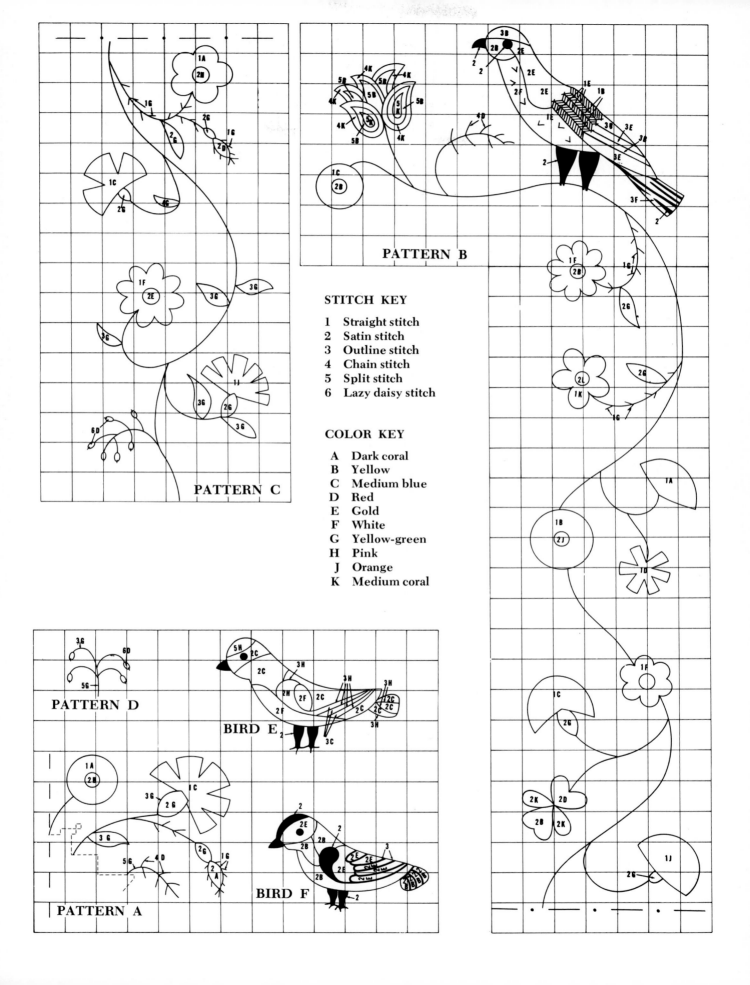

PATTERN C

PATTERN B

PATTERN D

PATTERN A

BIRD E

BIRD F

STITCH KEY

1　Straight stitch
2　Satin stitch
3　Outline stitch
4　Chain stitch
5　Split stitch
6　Lazy daisy stitch

COLOR KEY

A　Dark coral
B　Yellow
C　Medium blue
D　Red
E　Gold
F　White
G　Yellow-green
H　Pink
J　Orange
K　Medium coral

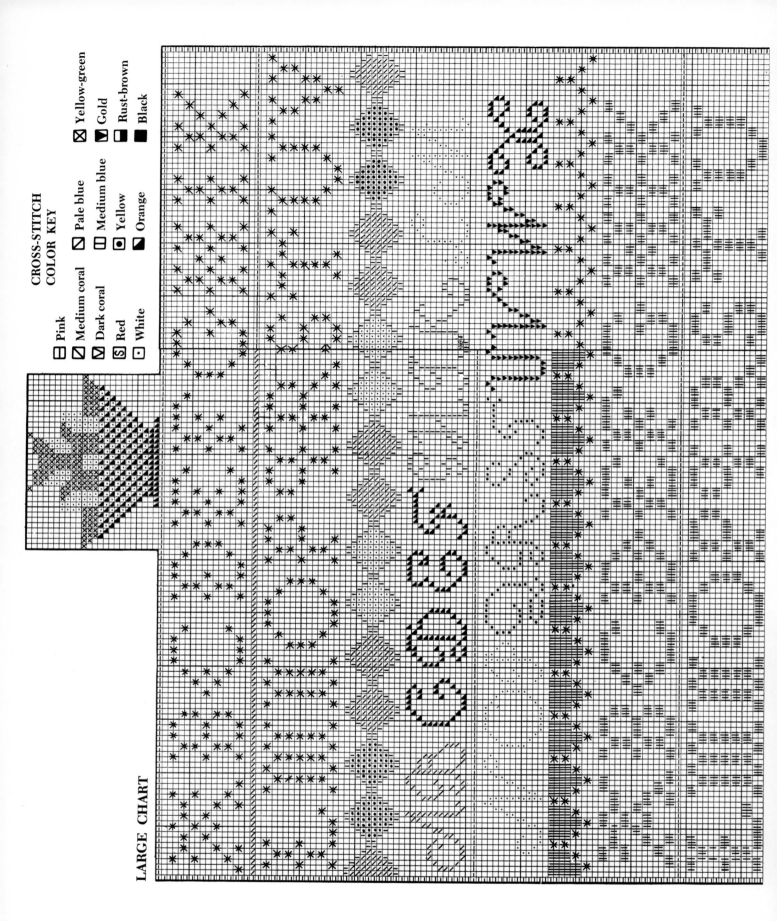

CROSS-STITCH
COLOR KEY

Pink
Medium coral
Dark coral
Red
White
Pale blue
Medium blue
Yellow
Orange
Yellow-green
Gold
Rust-brown
Black

LARGE CHART

16

Trace Pattern D four times. Pin one Pattern D at center top of each mound at bottom of panel and outline with white thread. Trace Birds E and F as given and make two reverse tracings. At points indicated by letters E and F on Tree Chart, pin the four birds in position all facing to center; outline with white thread as for other patterns.

Embroider all stems in green, using single strand of yarn in needle. Embroider main continuous stems in chain stitch; make offshooting stems in split stitch. Following numbers for stitches and letters for colors, embroider flowers and leaves, using single strand of yarn in needle. Work straight stitches radiating out from center point. Where outline stitch, split stitch, or chain stitch is indicated to fill an area, make rows of stitches close together, conforming to shape of area.

On birds, work satin stitch across areas in narrowest direction. Solid black areas are done with black yarn.

FINISHING: When embroidery is complete, stretch burlap over fiberboard, placing bottom of mounds along bottom edge of fiberboard. Push pins through burlap into edges of board, starting at center of each side and working toward corners. Stretch burlap smoothly and be sure threads of burlap are straight. Turn excess burlap to back of fiberboard and tape in place.

COLONIAL SAMPLER

Authentic colonial motifs—gentleman's house, pheasants, an urn—depict the life of a wealthy colonist under the Crown. Crosses are worked eight to the inch, following illustration as chart.

SIZE: Design area, 12¾" x 10".
EQUIPMENT: Embroidery scissors. Embroidery needles. Pencil. Ruler. Embroidery hoop (optional). **For Blocking:** Brown paper. Soft wooden surface. Square. Hammer. Thumbtacks.
MATERIALS: White hardanger cloth with 24 threads to the inch, 18" x 22". Six-strand embroidery floss: 1 skein each light coral, red, orange, light yellow, medium blue, brown, magenta, medium yellow-green, black; two skeins emerald green. **For Mounting:** Stiff white mounting cardboard, 11" x 14". Short straight pins. Masking tape. Wooden frame, 11" x 14" (rabbet size).

DIRECTIONS: Read Four Ways to Work Cross-Stitch on page 284. Work all cross-stitch using three strands of six-strand floss in needle. Each cross-stitch is made over three threads of the hardanger cloth. Bring floss to front between two threads of cloth, count up three threads and over three threads and put needle between two threads to back of cloth for half of cross-stitch; count threads in reverse for second half. Make the first half of every cross in

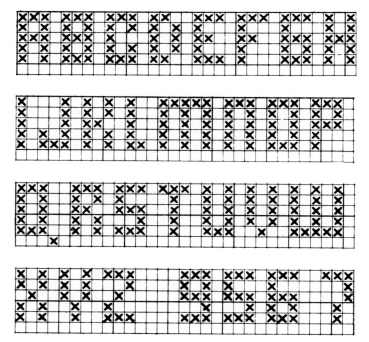

Alphabet and numbers for cross-stitching year and initials on Colonial Sampler.

same direction and all top stitches of cross in opposite direction.

Follow illustration as a working chart. In order to determine the number of threads to count between stitches, it may help to draw rule lines on the illustration, vertically and horizontally all the way across, between rows of crosses. Mark accurately over complete illustration. Each resulting square will indicate three threads of the cloth. For initials and date, use chart provided.

When embroidery is finished, block and mount finished piece following directions on pages 280–81.

HAPPY HEARTS SAMPLER

Traditional motifs—baskets, birds, a house—are brightened with a delightful verse for today. Sampler is worked completely in cross-stitch on a counted-thread fabric (24 threads to the inch). Variation in stitch size is achieved by making some crosses over two threads and some over one thread.

SIZE: 15⅜″ x 9⅞″, design area.

EQUIPMENT: Tape measure. Scissors. Pencil. Masking tape. Embroidery hoop (optional). Embroidery needle. **For Blocking and Mounting:** Soft wooden board. Brown wrapping paper. Rustproof thumbtacks. Turkish towel. Square. Ruler. Sewing and darning needles. Hammer.

MATERIALS: Off-white, even-weave linen with 23–24 threads to the inch, 22″ x 16″. Six-strand embroidery floss, 7-yard skeins: 1 each light green, rose, champagne, medium brown, black, light blue, gold; 2 skeins dark green; 3 skeins each of brick red and dark blue. **For Mounting:** Sewing thread to match linen. Heavy mounting cardboard. Small straight pins. Frame.

DIRECTIONS: Charts for design are given exactly as sampler is worked. Each square on chart represents one thread of fabric. Large crosses are worked over two threads; small crosses are worked over one. Use two strands of floss for small crosses; use three strands for large crosses.

Place linen on a smooth, hard surface. Using pencil, lightly mark on linen a 15⅜″ x 9⅞″ rectangle (area for embroidery). To prevent raveling, tape edges with masking tape.

Thread embroidery needle with an 18″–20″ length of floss, using number of strands indicated above. Read directions for working cross-stitch on even-weave fabric, page 284. Follow color key and charts to work cross-stitch sampler; repeat in reverse for second half. Follow separate charts to complete alphabets and to work poem.

To personalize sampler, use same style of letters as those used in verse to chart your name. Letters not used are in separate chart.

Block and mount following directions on pages 280–81. Frame as desired.

ABCDEFGHIJKLMN
OPQRSTUVWXYZ

& ABCDEFGHIJKLMNOPQRSTUVWXYZ

1974

clocks, crocks, ladderback chairs
tieback curtains, patchwork squares
samplers, quilts, pewter and pine
friends for dinner-hot mulled wine
pot roast, potatoes, cherry tarts
love, happiness, happy hearts

m. beams

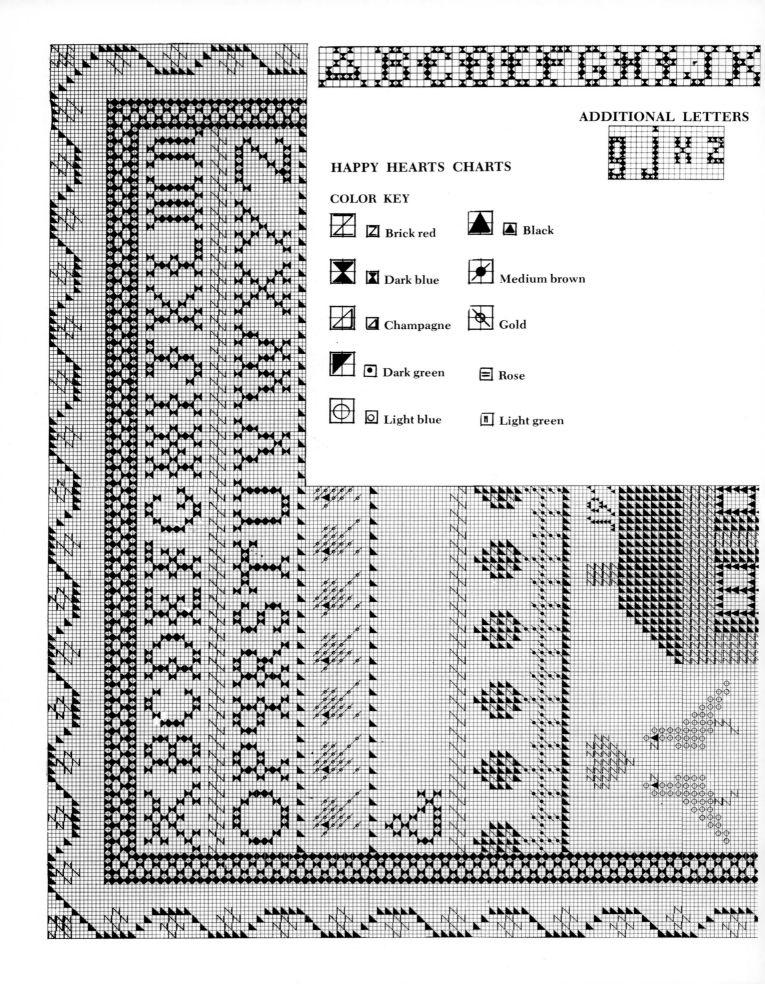

ADDITIONAL LETTERS

HAPPY HEARTS CHARTS

COLOR KEY

Brick red   Black

Dark blue   Medium brown

Champagne   Gold

Dark green   Rose

Light blue   Light green

LMNOPQRSTUVWXYZ

clocks, crocks, ladderback chairs
tieback curtains, patchwork squares
samplers, quilts, pewter and pine
friends for dinner·hot mulled wine
pot roast, potatoes, cherry tarts
love, happiness, happy hearts

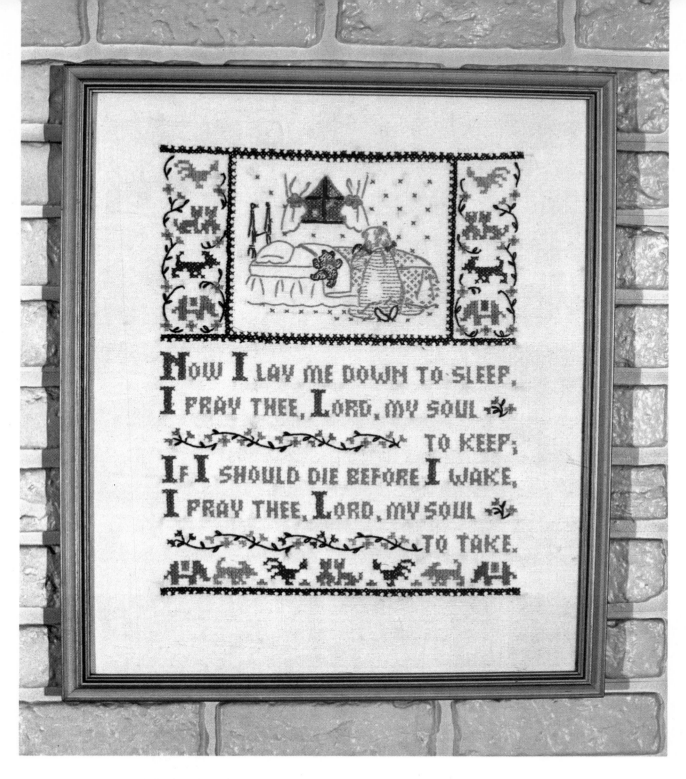

CHILD'S PRAYER SAMPLER

Sweet and familiar to generations of children, this nighttime prayer makes a charming cross-stitch picture for the nursery. The stitches are worked 10-to-the-inch over Penelope canvas with six-strand embroidery floss. The little bedtime scene, worked in a few simple stitches, is traced from the pattern given.

SIZE: 12¾″ x 9¾″, design area.

EQUIPMENT: Embroidery needle. Embroidery frame (optional). Penelope (cross-stitch) canvas, 10-mesh-to-the-inch, about 13″ x 10″. Sewing needle. Basting thread. Tweezers. Tracing paper. Pencil. Dressmaker's tracing (carbon) paper. Dry ball-point pen. **For Blocking:** Soft wooden surface. Brown wrapping paper. Ruler. Square. Rustproof thumbtacks. Hammer.

MATERIALS: White medium-weight linen, linenlike cotton, or quality muslin, 21″ x 18″. (**Note:** Even-weave fabric, 20 threads to the inch, may be used instead, eliminating the need for Penelope canvas. Each square on chart is then worked over two threads, yielding 10 stitches to the inch. (See page 284 for working embroidery on counted-thread fabric.) Six-strand embroidery floss: one skein of each of the following: deep bright blue, light bright blue, light green, dark green, bright pink, orange, light gold, purple, medium brown. Heavy mounting cardboard. Small straight pins. Masking tape. Frame.

DIRECTIONS: Center Penelope canvas on right side of fabric. Baste canvas in place on fabric (see directions for working cross-stitch over Penelope canvas on page 284).

Using three strands of floss in needle and referring to chart and color key, work all cross-stitches of border and prayer as indicated.

Using tweezers, remove Penelope canvas as indicated on page 284. Connect cross-stitch flowers with dark green stems worked in outline stitch (see stitch details, page 282). Work dark green leaves as indicated in lazy daisy stitch.

Using tracing paper, trace actual-size pattern for center panel. Center traced design in panel; insert dressmaker's carbon underneath tracing. Using dry ball-point pen, carefully trace entire design to transfer to fabric.

Using two strands of floss in needle and following illustration for color, and details on page 282 for stitches, embroider panel as follows: Work outlines of star, curtains, bed, bedposts, little girl's feet and hand, nightgown, and teddy bear in outline stitch. Work Teddy bear's body, little girl's hair, and nightgown in short straight stitches. Work moon crescent and bows on Teddy and little girl's hair in satin stitch. Work windowpane dividers and sash in chain stitch. Flowers on curtains have French knot center; work radiating straight stitches from knot for flower shape. Outline entire flower with outline stitch. Work cross-stitches where indicated.

When embroidery is finished, block and mount following directions on pages 280–81. Frame as desired.

ACTUAL-SIZE PATTERN FOR CENTER PANEL

CHILD'S PRAYER CHART

COLOR KEY

- ⊙ Dark green
- ⊟ Purple
- ◣ Light gold
- ⊠ Orange
- ⊘ Light bright blue
- ⦀ Bright pink
- ◥ Deep bright blue
- ⊟ Light green

APPLES SAMPLER

This delightful sampler design, celebrating the autumn harvest all year round, is similar to the Happy Hearts Sampler on page 20 in the use of traditional motifs.

SIZE: 12⅜" x 8⅞", design area.

EQUIPMENT: Tape measure. Scissors. Pencil. Embroidery hoop (optional). Embroidery needle. **For Blocking and Mounting:** Soft wooden board. Brown wrapping paper. Turkish towel. Square. Ruler. Rustproof thumbtacks. Sewing and darning needles. Hammer.

MATERIALS: Off-white, even-weave linen with 23–24 threads to the inch, 18" x 14". Six-strand embroidery floss, 7-yard skeins: 1 each light green, pale pink, champagne, navy, medium brown, black, rose, light blue; two each of brick red and dark green. **For Mounting:** Heavy mounting cardboard. Sewing thread to match linen. Small straight pins. Frame.

DIRECTIONS: Charts are given exactly as sampler is worked. Each square on chart represents one thread of fabric. Larger crosses are worked over two threads, smaller crosses over one thread. Use three strands of floss in needle for large crosses; use two strands of floss for small crosses. Place linen on a smooth, hard surface. Using pencil, lightly mark on linen a 12⅜" x 8⅞" rectangle (area for embroidery). To prevent raveling, tape edges with masking tape.

Thread embroidery needle with an 18"–20" length of floss, using number of strands indicated above. Read directions for working cross-stitch on even-weave fabric, page 284. Follow stitch detail, chart, and color key to work cross-stitch sampler.

To personalize sampler, use letters on this sampler and charts for Happy Hearts sampler (pages 22 and 23) for additional small letters.

Block and mount finished sampler following directions on pages 280–81. Frame as desired.

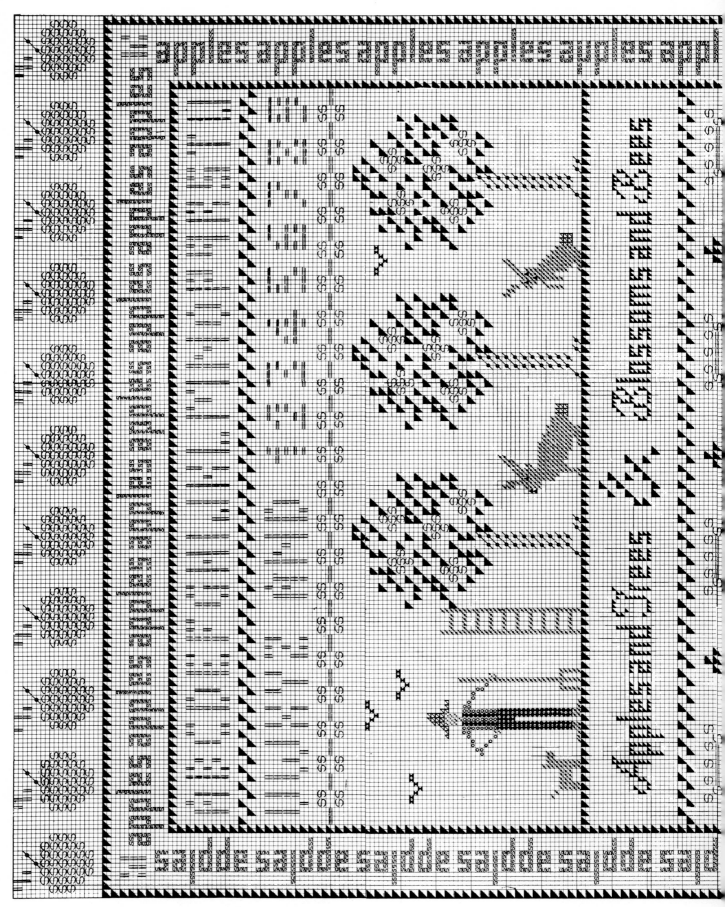

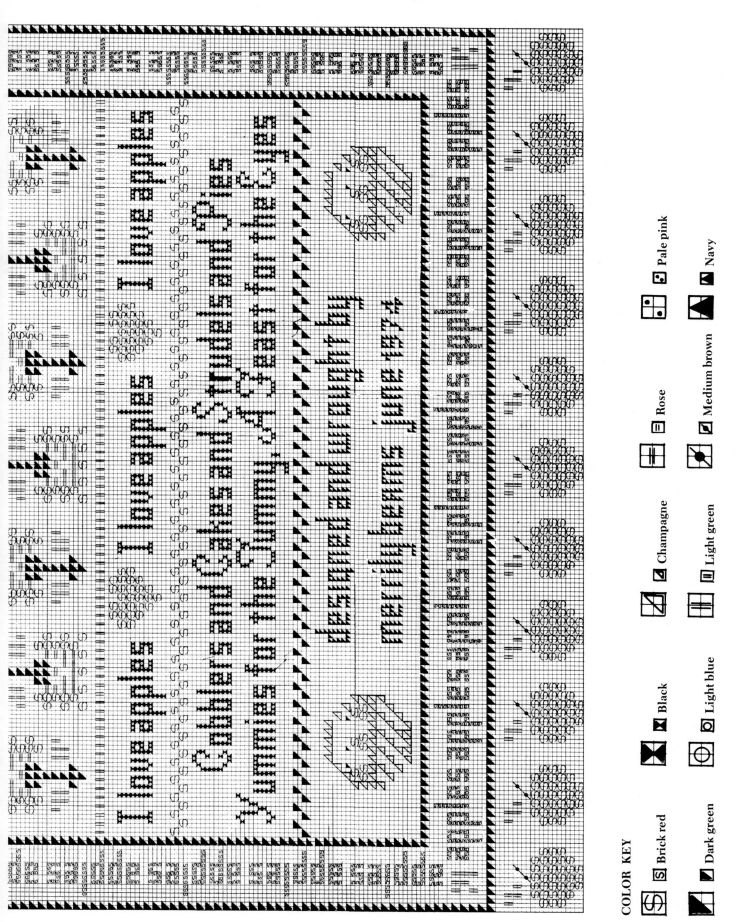

COLOR KEY

S Brick red	**☒** Black	**⊞** Champagne
	⊡ Light blue	**Ⅲ** Light green
◨ Dark green		**⊞** Rose
	◨ Pale pink	**◩** Medium brown
	◪ Navy	

29

GINGHAM SAMPLER

Traditional sampler motifs—birds, flowers, and an urn—are combined in a sampler that has a sprightly freshness perfect for a kitchen picture. As another idea, use the same easy cross-stitch-on-gingham design to make a pretty pillow for an Early American setting.

SIZE: 14″ x 12″, design area.

EQUIPMENT: Scissors. Sewing and embroidery needles. Basting thread. Embroidery hoop (optional). **For Blocking:** Soft wooden surface. Brown wrapping paper. Ruler. Square. Rustproof thumbtacks.

MATERIALS: Gold-and-white-checked gingham, 8 squares to the inch, 18″ x 16″. Six-strand embroidery floss (8.7-yard skeins): 1 skein each of light olive green, dark aqua, dark coral, cornflower blue; 2 skeins each of dark olive green, light aqua, light coral. **For Mounting:** Stiff mounting cardboard. Masking tape.

DIRECTIONS: Using sewing needle and basting thread, baste ¼″ hems all around fabric to prevent raveling. Read directions for working cross-stitch on gingham, page 284. Using four strands of floss in needle, work cross-stitches following chart and color key. When embroidery is finished, remove basting threads; block and mount as directed on pages 280–81. Frame as desired.

GINGHAM SAMPLER CHART

"GOD BLESS OUR HOME" SAMPLER

Surrounded by gaily colored motifs, the ever-popular cross-stitch message on page 33 is worked on even-weave fabric in the easy, counted-thread method.

SIZE: Varies according to material and embroidery. See Note.

EQUIPMENT: Scissors. Tape measure. Embroidery needle. Embroidery frame (optional). Masking tape. **For Blocking:** Rustproof thumbtacks. Soft wooden board. Brown wrapping paper. Turkish towel.

MATERIALS: Even-weave, round-thread white or cream-color fabric (see Note below). Six-strand embroidery floss: 1 skein each of medium yellow, gold, light yellow-green, dark emerald green, royal blue, lavender, purple, dark brown, medium gray, and black; 2 skeins each of light scarlet, rose pink, medium turquoise, and russet brown; 5 skeins of medium green.

NOTE: The fabric to be used must be evenly woven of round threads that can be counted individually. It is im-portant that the count of threads be the same horizontally and vertically. The number of threads to the inch and the number of threads over which you stitch will determine the finished size of your sampler. For example, if the fabric has about 30 threads to the inch and crosses are worked over three threads, the design area will be about 15″ x 11″. To calculate the size, multiply the number of crosses horizontally (109) and the number vertically (150) by the number of threads over which the crosses will be worked (3, 4, etc.); then divide the total of each side by thread count of fabric to obtain the dimensions. Many fabrics have a slightly different number of threads to the inch horizontally compared to vertically. Check your fabric for which way you want to work design.

DIRECTIONS: Cut even-weave fabric 3″ larger all

COLOR KEY

☑ Light scarlet	⊠ Gold	⊞ Medium turquoise	⊘ Russet brown
⊞ Rose pink	⊡ Light yellow-green	☐☐ Royal blue	⊻ Dark brown
⊡ Medium yellow	◪ Dark emerald green	⊟ Lavender	⊠ Medium gray
	⊠ Medium green	⊟ Purple	■ Black

around than finished design size. To keep the material from raveling as you embroider, bind the edges with masking tape, removing it when sampler is finished. Read directions for cross-stitch on page 284. To center the embroidery, fold the fabric in half lengthwise, then fold again crosswise; mark the center point with a pin.

To work embroidery, use four or six strands of floss in the needle, depending upon the size of crosses, for all colors except black. Use four strands of black if working the colors with six strands; use three strands of black if working colors with four. Use six strands for larger crosses, four strands or fewer for smaller crosses.

Determine the center point of the chart and the fabric. Begin working cross-stitch from the center, following the chart for colors and placement of design. Work each stitch over the same number of threads across and down, being careful to work all stitches in the same direction, with the ends of stitches touching.

Complete the sampler, if desired, by adding your initials and the date in block letters in positions indicated. Use two strands of black floss in the needle; make smaller crosses than in sampler.

Block and mount (see pages 280–81).

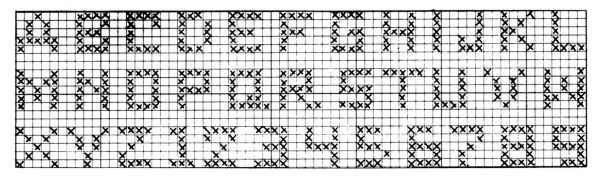

BIRTH SAMPLER

Red, white, and blue—fresh, clear colors for the nursery of a tiny girl or boy—predominate in this birth sampler which is the perfect "welcome" gift for baby. The border is worked in cross-stitch; the stork and his precious bundle are worked in other simple stitches.

SIZE: 15¾″x 14″, design area.

EQUIPMENT: Paper for pattern. Pencil. Ruler. Scissors. Tracing paper. Dressmaker's tracing (carbon) paper. Graph paper (10 squares to the inch). Masking tape. Embroidery and sewing needles. Embroidery hoop (optional). Penelope (cross-stitch) canvas, 10-mesh-to-the-inch, about 16″ x 15″. Basting thread. Tweezers. **For Blocking:** Brown paper. Soft wooden surface. Square. Hammer. Rustproof thumbtacks.

MATERIALS: Light blue linen fabric, 22″ x 20″. Six-strand embroidery floss (8-yard skeins): 3 skeins red; 2 skeins dark blue; 1 skein each of four shades of blue (from light to dark), ecru, bright and light orange, white, pale pink, light green, dark green. **For Mounting:** Heavy white cardboard. Straight pins. Frame, 15¾″ x 14½″, rabbet size.

DIRECTIONS: Following directions for working cross-stitch over Penelope canvas on page 284, baste canvas in place on blue linen. Only corner of border is given; repeat design as indicated in directions below.

Using four strands of floss in needle, begin working heart border. (**Note:** Rows of hearts on each side begin with one color and end with another.) Top and bottom borders each have 14 hearts pointing in same direction; side borders consist of 18 hearts each.

To Personalize: On graph paper, mark outline of area within inside border; each mesh of canvas is one square on graph. Using the alphabet and numbers on page 36 for Birth Alphabet Chart, make a chart for lettering as follows: Measure ⅜″ down from top of ruled-off area, and center the child's name. Measure ⅜″ up from bottom of ruled-off area, and center the birthdate.

When design is complete, remove basting. Cut away excess canvas around edges of design. Using tweezers, carefully draw out canvas threads following directions on page 284.

Using three strands of red floss in needle, center a French knot (see detail, page 36) in each "diamond" formed by cross-stitches on inner border.

Trace pattern for stork and baby. Having carbon paper between, center design within borders and tape pattern to fabric. Go over lines of pattern with a pencil to transfer design to fabric. Remove pattern and carbon.

To embroider, refer to stitch details on page 282. Using two strands of ecru, work body of stork in split stitch. Using four shades of blue to shade wing as illustrated, work wing in satin stitch with two strands of floss in needle. Using three strands of dark blue, outline wing in outline or stem stitch. Embroider clouds and grass freehand, following illustration. Use three strands of white for clouds, working them in outline or stem stitch.

Using two strands of bright orange in needle, work beak in satin stitch. Using three strands of bright orange, work stork's feet in outline or stem stitch.

Baby's hands, face, and feet are worked in split stitch, using two strands of pink. Using three strands of light orange, work French knots for hair. Using two strands of blue, work eyes in French knots. Using two strands of orange, work mouth in outline stitch, nose in straight stitch.

Using three strands of white, work outline of diaper in outline or stem stitch. Using three strands of floss in needle, work grass in outline stitch, alternating light green and dark green to give a shaded effect.

When embroidery is finished, block and mount following directions on pages 280–81. Frame as desired.

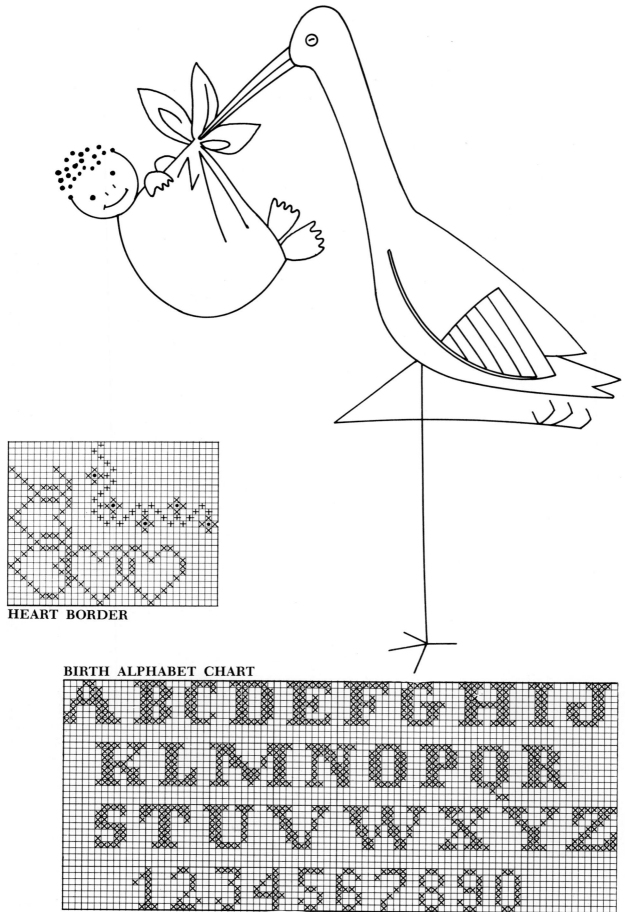

HEART BORDER

BIRTH ALPHABET CHART

"HOME SWEET HOME"

Flowers frame a calico scene that illustrates a sampler's sentiment. The center oval, with its tiny appliquéd house and picket fence, is quilted with small scattered stitches for an extra dimension. The embroidered touches are worked in six-strand floss. Framed, the picture measures approximately 13-3/4" by 12-1/2".

SIZE: 9½" x 8½", design area, including inside print borders.

EQUIPMENT: Paper for patterns. Tracing paper. Pencil. Ruler. Dressmaker's tracing (carbon) paper. Scissors. Hard lead pencil. Straight pins. Sewing and embroidery needles. **For Mounting:** Mat knife. Square. Metal straight edge.

MATERIALS: Heavy unbleached muslin, 21" x 22".

Scrap of batting. Cotton print fabrics: green floral print for inside borders, two strips each 10¼" x 1¾", two strips each 9" x 1¾"; blue floral print, ½" larger all around than mat board; small pieces of assorted prints as illustrated or as desired, which are suitable for the appliqués. Six-strand embroidery floss, 1 skein each of the following: bright pink, orange, medium green, light green, red, brown. Sewing thread to match fabrics. **For Mounting:**

HOME SWEET HOME

Heavy cardboard and mat board in size desired for finished piece. Rubber cement. Double- and single-faced masking tape.

DIRECTIONS: Trace actual-size pattern for each part of appliqué piece. Heavier lines on pattern indicate pieces to be cut out and appliquéd. Fine lines indicate what is to be embroidered.

To make background and inside border, fold each strip of green floral print in half lengthwise; turn in 1/4″ on each long edge; press. Turn 1/4″ under on each end; press.

Cut muslin background fabric 15″ x 16″. Overlap ends of green floral strips and pin strips into a rectangular border, centering the rectangle on the muslin background. With two strands of sewing thread in needle, use tiny running stitches to sew border strips along both sides of strips to the background fabric.

Place separate patterns on desired fabrics with carbon between; using hard-lead pencil, trace around outline to transfer design to fabric. Cut out individual pieces, adding 1/4″ all around each piece. Overlap top edge of grass appliqué 1/2″ over bottom of sky; turn under top edge of grass and sew to sky with tiny running stitches. Fold edges of other pieces under 1/4″; press.

To appliqué, pin pieces in place on grass-sky piece. Using double strand of matching sewing thread, stitch pieces to background with tiny running stitches spaced 1/4″ apart.

Following stitch details on page 282, work embroidery. Using three strands of floss in needle, work windows in red straight stitch, bushes in light green straight stitch.

Sky-grass piece forms an uneven oval. Cut a scrap of batting and a scrap of muslin size and shape of oval. Place batting on top of muslin; place appliquéd oval on top of batting; baste all together. Quilt background with double strand of matching sewing thread and tiny running stitches. Use a random pattern for quilting.

Baste oval appliquéd scene to the background muslin within the rectangular printed fabric border. The oval should be centered within the border but placed slightly closer to the bottom of the border.

Turn ¼″ seam allowance to wrong side of oval print frame, clipping where necessary to get a smooth curve; press. Pin oval frame over edges of oval appliqué. With two strands of sewing thread in needle, use tiny running stitches to sew oval frame along both edges to the background fabric and through the appliqué.

Trace patterns for embroidered corner floral motif and lettering. Center lettering pattern above oval appliqué within printed rectangular border. Insert carbon, and transfer the outline with hard-lead pencil to the fabric. Using two strands of brown floss, embroider letters in satin stitch. Using carbon, transfer corner motif to each corner within the printed rectangular fabric border. Work flowers and stems with full six strands of floss in satin stitch, using pink for flowers, orange for flower centers, and medium green for leaves.

To Mount: Cut 9¼″ x 10¼″ opening in center of mat board, using knife, square, and metal straight edge. Spread rubber cement over one surface of mat and cover with blue floral fabric. Pull excess fabric over outer edge to back of mat and cement in place to secure. Clip into center of fabric and cut out 1½″ away from inner edges of mat; fold fabric over to back and cement.

Following directions on page 281, mount finished muslin piece. Place double-faced masking tape around edge of mounting cardboard; place mat over picture and cardboard; press to secure. Frame as desired.

WEDDING AND ANNIVERSARY SAMPLERS

A wonderful way to remember happy occasions, the samplers on the next two pages will surely become the most cherished pictures in the home. "Wedding Day" would make a perfect wedding gift; "25 Years Wed" would be a charming remembrance for the silver anniversary. Worked mainly in cross-stitch, with a few other simple stitches, the samplers are slightly varied to show the possibilities for making something unique. "Wedding Day" has a two-color border with white bells and a bride and groom in traditional color. "25 Years Wed" repeats the border in one color and adds yellow wedding bells. The happy couple are worked in silhouette. Another idea: work the samplers all in white thread on a ground of blue.

SIZE: 13″ x 10″, design area.
EQUIPMENT: Sewing and embroidery needles. Basting thread. Embroidery frame (optional). Tweezers. Dressmaker's tracing (carbon) paper. Tracing paper. **For Blocking:** Soft wooden surface. Brown wrapping paper. Rustproof thumbtacks. Ruler. Square. Pencil.
MATERIALS: Medium-weight linen or linenlike cotton in color desired, 19″ x 16″. Penelope (cross-stitch) canvas, 10-mesh-to-the-inch, approximately 13″ x 10″, for main design. Needlepoint canvas, 16-mesh-to-the-inch, 6″ x 8″ for lettering. Six-strand embroidery floss (8.7-yard skeins): **Wedding Day:** 1 skein each of green, yellow, dark blue; 2 skeins white, rose, medium blue. **25 Years Wed:** 1 skein each orange, pink, brown, olive green; 2 skeins yellow, 3 skeins white.

DIRECTIONS: Baste Penelope canvas to fabric as directed on page 284. Following chart and color key, use three strands of floss in needle to work cross-stitch border and center design. When embroidery is complete, use tweezers to remove Penelope canvas.

To personalize sampler, baste needlepoint canvas in place: tops of letters in date will be 1½″ above center design; tops of letters in name begin ½″ below center design. Alphabet and number chart is provided. Using two strands of floss in needle, work names and dates in cross-stitch.

When embroidery is complete, use tweezers to remove canvas.

Trace patterns on page 44 for facial features on both samplers, ferns on Wedding Day, and ball of yarn, logs,

WEDDING CHART

COLOR KEY ⊡ White   ◣ Yellow   ⊠ Medium blue

⊟ Rose   ⊠ Dark blue

WEDDING/ANNIVERSARY ALPHABET

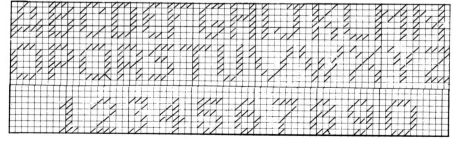

ANNIVERSARY CHART

COLOR KEY ▨ Pink   ▨ Brown   ⊡ White

▥ Yellow   ⊟ Olive green

fire, and hurricane lamps on 25 Years Wed. Place tracing on fabric in correct position; insert dressmaker's carbon in between and trace entire design to transfer.

Following stitch details on page 282, and illustrations for colors, complete embroidery on sampler as follows: **Wedding Day:** Work orange-blossom leaves in lazy daisy stitch. Work fern stems, facial features, and bouquet streamers in outline stitch. Work fern leaves and bell top

in straight stitch. **25 Years Wed:** Work hurricane lamps, fire's flames, clock top, and yarn in outline stitch. Work andirons and clock's hands in straight stitch. Work flowers on her chair with lazy daisy petals and French knot centers. Work French knots in squares on his chair and at top of clock. Work fireplace logs in satin stitch.

When all embroidery is finished, block and mount following directions on pages 280–81. Frame as desired.

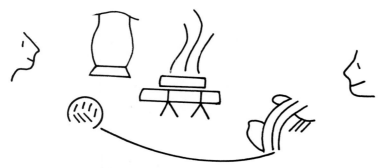

**ACTUAL-SIZE PATTERNS
FOR ANNIVERSARY SAMPLER**

LEG

**ACTUAL-SIZE PATTERNS
FOR WEDDING SAMPLER**

FRIENDSHIP SAMPLERS

Warm sentiments make a delightful pair of samplers that glow with inspiration. The stitches are worked with cotton embroidery floss on fabric that is trimmed with a velvet ribbon.

SIZES: Wealth, 10″ x 8″; Stay, 5½″ x 6½″.

EQUIPMENT: Pencil. Dry ball-point pen. Heavy-weight artist's tracing paper. Dressmaker's tracing (carbon) paper. Embroidery and sewing needles. Embroidery hoop. Thread. Masking tape. Staple gun.

MATERIALS: Wealth: Tightly woven medium-weight fabric in a light color (we used beige), 12″ x 10″. Canvas stretchers, 10″ x 8″, or a piece of wood, 10″ x 8″ x ½″. Bright blue velvet ribbon, ⅞″ wide, 37″. Six-strand embroidery floss (8.7-yard skeins): 2 skeins lime green; 1 skein each of the following: yellow, dark blue, black, dark green, bright blue, bronze, white. **Stay:** Tightly woven medium-weight fabric in a light color (we used beige), 9″ x 8″.

Canvas stretchers, 5½″ x 6½″, or a piece of wood 5½″ x 6½″ x ½″. Dark green velvet ribbon, ⅞″ wide, 25″. Six-strand embroidery floss: 1 skein each of the following: dark green, lime green, black, light green, dark yellow.

DIRECTIONS: Read embroidery directions on page 280. Trace actual-size patterns. Bind raw edges of fabric with masking tape to prevent raveling. Place dressmaker's tracing paper over right side of fabric to be embroidered. Center traced pattern over dressmaker's carbon. With ball-point pen, lightly trace outlines of pattern to transfer design. Insert fabric in embroidery hoop. For stitch details, see page 282.

To Block: Place finished embroidery face down on

ALL THE WEALTH
OF THE WORLD
COULD NOT BUY
YOU A FRIEND
OR PAY YOU FOR
THE LOSS OF ONE

C.O. PRENTICE

Stay
IS A CHARMING WORD
IN A FRIEND'S VOCABULARY

AMOS BRONSON ALCOTT

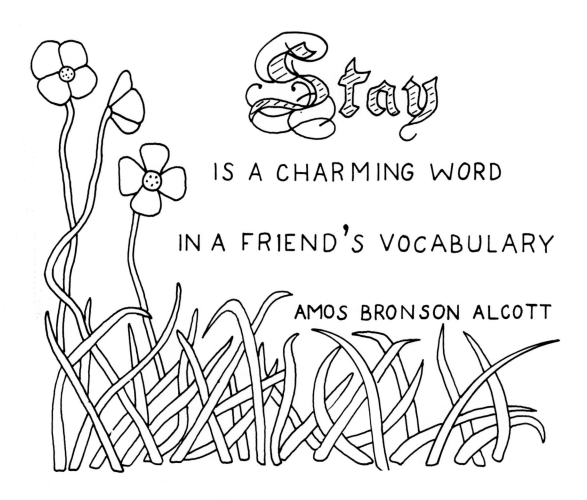

IS A CHARMING WORD

IN A FRIEND'S VOCABULARY

AMOS BRONSON ALCOTT

padded ironing board. Steam-press wrinkles and puckers out gently.

To Mount: Press raw edges of fabric under ½". Center fabric, right side up, over canvas stretcher (or wood). With staple gun, staple fabric to sides of canvas stretchers. Stitch two ends of velvet ribbon together on wrong side, taking ½" seams. Trim seam allowance close to stitching. Slip ribbon over sides of stretchers; slip-stitch ribbon in place. Stitch corners of ribbon together on back so they lie flat.

WEALTH

Using two strands of bright blue floss, embroider the name "C.D. Prentice" in backstitch. With four strands of bright blue, work remaining words in backstitch. The remaining areas to be embroidered are worked in four strands of embroidery floss. With white, work flower petals in satin stitch; with yellow, work flower centers in French knots. With green, work flower stems in outline stitch. Work berry seeds as follows: With bright blue, make one seeding stitch; with dark blue, make one seeding stitch next to the first stitch. With black, backstitch around outline of berry; then fill in background of berry in seeding stitch. With green, work stems

of berries in outline stitch. With bronze, work stems of leaves in outline stitch and center areas of leaves in long and short stitch. With bronze, embroider outline of main stem in outline stitch; then work thorns in satin stitch. Using lime green, fill remainder of stem with several rows of outline stitch. Work all leaves as follows: With green, work middle areas in long and short stitch. With lime green, work outer areas in long and short stitch as shown.

STAY

Using four strands of black floss, embroider the word "stay" in satin stitch; using two strands of black, work curved lines around the word in backstitch. With two strands of black, embroider the name "Amos Bronson Alcott" in backstitch; with four strands of black, work remaining words in backstitch. Using two strands of light green, embroider stems of flowers in satin stitch. The remaining areas to be embroidered are worked with four strands of floss. With dark yellow, work center flower in satin stitch. Work petals of other two flowers in satin stitch, and the centers in French Knots. Work the grass in split stitch, alternating the colors dark green and lime green for each blade of grass.

ALL THE WEALTH
OF THE WORLD
COULD NOT BUY
YOU A FRIEND
OR PAY YOU FOR
THE LOSS OF ONE

C.D. PRENTICE

KINDNESS SAMPLER

Cross-stitch a delicate bouquet and a meaningful message for a lovely sampler. The two colors of embroidery floss are worked over 10-to-the-inch Penelope canvas from the chart given.

SIZE: 20⅛″ x 16″, design area.

EQUIPMENT: Ruler. Pencil. Scissors. Embroidery and sewing needles. Embroidery hoop or wooden pic-

ture frame, 23″ x 19″. Rustproof thumbtacks. Basting and pastel-colored thread. Penelope (cross-stitch) canvas, 10-mesh-to-the-inch, about 23″ x 19″. Felt-tipped pens:

Kindness in words
creates confidence,
Kindness in thinking
creates profoundness,
Kindness in giving
creates Love.

pink and green. Tweezers. **For Blocking:** Brown paper. Soft wooden surface. Square. Hammer.

MATERIALS: White or off-white linen fabric, 29″ x 25″. Six-strand embroidery floss (8.7-yard skeins): pink, 9 skeins; green, 5 skeins. **For Mounting:** Heavy white cardboard. Straight pins. Masking tape. Frame, 23″ x 19″ rabbet size.

DIRECTIONS: With pink and green felt-tipped pens, mark design on canvas. Each square of chart represents one mesh of canvas; mark stitch placement in center of mesh. Starting 1½″ from top of canvas, mark flower and heart designs in pink and motto in green.

See directions for preparing canvas and cross-stitching on page 284. Work crosses over mesh of canvas, using four strands of floss in needle throughout. Work the motto in green and the flower and heart designs in pink. Each X on the chart represents one cross-stitch.

When embroidery is finished, block and mount following directions on pages 280–81.

DRAWNWORK SAMPLER

Create a different kind of sampler—in drawnwork embroidery! The threads are drawn from fabric following a pattern, then the remaining threads are grouped and stitched. Although traditionally made on fine fabric, this sampler is worked on burlap for a larger, bolder look.

SIZE: 20¼″ x 17″.

EQUIPMENT: Large-eyed embroidery needle. Pencil. Ruler. Pointed scissors.

MATERIALS: Burlap, 36″ wide, white, ¾ yard. Tapestry yarn, 8.8-yard skeins: burnt orange, 3 skeins; brown, 4 skeins.

DIRECTIONS: Read directions for Drawnwork on following pages. Practice hemstitching and needleweaving stitches shown. Cut the fabric to measure 22″ wide, with selvage at side. With pencil, mark a rectangle 23¾″ x 20″ on back of fabric. Count 23 threads down, 23 threads in from two upper corners of penciled outline; draw a single thread to mark start of border. Repeat at bottom corners. Begin at upper left corner: cut 13 threads both ways from the angle. Raise the cut threads one by one with point of needle and draw all the 13 threads both directions of the material, cutting them again where they meet the drawn thread at the opposite corners. Repeat in all corners until border is formed. Hemstitch all around with matching thread. Using brown yarn, work plain hemstitching along both edges around border, putting needle under four upright threads when working across, four cross threads when working down. Work each corner following stitch detail.

Measure 1¾″ down, 1¾″ in from inner edges of border; mark a rectangle 14½″ x 10½″. Within this area, work seven bands of hemstitching and needleweaving spaced about ¾″ apart. Work stitches shown in our sampler or plan your own design. In working the hemstitching on burlap (a coarser fabric than linen), draw out one thread instead of two for single rows, and fewer threads for wide patterns than called for in the directions for linen. Sampler can be mounted and framed, or used as a wall hanging. For wall hanging, make ½″ side hems and 1″ top and bottom hems; hang on wooden dowels or rods.

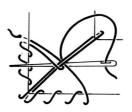

GENERAL DIRECTIONS FOR DRAWNWORK

NEEDLEWEAVING: Choose coarse or fine linen or other fabrics from which threads can be drawn easily. Use pearl cotton or all strands of six-strand cotton for finer fabrics. Heavier embroidery yarns may be used on coarse fabrics. Use a blunt needle for weaving.

Draw out enough threads to make desired border (see individual instructions). Needleweaving is easier to do when both edges of drawn section are hemstitched first. Use thread to match fabric for hemstitching. Take an equal number of vertical threads in each stitch (usually 3, 4, or 5) according to weight of fabric being used. Then do needleweaving on right side of fabric over and under each group of threads divided by hemstitching—never split these groups. Always be sure that weaving threads are close together so they cover vertical threads of drawn section of fabric.

To begin work, fasten end of thread by placing it along first group of threads and working over it. To end off, run

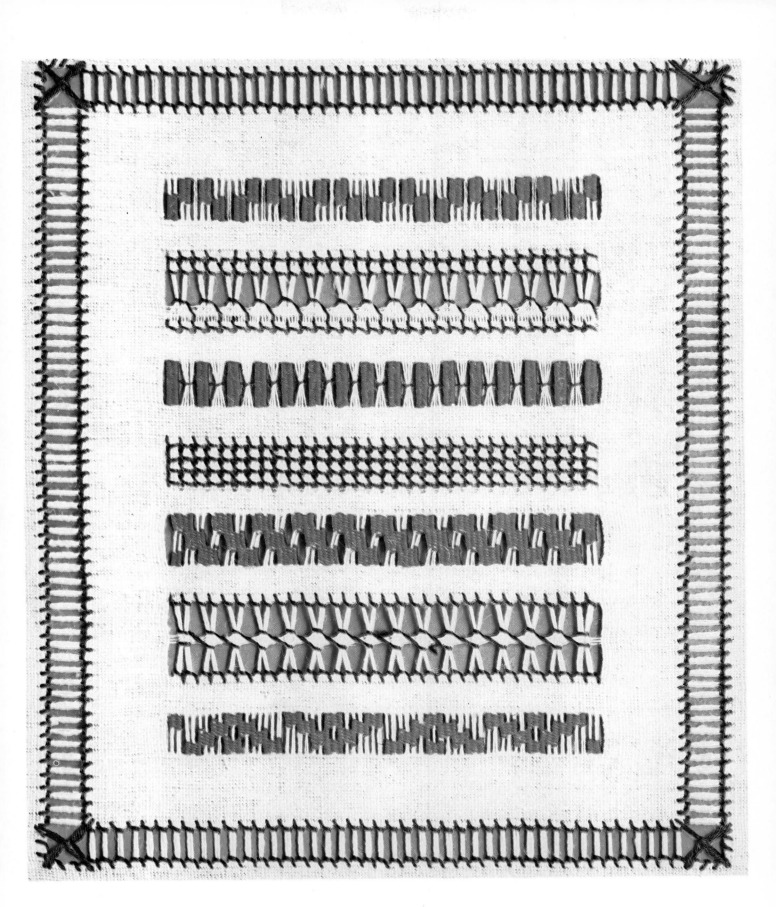

needle back into weaving for about four rows and cut thread close to work.

Practice the following six basic formations before starting to work borders.

Vertical Bars (Fig. 7): Fasten thread at lower right and work closely around first group from bottom to top. End off thread. Make each bar separately in same way.

Zigzag Bars (Fig. 8): Fasten thread at bottom right and work one vertical bar, but do not end off. Work 2 stitches around first bar and next group of threads at same time, then work down second group of threads. Work 2 stitches around bar just made and next group of threads at same time. Continue in same way.

Double Bars (Fig. 9): Fasten thread at lower right of drawn area, weave under first group of threads and over second group. Then weave under second group and over first group. Continue weaving closely under and over first and second groups from bottom to top. End off thread. Make each double bar separately.

Broken Double Bars (Fig. 10): Fasten thread at lower right and weave double bar same as above, halfway up drawn section; then weave under first group, over second and under third. For second half of bar, weave over third group of threads and under second, then back over second group and under third. Continue weaving over and under third and second groups to top. End off thread. Start next broken bar at bottom, weaving third and fourth groups of threads halfway up and continuing to top on fourth and fifth groups. Work across in same manner. First bar is finished by working to top of drawn section.

Alternating Blocks (Fig. 11): Fasten thread at lower right, weave under first group of threads, over second group, under third, over fourth. Then weave back under fourth, over third, under second, over first. Continue weaving in this manner halfway up drawn section. Then weave under first group, over second, under third, over fourth, under fifth, over sixth. Weave back under sixth, over fifth, under fourth and over third. Continue weaving to top on third, fourth, fifth and sixth groups of threads. Fasten off threads. Start next block at bottom on fifth, sixth, seventh and eighth groups of threads and weave halfway up. Then weave on seventh, eighth, ninth and tenth groups of threads to the top. Continue across in this manner. Finish first 2 groups of threads as a double bar.

Pyramids (Fig. 12): Fasten thread at lower right, weave under and over first 8 groups of threads and back under and over to first group. Weave back and forth for one-quarter depth of drawn section. Then weave over and under one group fewer of threads on each side (6 groups) for second quarter of depth. Weave under and over one fewer group on each side (4 groups) for third quarter of depth. Weave over and under 2 center groups for last quarter, to top of drawn section. End off thread. Start next pyramid upside down at bottom of drawn section. Weave under and over 2 groups of threads for first quarter; over and under 4 groups for second quarter; under and over 6

groups for third quarter; over and under 8 groups for last quarter. End off thread. Continue across, forming pattern of pyramids and inverted pyramids.

Many interesting designs can be made with these basic formations of woven thread groups.

HEMSTITCHING: Any linen or cotton fabric with a plain weave may be used for hemstitching. To draw out threads, insert a pin under one thread near edge of fabric and pull it up; then carefully draw the thread from fabric all the way across. Try to ease it out without breaking it. Hemstitching is done on wrong side of fabric, from left to right. Use a matching or contrasting embroidery thread, such as one or two strands of six-strand cotton for finer fabrics. Heavier embroidery yarns may be used on coarse fabrics. Use an embroidery needle.

Plain Hemstitching: Draw out 2 or 3 threads across fabric, depending on its coarseness. Secure thread at left edge of drawn section without making a knot by taking a few stitches over end of thread. Put needle under next 3 or 4 upright threads of drawn section from right to left (Fig. 1). Pull thread taut, insert needle in second row of threads above drawn section (Fig. 2) and pull thread tight. Continue across, as in Figs. 1 and 2, always picking up same number of threads. Secure thread at end. Bottom edge of drawn section may be hemstitched also.

A hem may be made at same time hemstitching is done. Turn fabric over twice to make hem desired width, and baste. Draw out threads just below edge of hem. Starting at left, hemstitch as in Figs. 1 and 2, inserting needle in second row of threads above and through bottom edge of hem. Repeat these two steps across, catching edge of hem and picking up same number of threads each time.

For a more decorative border (Fig. 3), pull out about 8 threads and work across in same manner as Figs. 1 and 2, picking up 6 threads at a time. To hemstitch lower edge of drawn section and make zigzag design, pick up first 3 threads only, then continue across, picking up 6 threads at a time (Fig. 3).

To make twisted groups of hemstitched threads (Fig. 4), pull out 10 or more threads and work plain hemstitching evenly at top and bottom of drawn section, picking up 4 threads at a time. Turn work over to right side, secure thread at right-hand edge in middle of drawn section. Pick up second group of threads at left, with needle pointing from left to right. Bring this group of threads over and to the right of first group by inserting needle under first group and turning it to the left, keeping second group on needle (Fig. 4). Continue across in same manner, always picking up second group of threads first.

Italian Hemstitching: This is based on the same two steps as plain hemstitching, except that in the second step the needle points downward instead of upward, unless otherwise stated.

To make border shown in Fig. 5, baste hem. Draw out 2

HEMSTITCHING

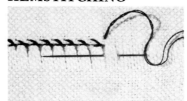

Figure 1

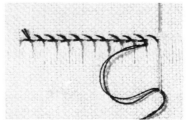

Figure 2

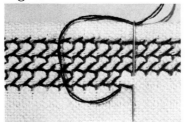

Figure 3

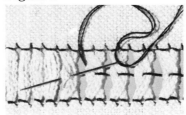

Figure 4

Figure 5

Figure 6

NEEDLEWEAVING

Figure 7

Figure 8

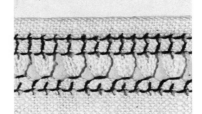

Figure 9

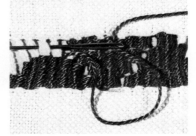

Figure 10

Figure 11

Figure 12

threads, just below hem, skip 3 threads, draw out next 2 threads, skip 3, etc., for desired width. Make first row of hemstitching, picking up 4 threads at a time. With needle pointing downward for second step, insert needle in hem first, 2 threads up from fold, then through all thicknesses and out at drawn section. Continue across in same manner. To make succeeding rows, insert needle in space between groups of threads of preceding row.

A wide decorative border, the right side of which is shown in Fig. 6, is worked as follows: Baste hem. Draw out 2 threads just below hem, skip 3 threads, draw out 10 threads, skip 3 threads, draw out 2 threads. Work first two rows of hemstitching as shown in Fig. 5, picking up 4 threads at a time. On next row, fasten thread at base of wide drawn section and work a row of plain hemstitching, picking up 8 threads at a time. On last row, fasten thread in last drawn section and work a row of hemstitching like second row, inserting needle in space between groups of threads and at base of groups.

Florals

VICTORIAN WOOL PICTURES

Wool flowers, puffed and padded, make the unusual embroidery of two Victorian pictures—the symmetrical bouquet and the floral wreath. Petals and leaves are constructed by sewing strands of yarn together, then using the resulting yarn piece in various ways as shown, sometimes building extra dimension with padding. The flowers, leaves, and strawberries are sewn on a black fabric background. The stems and smaller flowers are made with embroidery stitches. The cherries in the wreath are from ball fringe.

SIZES: Floral Bouquet, 17″ x 14″; Wreath, 16″ square.

EQUIPMENT: Paper for patterns. Tracing paper. Pencil. White dressmaker's tracing (carbon) paper. Stiff cardboard. Scissors. Ruler. Dry ball-point pen. Sewing needle. Large-eyed embroidery needle. Tack hammer for framing pictures.

MATERIALS: Black suede cloth or good-quality felt, 24″ square for Wreath Design; 26″ x 22″ for Bouquet Design. Tapestry yarn (8-yard skeins): 2 skeins of white for each picture, and 1 skein of colors listed in Color Keys for each, except that Wreath Design requires 2 skeins olive green, light olive, deep green, and dark green. Sewing thread to blend with each color group of yarns (see Color Keys). White cotton flannel for stuffing. Carpet thread. **For Wreath Design:** Red pompons from ball fringe, 6. Gold silk or metallic thread. **For Framing:** Heavy mounting cardboard, 20″ square for Wreath Design; 22″ x 18″ for Bouquet Design. Straight pins. Masking tape. Wide shadow-box frame with glass, rabbet size the same as mounting boards. Brown wrapping paper.

DIRECTIONS: The three-dimensional effect of these pictures is achieved by forming separate flowers, petals, and leaves from strands of yarn sewn together and then sewn onto the background fabric. Stems and other flowers are embroidered flat, directly on the background.

Flowers, petals, and leaves made separately are indicated by a letter A–H on patterns. However, all leaves in an area and similar petals of a flower have not been lettered, but are to be made the same as others. The Stitch Key with each pattern indicates the type of leaf or petal. (see figures). The numbers on patterns indicate color combinations of yarn to use for leaves, flowers, and petals (see Color Keys). Arrange colors of yarn strands from light to

dark, so that when strands are folded, either the light or the dark will be at center. Colors and combinations may be changed to suit your own scheme. Try different combinations as you practice making the petals and leaves. To make petal and leaf shapes, follow directions and details.

To prepare yarn for making all separate pieces, cut strands of yarn to length given in individual directions. Work over a small piece of cardboard and sew with thread and a sewing needle (see Fig. 1). Hold strands side by side and tack together with thread in a color that blends with color combination of yarn. Hold strands flat and taut over cardboard as shown in Fig. 1. Carefully sew through each strand from right to left, then from left to right, making each row of stitching about ⅛″ apart. Do not pull thread tight, but have it snug enough to keep strands of yarn close together and flat. Continue stitching through strands along complete length (front and back of cardboard). Form each petal and leaf shape with these stitched strips of yarn.

A—Straight Leaf Strip: Cut number and colors of yarn strands indicated in Color Key, long enough to form complete folded arrangement on pattern for Wreath Design. Sew together as in Fig. 1. Turn under ends of strands and tack. Place strip over pattern, fold and tack to conform with shape on pattern. Tack to black fabric wherever necessary to hold in place.

B—Tulip-Shape Stuffed Petals: For each petal, cut number and colors of yarn strands indicated in Color Keys, and sew together, Fig. 1; cut strands twice the length of petals on patterns, plus 2″. Fold strands in half, keeping them flat, and using one finger to hold curve at fold, Fig. 2. Sew across strands near ends; sew center strands together.

Form a roll, Fig. 3, by cutting long strips of cotton flannel and rolling tightly to make about ½″ diameter. Measure the length of each petal on pattern; cut flannel strips to that width and roll. Wrap white thread around roll and knot thread. Sew across one end for top to make it round. Place sewn strands of yarn over flannel roll, covering top and sides, with folded end of strands over rounded end of roll. Tack in place; turn ends to back and tack, see Fig. 4.

C—Tulip-Shape Unstuffed Petals: Make as for stuffed tulip petals, omitting the flannel roll, and turning ends in. Unstuffed petals are placed over stuffed petals to form flower, see Fig. 5.

D—Leaves: Cut number and colors of yarn strands indicated in Color Keys, about 2½″ long, and sew together, Fig. 6. Fold in half, keeping all strands flat so a point is formed by strands underneath, Fig. 7. Sew ends together tightly. Turn leaf over and tack to black background at tip and bottom; turn ends under leaf and make a straight stem stitch with yarn, Fig. 8.

E—Leaves with Stitched Tip: Make as for Leaves D. At folded tip, stitch across strands ⅛″ from tip, pulling thread tight; knot. Sew to background as for leaves D.

F—Flower with Small Petals: For each petal, cut number and colors of strands indicated in Color Keys, 2″ long. Make 54 small petals as for Leaves D, but do not tack to background. Cut a cardboard circle slightly smaller than circles F on patterns; pad with a few layers of flannel to make a slight mound. Cover with a larger flannel circle and gather edge of flannel to cover padded mound smoothly. Starting around outside edge, tack a round of petals to mound with points out. Tack another round of petals inside and overlapping last round, with points of petals between those of last round. Make five rounds of petals to center. Sew a small pompon at center.

G—Padded Rose: Cut long strands of yarn in colors and numbers indicated in Color Keys; sew together, Fig. 9. For padding, cut a circle of flannel about 4″ in diameter. Gather around circle with small running stitch and stuff circle with pieces of flannel to make a plump mound a

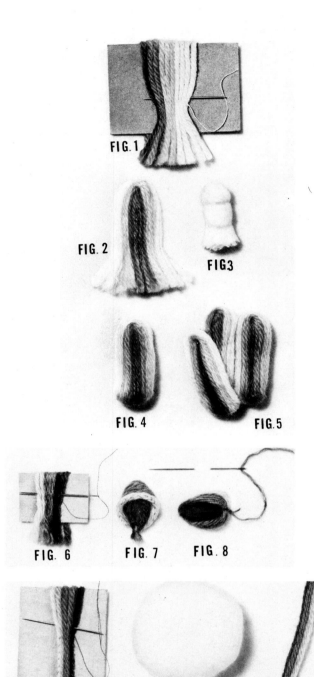

FIG. 1

FIG. 2

FIG 3

FIG. 4

FIG. 5

FIG. 6

FIG. 7

FIG. 8

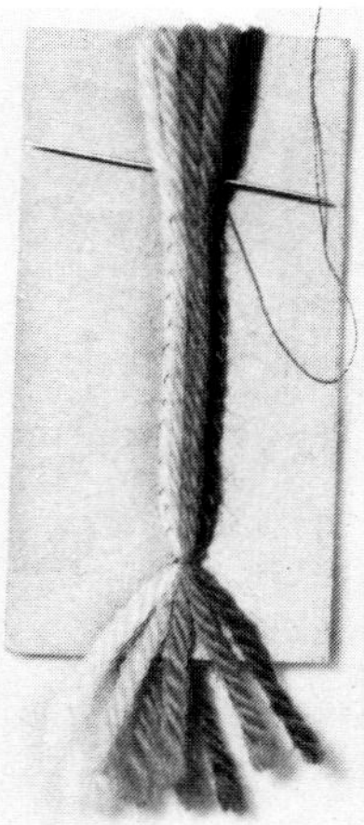

FIG. 9

FIG. 10

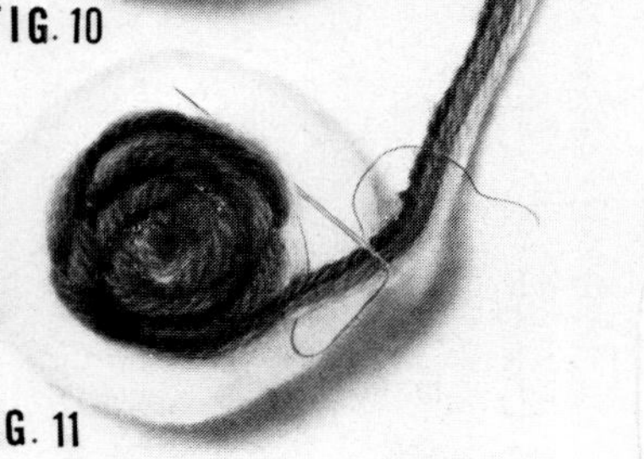

FIG. 11

COLOR KEY

No. 1 Leaves	**1 strand dark blue-green** **2 strands olive green** **2 strands light olive** **2 strands dark gold**
No. 2 Leaves	**1 strand dark blue-green** **2 strands dark green** **2 strands medium green** **2 strands pale olive**
No. 3 Leaves	**2 strands deep green** **2 strands olive green** **2 strands light olive** **1 strand pale green**
No. 4 Leaves	**2 strands deep green** **3 strands dark green** **2 strands light green**
No. 5 Flower	**1 strand dark brick red** **1 strand medium brick red** **2 strands light brick red** **1 strand pale brick red** **1 strand white**
No. 6 Flower	**1 strand burnt orange** **2 strands light orange** **3 strands yellow** **3 strands white**
No. 7 Flower	**1 strand dark brick red** **1 strand scarlet** **1 strand coral** **2 strands salmon** **1 strand pale brick red**
No. 8 Flower	**2 strands white** **4 strands pale brick red** **1 strand salmon**
No. 9 Flower	**2 strands maroon** **2 strands pink** **3 strands white**
No. 10 Flower	**1 strand deep blue** **1 strand royal blue** **1 strand light blue** **3 strands pale blue**
No. 11 Flower	**1 strand deep red** **1 strand dark brick red** **3 strands burnt orange** **1 strand light orange**
No. 12 Flower	**8 strands white** **1 strand light blue**

Techniques for making flowers and leaves: ***Top detail shows how strands of yarn are laid around cardboard and sewn together, then spread out to be sewn down center; piece is used for flat petal or sewn over flannel cylinder. Middle detail shows strands turned inside out for leaves. In bottom detail, long strands of sewn-together yarn are couched in a spiral on a cotton-stuffed flannel form.***

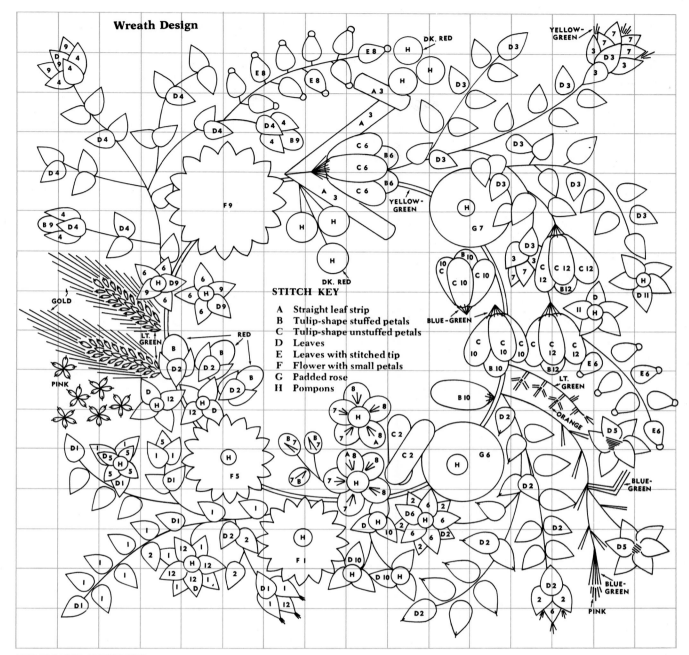

Wreath Design

YELLOW-GREEN

DK. RED

STITCH KEY

A Straight leaf strip
B Tulip-shape stuffed petals
C Tulip-shape unstuffed petals
D Leaves
E Leaves with stitched tip
F Flower with small petals
G Padded rose
H Pompons

GOLD

LT. GREEN

RED

PINK

DK. RED

YELLOW-GREEN

BLUE-GREEN

LT. GREEN

ORANGE

BLUE-GREEN

BLUE-GREEN

PINK

WREATH DESIGN

little smaller in diameter than pattern circles G. Pull gathers together and knot thread, Fig. 10. Starting at center top, attach end of sewn yarn strands to mound, wind strands around center, tack to flannel mound about every ½"; overlap each round slightly to cover top and sides of mound, Fig. 11. If sewn strands are not long enough to cover mound completely, make another strip the same and add to end of first strip at a tacking place on mound. Sew rose to background around bottom edge. Make a small yarn pompon. Sew pompon to center of rose.

H—Pompons: (**Note:** Cherries on Wreath Design are pompons from ball fringe.) For all other small pompons, use two colors of yarn. Most of the pompons are white and yellow; some are yellow and brown, or they may be all yellow. Cut two strands of tapestry yarn 36″ long. Split each into four single-ply pieces. Cut a strip of cardboard ½″ wide. Cut a 6″ piece of carpet thread and lay it along one edge of the cardboard. Wind the four split strands of one color yarn around cardboard and thread, and wind two split strands of second color yarn around, on top of first color. Tie all strands together very tightly with the carpet thread; cut strands on opposite side. Fluff out pompon and trim yarn ends to a small pompon ⅜" to ½" in diameter.

To Transfer Designs: Enlarge patterns by copying on paper ruled in 1" squares. Trace patterns. Using white carbon paper on top of black fabric and a dry ball-point pen, go over main outlines of large flowers and stems.

To Work Designs: Following pattern and Color and Stitch Keys, make each three-dimensional piece. Using pattern as a guide, place pieces on background and tack in place with thread. When all pieces are sewn to background, embroider remaining parts of designs following colors marked on patterns (see stitch details on page 282).

To do embroidery, split tapestry yarn into four single-ply pieces and use a single ply (or use other fine yarn). Stems are outline stitch. Loop petals are lazy daisy stitch. Lines close together in an area are satin stitch; remaining lines are straight stitch.

To Frame: Stretch finished picture on mounting board. Insert pins through fabric into edges of mounting board, beginning at center of each side and working to corners (see mounting directions on page 281). Hammer pins into mounting board. Turn excess fabric to back and tape smoothly in place. Insert and secure picture in shadow-box frame with glass. Seal back by gluing wrapping paper tautly across back of frame.

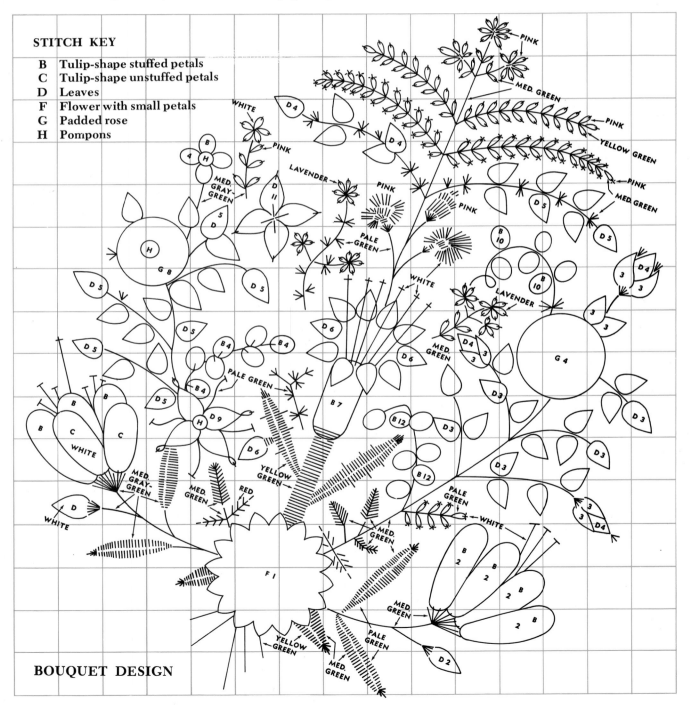

STITCH KEY

B	Tulip-shape stuffed petals
C	Tulip-shape unstuffed petals
D	Leaves
F	Flower with small petals
G	Padded rose
H	Pompons

BOUQUET DESIGN

COLOR KEY

No. 1 **Flower**	3 strands lavender 2 strands medium purple 2 strands plum		**No. 7** **Flower**	Three groups of— 2 strands salmon 2 strands pale brick red 1 strand white
No. 2 **Flower**	1 strand coral 4 strands gold 4 strands pale gold		**No. 8** **Flower**	3 strands pale brick red 3 strands white
No. 3 **Leaves**	3 strands dark green 3 strands medium green 1 strand light olive		**No. 9** **Flower**	2 strands dark gray-blue 2 strands medium gray-blue 2 strands light gray-blue 1 strand white
No. 4 **Flower**	1 strand medium rust 6 strands dark rust		**No. 10** **Flower**	6 strands medium purple
No. 5 **Leaves**	2 strands light gray-green 4 strands medium gray-green 1 strand dark gray-green		**No. 11** **Flower**	2 strands white 2 strands pale gold 3 strands gold 1 strand coral
No. 6 **Flower**	1 strand coral 2 strands salmon 3 strands pale brick red 1 strand white		**No. 12** **Flower**	6 strands lavender

VICTORIAN EMBROIDERED PARROT

An exotic parrot perched on a branch of brilliant blooms typifies the Victorian interest in naturalistic design. This "woolwork" picture is an old one, embroidered in cross-stitch on black monk's cloth. The parrot would also make a charming subject for a Victorian sofa pillow.

SIZE: Design area approximately 18½″ square.

EQUIPMENT: Large-eyed embroidery needle. Cross-stitch canvas (for linen). Hoop (optional). **For Blocking:** Rustproof thumbtacks. Soft wooden surface. Brown wrapping paper. Ruler. Square. Pencil.

MATERIALS: (**Note:** As black monk's cloth is not available, directions are given for working on linen, using Penelope (cross-stitch) canvas as stitch guide.) Black linen or linenlike fabric, 28″ x 28″, and Penelope (cross-stitch) canvas, 10-mesh-to-the-inch (design area about 18½″ square). Crewel wool or six-strand embroidery floss in colors listed in Color Key, 8-yard skeins, one skein each except for those with larger amounts given in parentheses. Heavy cardboard or ¼″ plywood for mounting, 23″ square. Masking tape.

DIRECTIONS: Read embroidery directions on page 280 and cross-stitch directions on page 284, referring to section on Penelope canvas. Antique picture was worked on black monk's cloth with wool. The stitches were counted and worked directly on the monk's cloth, using the even weave of the fabric as a guide; each cross-stitch covers one square of the weave. However, since black monk's cloth is not available, work picture in cross-stitch on linen over cross-stitch canvas.

Baste cross-stitch canvas, centered, over fabric first. Make basting stitches horizontally and vertically across center of fabric, then diagonally in opposite directions, then around sides. Work cross-stitches over canvas and through linen, following chart and Color Key. Leave background free. Be careful not to pull stitches too tightly, so that fabric is kept flat. An embroidery hoop will help to keep the fabric taut and stitches even. Work bottom half of all crosses in one direction, top half all in opposite direction. Make ends of adjoining crosses meet in same mesh of fabric (see cross-stitch detail on page 282). When cross-stitching is complete, pull away strands of canvas horizontally and vertically, one at a time, leaving the cross-stitches on the linen (see detail).

To block and mount, see pages 280–81.

COLOR KEY

⬡ Pale gray-green (2)	▮ Deep olive green	⊟ Gold
⬈ Medium gray-green (2)	⊟ Pale cocoa	▼ Antique gold
⬑ Dark gray-green (3)	⋁ Light cocoa	⋅ Pale mauve
⊠ Apple green	▪ Medium cocoa brown	⧄ Light mauve
⊠ Medium bright green	◤ Dark cocoa brown	⊠ Medium mauve
⬛ Deep green	⊞ Light red-brown	Ⓢ Dark mauve
⋮ Pale yellow-green	◩ Medium red-brown	⌐ Lavender
⊠ Light olive green	▼ Dark red-brown	‖ Purple
⊡ Olive green	⬅ Tan	▪ Deep purple

◆ Light blue
ⓦ Medium blue
◨ Dark blue
▢ Light coral
ⓨ Medium coral
⊟ Red
◪ Maroon

WILD FLOWER PRINTS

The natural beauty of wild flowers is captured with just a few simple stitches, chosen to portray the essence of each flower. From top left, the set consists of violets, bunchberry, wild rose, buttercups, clover, lady's slipper (or moccasin flower), and jack-in-the-pulpit. The thistle print that follows, shown in closer view, completes the set. Directions for all eight flower prints are given below; actual-size patterns with close-ups of suggested stitches are included.

EQUIPMENT: Scissors. Tracing paper. Pencil. Dressmaker's tracing (carbon) paper. Embroidery needle. Dry ball-point pen. Masking tape. **For Blocking:** Soft wooden surface. Brown wrapping paper. Square. Hammer. Rustproof thumbtacks.

MATERIALS: Linen, 12″ x 9″, for embroidery for each picture. Six-strand embroidery floss: for stems and leaves, light and dark green; for blossoms, colors as shown.

DIRECTIONS: Read directions for embroidery on page 280. Trace actual-size patterns. Transfer designs to linen, using dressmaker's carbon and dry ball-point pen.

Using four strands of six-strand embroidery floss in needle, work designs with simple embroidery stitches, such as straight, running, outline, lazy daisy, long and short, satin, backstitch, chain, French knot, blanket, and featherstitch. Work stitches in a loose, free manner.

To block and frame, see pages 280–81.

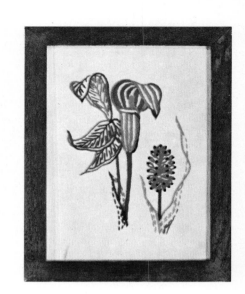

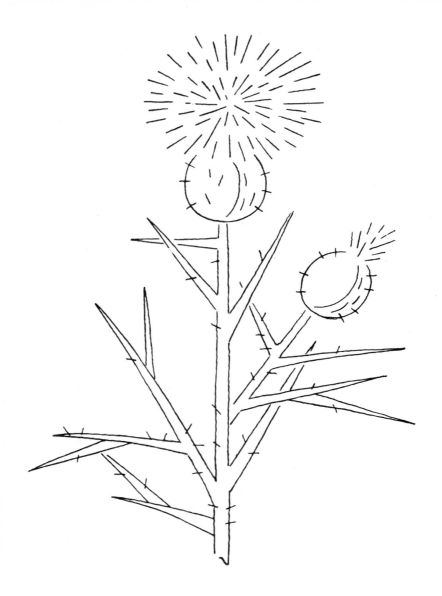

ASTERS IN A BASKET

Embroider a basket full of blooms on burlap with just two simple stitches and a variety of yarns. Choice of yarn is important in expressing the character of the flowers and the texture of the basket. Crisp asters are bold, straight stitches worked in a clear yellow and harmonizing colors of knitting worsted and a tweed yarn. Delicate Queen Anne's lace is created by working straight stitches in a loopy mohair. Basket is made with running and straight stitches of heather-tone yarn; background shows through "weave."

SIZE: 21¼" x 18".

EQUIPMENT: Paper for planning design. Tracing paper. Dressmaker's tracing (carbon) paper. Dry ballpoint pen. Masking tape. Pencil. Ruler. Scissors. Large-eyed embroidery and rug needles. Stapler. **For Framing:** Backsaw and miter box. Hammer. Flat paint brush.

MATERIALS: Dark gold burlap, 26¼" x 23". Knitting yarns in various weights and textures, such as mohair, knitting worsted, nubby, looped, and tweed yarns, in yellow and harmonizing colors. Canvas stretchers, 21¼" x 18". Pine stripping, ¼" thick, 1" wide, 7 ft. Small finishing nails. Wood stain in desired color. Heavy paper for backing picture. All-purpose glue.

DIRECTIONS: See embroidery directions on page 280. Assemble canvas stretchers to make frame 21¼" x 18". Stretch burlap over frame, being sure threads are straight; bring excess fabric to back and staple. Plan design on paper to fit the area of picture, using your own ideas for flower effects or following illustration. Sketch a semi-circular basket about 7½" wide and 4" deep; sketch circles for flowers (about 2½" in diameter) closely, with some overlapping others. Trace design. Tape tracing to fabric, with carbon between, placing it slightly below center. Go over lines of design with dry ball-point pen to transfer it to fabric.

To embroider, use the medium yarns, such as knitting worsted and sport yarn, double in the needle; finer yarns may be used with three, four, or more strands in the needle. The best effect is achieved if a wide variety of textured yarns is used, in tweed, heather, and solid colors. Embroider flowers in straight stitches fanning out from center, with a long stitch across center. Using a dark heather-tone yarn, outline basket first with long running stitches. Then take running stitches across basket in lines ¾" apart. Take long diagonal stitches across basket in two opposite directions, then vertical stitches.

When embroidery is finished, restretch burlap if necessary, to make it taut. Fold corners of fabric neatly and staple fabric to back of canvas stretchers. Measure and cut four pieces of pine stripping to fit around sides of picture, with mitered corners. Stain; let dry. Fit around picture and nail to canvas stretchers at corners and center of sides with finishing nails. Cut heavy paper slightly smaller than picture frame and glue across back of frame.

FRENCH KNOT FLOWERS

Here is a picture that has been worked in only two stitches—straight stitch and French knot. It illustrates how stitches can express the flowers, stems, and grasses in a meadow. The choice of yarn texture and color help portray various stages of meadow life: knitting worsted and bulky yarns for freshly blooming flowers; heather yarns and mohairs for flowers going to seed; soft, pale mohair for the faded undergrowth.

SIZE: 28" x 19".

EQUIPMENT: Paper for planning designs. Pencil. Scissors. Large-eyed embroidery and rug needles. Tape measure. Stapler. Hammer.

MATERIALS: Yellow burlap (or color desired), 34" x 24". Canvas stretchers (two 28" and two 19"). Knitting yarns in various weights and textures, such as knitting worsted, sport yarn, mohair, tweed and heather yarns, bulky yarns, in colors shown or as desired. Staples. Escutcheon pins (small brass-head nails). Heavy paper for backing picture. All-purpose glue.

DIRECTIONS: Only straight stitch and French knots are used for this picture.

Before starting, plan the design on paper, following the illustration or using your own ideas. Use medium-weight yarns, such as knitting worsted and sport yarn, double in the needle.

Canvas stretchers can be purchased in lengths from about 8" to 60", and the various lengths can be interchanged to make any size frame desired. Cut burlap for background about 3" larger all around than frame. Stretch burlap evenly over frame, bringing edges to the back; staple burlap to back of frame, keeping it taut. Be sure design area is planned to fit within inner area of canvas stretcher frame. Embroider on burlap, keeping design inside frame area.

Embroider stems first with long straight stitches, using sport yarn or knitting worsted double in the needle. Catch yarn under a thread of burlap at 2" or 3" intervals to hold yarn in place. Embroider flowers in French knots, using various colors and weights of yarn. Place French knots on both sides of stems as shown and top each stem with a French knot. After stems and flowers are complete, fill in bottom portion between and over stems with pale mohair, using straight stitches; mohair should be double in the needle.

When embroidery is finished, restretch burlap, if necessary, to make it taut. Hammer escutcheon pins into sides of each corner to hold corner folds neatly. Cut heavy paper slightly smaller than the picture frame; glue paper to back of frame.

GARDEN POTPOURRI

The colorful garden of flowers shown on the next page is actually an embroidery stitch sampler of more than 30 stitches! The design is based on a simple scheme of diagonals and circles embroidered on monk's cloth in a variety of yarns.

SIZE: 15" x 13¾".

EQUIPMENT: Tracing paper for pattern. Pencil. Dressmaker's tracing (carbon) paper. Dry ball-point pen. Scissors. Embroidery needles. Sewing needle and black thread. Ruler. Compass. Tack hammer (for mounting).

MATERIALS: Linen, homespun, or monk's cloth 21" x 20". Embroidery yarns such as three-ply Persian, crewel, knitting worsted, six-strand embroidery floss. Fiberboard ¼" thick for mounting. Straight pins. Masking tape.

DIRECTIONS: Read embroidery directions on page 280. Picture may be worked using stitches shown, or you can create your own flower-strewn picture and embroider with the stitches you like best.

To plan a design similar to this one, follow diagram and directions. Mark picture area on paper, 15" x 13¾". Using ruler and following diagram, mark the lines for diagonal background bands. The width of the diagonal bands varies from ½" for narrowest to 1" for widest, with most of them about ¾" wide. Using a compass, mark circles for flowers, ranging from ¾" diameter for smallest to 3¼" diameter for largest. Scatter the flower circles approximately as shown, overlapping edges of some. When

arrangement seems satisfactory, erase the diagonal lines that are under the flower circles to get a clearer view of design.

Bind raw edges of fabric with masking tape to prevent raveling. Mark embroidery area outline 15″ x 13¾″ on fabric with running stitch and black thread, being sure lines are straight with weave of fabric. Pin pattern on fabric matching outlines, and insert dressmaker's carbon between. Go over lines of pattern with dry ball-point pen to transfer design to fabric.

For embroidery, use Persian yarn split to two plies for most stitches, one ply for very fine stitches. An interesting texture may be obtained by combining Persian yarn with six-strand floss or knitting worsted in two-color stitches,

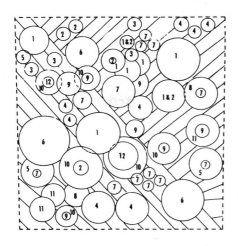

1 Straight stitch
2 French knots
3 Woven spider web
4 Turkey work
5 Couching
6 Satin stitch
7 Whipped spider web
8 Burden stitch
9 Split stitch
10 Lazy daisy
11 Bullion stitch
12 Trellis filling

such as the cloud filling, couching, and burden stitch. For large French knots, use knitting worsted or the full three strands of Persian yarn double; for small French knots use one or two strands of Persian yarn.

Embroider flowers first, following diagram and stitch key, using colors shown or as desired. Embroidery stitch details are on page 282. When flower embroidery is complete, fill in diagonal bands for background, using various shades of green. Embroider bands in a variety of stitches,

such as long and short stitch, cloud filling, chain stitch in touching rows, buttonhole stitch, herringbone stitch, French knots, Van Dyke stitch, zigzag chain, straight featherstitch, seeding stitch, open Cretan stitch, split stitch, closed Roumanian stitch, sheaf stitch, fishbone stitch.

When embroidery is complete, mount, following directions on page 281.

FRUIT AND FLOWER PANEL

A cheerful trio of fruit and flower arrangements is stitched on pale linen and mounted on wooden stretchers for a bright, country-look panel.

MOUNTED SIZE: 12″ x 26″.

EQUIPMENT: Paper for pattern. Pencil. Ruler. Scissors. Tracing paper. White dressmaker's tracing (carbon) paper. White pencil. Dry ball-point pen. Masking tape. Embroidery frame or hoop. Sewing and embroidery needles. Staple gun.

MATERIALS: Medium blue tightly woven linen-type fabric for embroidery, 17″ x 31″. White sewing thread. Persian three-ply yarn (8.8-yard skeins): See color key for colors and number of skeins (in parentheses). Wooden canvas stretchers, 12″ x 26″ (available at art supply stores). Staples.

DIRECTIONS: Lightly mark exact area of picture, 12″ x 26″, in center of blue fabric. Leaving at least 2½″ of fabric beyond marked outline, follow thread of fabric with sewing needle and white thread and take ¼″ running stitches over marked lines to mark guidelines around entire picture.

Enlarge pattern by copying on 1″ squares. Trace pattern. Place tracing on fabric with dressmaker's carbon paper between, matching pattern borders to stitched outline. Tape tracing and carbon to fabric to hold in place. Using dry ball-point pen, transfer all design lines to fabric. Remove tracing and carbon. To keep lines clear while embroidering, use sharp white pencil to clarify design lines as needed.

Stretch fabric in embroidery frame or hoop. To embroider, use two plies of the three-ply yarn in needle. Embroider pictures following stitch and color keys and stitch details (on page 282). Fine lines in design areas indicate directions of stitches.

To finish, place embroidery face down on padded ironing board. Steam-press wrinkles and puckers out gently.

To mount, assemble canvas stretchers to 12″ x 26″. Center fabric, right side up, over canvas stretcher frame. With staple gun, staple fabric to sides of canvas stretcher. Turn raw edges of fabric under; staple to back of canvas stretcher.

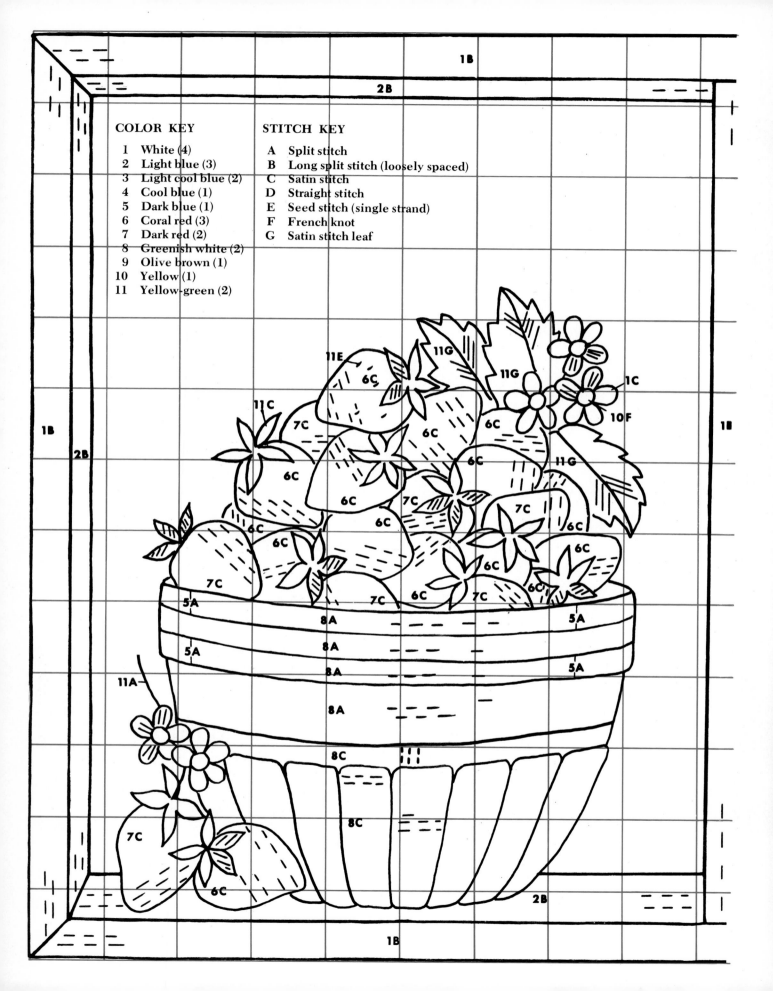

COLOR KEY

1 White (4)
2 Light blue (3)
3 Light cool blue (2)
4 Cool blue (1)
5 Dark blue (1)
6 Coral red (3)
7 Dark red (2)
8 Greenish white (2)
9 Olive brown (1)
10 Yellow (1)
11 Yellow-green (2)

STITCH KEY

A Split stitch
B Long split stitch (loosely spaced)
C Satin stitch
D Straight stitch
E Seed stitch (single strand)
F French knot
G Satin stitch leaf

POSY WALL HANGING

In an original and practical design, the embroidered felt flower has a mirror center and a flowerpot pocket to hold a comb and lipstick for quick touch-ups before dinner guests arrive. Nine embroidery stitches are used to add textural interest to the flower and flowerpot.

SIZE: 22″ x 10″, design area.

EQUIPMENT: Ruler. Pencil. Paper for patterns. Tracing paper. Scissors. Large-eyed embroidery needle. Dressmaker's tracing (carbon) paper. Tracing wheel. Small flat paintbrush. Hammer. Wire-cutting pliers.

MATERIALS: Homespun fabric, dark blue, 26″ x 14″. Felt, 9″ x 12″ pieces: one piece each bright pink, cerise, chartreuse, light yellow-green, medium yellow-green, dark green. Pearl cotton No. 5, one ball each of the colors listed in color key. Unframed mirror 8″ in diameter. Sewing thread to match felt. Heavy mounting cardboard 22½″

x 11¾″. All-purpose glue. Plywood or hardboard, ⅛″ thick, 26½″ x 15½″. Blue enamel paint. Small nails.

DIRECTIONS: Enlarge patterns for felt pieces (heavy outlines) by copying on paper ruled in 1″ squares; complete half- and quarter-patterns indicated by long dash lines. Trace patterns. Heavy lines indicate felt pieces, finer lines are embroidery. Letters and numbers indicate stitches and colors.

Using dressmaker's carbon and tracing wheel, transfer pattern pieces to felt as follows: piece L on bright pink (cut pattern in half on half-pattern line and carefully fit

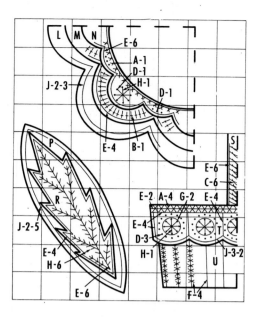

STITCH KEY

  A **Crossed blanket**
  B **Roumanian**
  C **Open Cretan**
  D **French knot**
  E **Outline stitch**
  F **Cross-stitch**
  G **Chain stitch**
  H **Straight stitch**
  J **Threaded herringbone**

COLOR KEY

  1 **Pink**
  2 **Rose**
  3 **Light yellow-green**
  4 **Medium yellow-green**
  5 **Dark yellow-green**
  6 **Emerald green**

and mark two semicircles on the 9″ x 12″ felt); piece M on cerise; piece N on light yellow-green; two pieces P on chartreuse; two pieces R on medium yellow-green; pieces T and U on dark green. Do not cut out felt pieces until embroidery is complete. Mark stem ¾″ x 9″ on medium yellow-green felt. Cut the pink pieces on half-pattern line and cut out centers; place edges together to form a complete circle; tack straight edges together so circle can be embroidered in a continuous line. With contrasting thread and running stitch, sew over outlines of each felt piece.

Following stitch and color keys and finer lines on patterns, embroider each piece, except crossed blanket stitch on inner edge of piece N and top edge of piece T. When embroidery is finished, cut out felt pieces on outlines just outside embroidery; cut out centers of pieces M, N. Place felt pieces together as indicated on pattern;

baste. Slip-stitch pieces in place, using matching thread. On inner edge of flower and top edge of pot, work crossed blanket stitch through all thicknesses of felt pieces.

Place felt pieces on blue homespun as shown; baste. Slip-stitch felt pieces to homespun background fabric with matching thread; leave center and one side of flower open to insert mirror; leave top of pot open for pocket. Insert mirror and slip-stitch opening closed.

Stretch homespun background over mounting board, being sure the threads of fabric are straight. Fold excess fabric to back and glue in place. Paint plywood board with two coats of enamel. When dry, center mirror panel on plywood and fasten with small nails near the four corners of mirror panel. Hammer nails in through front of mirror panel, into plywood. Carefully lift homespun up over nail heads, letting heads slip through fabric to inside. Snip off nail points on back with wire-cutting pliers.

TWO FRUIT PICTURES

Luscious red cherries and a ripe red apple are yarn-embroidered in easy stitches to make two companion kitchen hangings. The "scrollwork" on the frames is really painted macaroni!

SIZE: 13⅛″ x 11⅜″, framed.

EQUIPMENT: Paper for patterns. Pencil. Ruler. Tracing paper. Dressmaker's tracing (carbon) paper. Tracing wheel. Large-eyed embroidery needle. Embroidery hoop. Scissors. **For Blocking:** Brown wrapping paper. Square. Rustproof thumbtacks. Soft wooden surface. **For**

Framing: Saw. Hammer. Small piece of wire screen. Small paintbrush.

MATERIALS: For Each: Natural-color coarse linen or cotton fabric, 14″ x 12″. Crewel wool, tapestry yarn, or knitting worsted for embroidery: bright and medium red, light and medium yellow-green, light and medium blue-

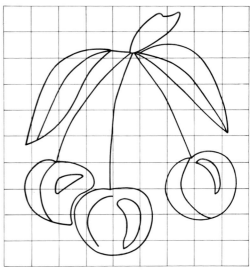

Copy on paper ruled in 1″ squares.

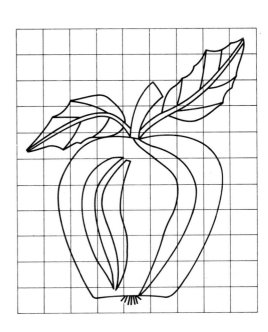

green, light and medium brown. Carpet tacks. Tape. **For Framing:** Wood or heavy cardboard, ⅛″ thick, 12¾″ x 10¾″. Pressed board, ½″ thick, 17⅜″ x 14¾″. Wood stripping, ¼″ thick, ⅞″ wide, 10′. Small finishing nails. Wood glue. Shellac. Macaroni: small elbows and wagon wheels. Flat white paint, spray can, and small jar.

DIRECTIONS: Enlarge patterns by copying on paper ruled in 1″ squares. Trace patterns. Center tracing on fabric with carbon between. Go over design carefully with tracing wheel to transfer.

Place fabric in hoop. Embroider, using one or more kinds of yarn. Make apple and cherries bright red with medium red accents. Make apple leaves light yellow-green with medium yellow-green veins; make stems and bottom of apple medium brown. Embroider cherry stems and half of leaves in medium yellow-green, and half of leaves in light blue-green, with dividing line medium blue-green; make twig at top light brown. See stitch details on page 282. For cherry picture, work the stems in outline stitch. Outline cherries, leaves, and twig and fill each in with rows of split stitch. For apple picture, work leaves, stem, and leaf veins in rows of outline stitch. Outline apple and fill in with rows of split stitch. Work bottom end of apple in straight stitches.

When embroidery is finished, block and mount, following directions on pages 280–81, using finishing nails if mounting on wood.

Frame: For each picture, saw stripping into four pieces: two 15¼″, two 17⅜″ long. Glue and nail these pieces around outside of pressed board with butt joints. Saw remaining stripping into four pieces: two 11⅜″, two 12⅞″. Glue and nail them together with butt joints to make frame 13⅛″ x 11⅜″. Place this frame in center of larger frame; toenail and glue smaller frame in place on larger frame.

Shellac entire frame and let dry. Spray-paint frame. Place wagon-wheel macaroni in each corner, centered between the two frames. Make pattern with four elbows back to back on each side of wheels. Fill in area between the frames with alternating pattern of wheel and four elbows (see illustration). Mark placement. Remove these macaroni, place on piece of wire screen; dip in white paint until macaroni is well coated with paint; let dry. Touch up any spots missed with paintbrush. When dry, glue on frame as previously arranged. Spray entire frame with paint; let dry. Push picture into center frame; nail picture in place at thickly embroidered area. Lift embroidered fabric carefully to cover the nailheads.

ROOSTER, FLOWERS, AND FRUIT PANEL

A bright addition to any kitchen wall, embroidered felt and fabric pieces are appliquéd to a cheery background in an easy-to-make collage.

SIZE: 23″ x 16″.

EQUIPMENT: Scissors. Pencil. Paper for patterns. Ruler. Needle. Compass.

MATERIALS: Upholstery or other heavy fabric, deep blue, orange, each 23½″ x 16½″. Orange cotton fabric 13″ x 14″. Felt: small amounts of hunter, emerald, and Kelly green; chartreuse; red; bright and pale yellow; orange; light blue. Sewing thread: blue, yellow, green, red, orange. Pale yellow embroidery floss. Fine wool yarn for embroidery: white, russet, coral, pale yellow-green, dark olive green, Kelly green, purple, blue, orange.

DIRECTIONS: See directions for appliquéing on page 284. Refer to stitch details on page 282. Enlarge patterns by copying on paper ruled in 1″ squares; complete half-patterns indicated by long dash lines. Cut piece of orange fabric 10″ x 13″; cut section 1½″ x 6¼″ from right-hand corner of one 13″ edge as shown. Cut 4″-diameter circle of orange fabric. Cut rectangle of blue felt 10″ x 5″. Appliqué these pieces, turning edges of large orange piece under ¼″, to right side of blue upholstery fabric as shown, with

buttonhole stitch, using matching sewing thread. Do not turn edges of felt under when appliquéing. Cut rooster of Kelly green felt; cut feet, wattle, and comb of red; cut wing of yellow felt. Appliqué rooster on orange rectangle as shown. Sew feet, wattle, and comb in place. Sew on rooster. Make eye in satin stitch with purple yarn. Trim neck with row of chain stitch in orange yarn, row of couching with pale yellow floss, row of zigzag straight stitches in orange yarn, and another in purple yarn. Work chain stitch with purple yarn around wing, then outline stitch with orange yarn, outline stitch again with blue yarn, and last, chain stitch with yellow floss. For tail feathers, work curved rows in thorn stitch with yellow floss. With olive green yarn, make a vertical line of chain stitch from bottom of orange circle to 1″ above bottom of orange rectangle. Cut two medium leaves of chartreuse, two large of hunter green, one small of emerald green, and one small of pale yellow felt; sew in place. Embroider veins in straight stitches with blue, yellow-green, and Kelly green yarn as shown. Cut flower of pale yellow and center of

Wall hanging patterns; enlarge on 1″ squares.

bright yellow felt; sew onto orange circle. Work chain stitch around center with russet yarn. Make straight stitches on petals radiating from center, alternating long stitch in yellow floss, and short stitch in white yarn. Cut butterfly of pale yellow felt, apple of red felt, apple leaves of hunter and emerald green, pear of orange felt, pear leaves of hunter green and chartreuse; sew to blue rectangle and background as shown. Work butterfly an-tennae in chain stitch with white yarn on one side and coral yarn on other side. Make two rows of chain stitch with white yarn on one side of butterfly.

Place blue and orange fabric with right sides facing and sew together ½″ from edges along sides and bottom. Turn to right side, push out corners neatly. Turn edges of opening in ½″ and slip-stitch closed. Sew loop on back near each top corner and center for hanging.

Designs From Nature

WINTER MOON WALL HANGING

A winter woodland scene of graceful pines and tall, slim trees silhouetted against a yellow moon is appliquéd and embroidered in bold black-on-black on a white background. The moon and three large trees are appliquéd; the distant trees are worked in running stitches. The pine branches are done in chain and outline stitches; pine needles are long and short "freehand" stitches. The tree bark effect is created by couching long strands of knitting worsted and rug yarn.

SIZE: 40″ x 35″.

EQUIPMENT: Large sheet of paper for pattern. Tracing paper. Yardstick. Pencil. Scissors. Large- and small-eyed embroidery needles. Dressmaker's tracing (carbon) paper. Dry ball-point pen. Staple gun. Hammer. Straight pins.

MATERIALS: White cotton fabric, 39″ wide, 1¼ yards. Black cotton fabric, 36″ wide, ¼ yard. Lemon-yellow cotton fabric, 7″ square. Sewing thread: black, yellow. Black knitting and embroidery yarns, small amounts of each as follows: wool rug yarn, knitting worsted, fingering yarn or crewel wool, heavy crochet cotton, six-strand embroidery floss. Canvas stretchers, 40″ x 35″. Scraps of ¼″ x 1″ pine strips for bracing. Small wire brads. Staples.

DIRECTIONS: Enlarge pattern by copying on paper ruled in 1″ squares. Trace pattern. Make a separate pattern for each tree trunk numbered 1, 2, and 3; cut these out of black fabric.

Cut white fabric 44″ x 39″. With dressmaker's carbon and dry ball-point pen, transfer tree trunks and branches onto the white fabric, placing tops of trees 2″ down from one 39″ edge, and leaving equal margins at sides. Baste the three fabric tree trunks in place. Cut moon 6¼″ in diameter from yellow fabric; baste moon behind smallest tree as shown. Sew in place with blind stitches, using black thread for trees and yellow for moon. Outline foliage on boughs using black thread and running stitch.

Refer to stitch details on page 282. For bark texture on fabric tree trunks, couch long strands of rug yarn and knitting worsted along the length of the trunks, using regular couching stitch and large herringbone stitch to couch some strands, use crochet cotton or fine yarn for couching.

Embroider remaining tree trunks given in pattern in outline stitch, using fine yarn for larger ones and two or three strands of six-strand embroidery floss for the smaller ones. Fill in trunks with vertical rows of outline stitch 1⁄16″ apart, or leave some unfilled.

Remainder of trees shown in illustration, but not given in pattern, are either one or two rows of outline stitch, using two strands of embroidery floss, or running stitch with one strand of floss for the most distant trees. Place these trees following illustration.

All branches are embroidered. To work them, use knitting worsted for the thickest ones, making chain stitch for the heaviest part and tapering with outline stitch out to tips. Use fine yarn and outline stitch for medium branches and two strands of embroidery floss in outline stitch for finest branches. On the foliage boughs, the branches are indicated on the pattern by heavy lines at top edge of foliage that extend onto fabric tree.

To embroider branch foliage, long and short stitches were used to fill in the outlined areas, with straight stitches jutting out at angles over the outline to resemble pine boughs. Use knitting worsted for long-and-short-stitch areas and for pine needles on larger boughs. Use fine yarn or six strands of embroidery floss for the smaller boughs. Remove thread outlines from foliage.

Assemble canvas stretchers to make a rectangle 40″ x 35″. To prevent wood from showing through, cover front and sides of canvas stretcher frame with strips of white fabric. These may be glued on. Nail a bracing strip across each corner on back of stretchers. Stretch embroidered piece across frame, with tops of trees at top of one 35″ length. Keep fabric taut, but do not pull out of shape; use straight pins to hold fabric along side edges while straightening and stretching it on frame. In order to achieve the desired effect in the picture, it is important to mount the fabric straight on the frame. To do this, pin the center of opposite sides first to center points of frame; then centers of top and bottom. Continue stretching opposite sides evenly from center to corners. When piece is evenly stretched on frame, fold edges of fabric to back of frame and staple securely in place all around; remove pins.

Pattern for Winter Moon Hanging and tree trunks; enlarge on 1″ squares.

GROWTH WALL HANGING

This stunning wall hanging bursts forth with energy as new growth emerges from earth. An appliquéd sun radiates in swirls of couched yarn. The strata are embroidered in chain and outline stitches; the seeds and buds are worked in French knots, the roots in outline, and the seedlings with straight stitches.

SIZE: 48″ x 28″.

EQUIPMENT: Paper at least 48″ x 28″. Yardstick. Pencil. Large and small embroidery needles. Hammer. Miter box. Backsaw. Dressmaker's tracing (carbon) paper, dark and light.

MATERIALS: Heavy pink cotton fabric 38″ x 34″. Heavy olive green cotton fabric 18″ x 34″. Light orange cotton fabric 19″ diameter. Medium olive green fabric 26″ long, about 6″ wide. Rug yarns (about ½ skein each): orange, bright pink, medium and dark rust. Lightweight wool yarn, such as three-ply crewel wool: bright pink, medium bright green, light olive green, medium olive green, dark olive green, dark blue, turquoise, purple. Sewing thread: orange, pink, rust. Canvas stretchers: two 28″ and two 48″. Rustproof thumbtacks. Pieces of pine stripping for bracing: four about 10″ long, one 28″ long. Small brads. All-purpose glue. **For Frame:** Narrow walnut picture molding 1½″ deep, with rabbet, 13-foot length.

DIRECTIONS: Seam one 34″ edge of pink fabric to 34″ edge of heavy olive green fabric. The picture can be worked by following the illustration, in your own interpretation. Or, if you wish to make a pattern, rule lines over the illustration ¼″ apart horizontally and vertically. To enlarge to actual size, rule 1″ squares on paper 48″ x 28″ and transpose lines of design from ¼″ squares to 1″ squares. Transfer design to fabric with dark and light carbon paper.

Cut sun, which is approximately 18″ in diameter, from light orange fabric. Baste in place on pink portion of background and slip-stitch to background without turning in edges. Following illustration for color, couch pink and orange rug yarn on and around sun. (See stitch details, page 282.) Over outer couching, work wide herringbone stitch. Below sun, work sprouting seedlings in straight stitches with French knots at tips. Cut medium olive green fabric for stratum below seedling roots and machine-stitch in place across dark olive background in rows following contour of piece. Embroider two rows of purple chain stitch across this stratum at right side. Embroider roots in light and dark olive green outline stitch. Work the various strata below in rows of chain stitch and rows of outline stitch. Couch rust rug yarn strata on background. Work seeds in strata in light olive green French knots.

Join the canvas stretchers to make frame 48″ x 28″. Stretch embroidery over frame; bring excess fabric to back; thumbtack all around with tacks ½″ apart.

To brace frame, nail one 10″ piece of pine stripping diagonally across back of each corner of frame. Nail 28″ brace horizontally across center back. Attach picture wire for hanging to top braces.

Picture may be hung unframed or, as shown, with a narrow frame. To make frame, measure and cut walnut picture molding for top, bottom, and sides, mitering ends with miter box and backsaw. Glue and nail pieces together. Insert picture in frame and hold in place with brads hammered through back of frame rabbet and into stretchers, on top, bottom, and sides.

MIDNIGHT SUN PICTURE

The midnight sun rides above the horizon, an aurora borealis flashes across the sky in an original design symbolic of the Arctic summer. Triangles and quadrangles in combinations of warm and cool colors are appliquéd to a heavy cotton background; zigzag lines in varied hues are worked in outline stitch.

SIZE: Approximately 23½″ x 18″.

EQUIPMENT: Pencil. Ruler. Compass. Scissors. Straight pins. Sewing and embroidery needles. Steam iron.

MATERIALS: Tightly woven cotton fabric: medium gray, 10¼″ x 22″, navy blue, 12″ x 20″, and medium blue, 7″ x 20″, for background; scraps of bright-colored fabric for design in colors illustrated. Large piece of thin, easy-to-cut cardboard. Sewing thread to match fabrics. Small amounts of six-strand embroidery floss: lavender, pink, light green, and light yellow. Heavy mounting cardboard, 23½″ x 18″.

DIRECTIONS: Place three background pieces of fabric out flat, gray at top, navy in middle, medium blue at bottom. Overlap and arrange on diagonals as illustrated, to form a rectangle 27½″ x 22″. With right sides facing, pin together where they meet and then sew across; cut away excess fabric.

For sun design, mark 13″-diameter circle on cardboard with pencil; from same center, mark 9″- and 6″-diameter circles. Make circles slightly uneven for interesting effect (see illustration). In small center circle, mark off 9 uneven triangles; mark next section into 13 uneven quadrilateral areas. Mark outer section with zigzag lines, making about 33 triangular areas. Cut center circle and two rings out of cardboard, taking care not to cut perfect circles as the unevenness adds to the design. Then cut into individual areas. Following appliqué directions on page 284, mark outline of cardboard on fabric and mark seam allowance all around, ¼″ wide. Cut fabric for each piece in same manner. Replace cardboard on wrong side of fabric; press seam allowances up. Fit all pieces together. Sew together by hand with slip-stitch; start with center pieces and work out. Then appliqué entire piece to background; see illustration for placement.

On cardboard, mark a strip 20″ long, about 2″ wide, making outer lines uneven to create effect illustrated. Then divide into 11 quadrilateral areas. Cut out cardboard pieces and fabric as for sun; sew together, then sew to background.

With three strands of pastel floss in needle, work uneven zigzag lines of outline stitch as illustrated.

Mount on cardboard, 23½″ x 18″.

Animal Personalities

SPRING PICTURE

CREWEL MOTIFS

Lively motifs in exciting crewel embroidery depict the delights of spring and fall. Stitch a 13″ square pillow or picture on monk's cloth as shown, or use the individual motifs to decorate bags, belts, pincushions— anything! Some of the stitches: padded satin, bullion, French knots, outline.

SIZE: 13″ square as shown.

EQUIPMENT: Paper for patterns. Tracing paper. Pencil. Dressmaker's carbon paper. Ruler. Embroidery needles. Embroidery scissors. **For Blocking:** Brown wrapping paper. Soft wooden surface. Thumbtacks. **For Mounting:** Mat knife (or single-edged razor blade). Masking tape. Tack hammer.

MATERIALS: White fine monk's cloth or other even-weave fabric, 18″ square for each picture as shown (or size to accommodate motifs desired plus 3″ extra all around). Persian yarns (3-ply), small amounts of colors listed in color keys. Heavy mounting cardboard for each picture as shown, 13″ square. Straight pins. Frame as desired.

DIRECTIONS: Enlarge patterns by copying on paper ruled in 1″ squares. Trace all designs or individual motifs as desired. Place tracings on fabric in positions desired,

with dressmaker's carbon between. Transfer motifs to fabric by tracing over lines of patterns; remove patterns and carbon.

Embroidering: Split the 3-ply yarn (or use single crewel strands) into single strands and use one strand in needle for all embroidery except French knots on goldenrod motif (use two strands in the needle for this). Work embroidery in colors and stitches indicated by letters and numbers on patterns. For direction of stitches and blending of colors, refer to color illustrations on pages 94 and 95. Follow stitch details on page 282 for embroidering. Be sure embroidery covers all transfer lines, but in order to keep shapes, do not go outside lines any more than necessary.

For the birds and animals, work the stitches in each part of the body to give realistic shaping (see illustrations).

On flowers where bullion stitch is used, make one stitch

FALL PICTURE

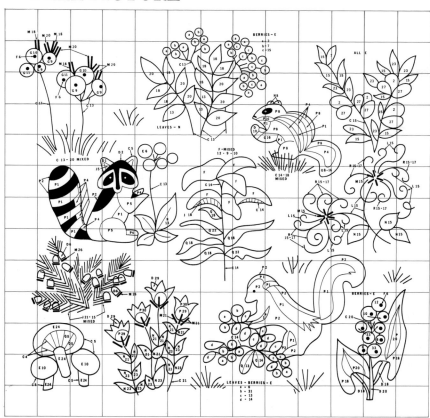

COLOR KEY FOR FALL PICTURE

1   Creamy white
2   Black
4   Medium gray-brown
5   Deep sand
6   Red
7   Dark blue
8   Dark copper
9   Deep golden yellow
10 Gold
11 Light gold
12 Bright yellow
13 Medium yellow-green
14 Forest green
15 Medium blue-green
16 Pale gold
17 Light green
18 Dark chartreuse
20 Medium chartreuse
21 Bright green
22 Light yellow-green
23 Light bright green
24 Pale chartreuse
26 Purple
27 Royal blue
29 Light blue
30 Light aqua
31 Dark red
33 Light orange

STITCH KEY

A   Chain stitch
B   Lazy daisy stitch
C   Outline stitch
D   Satin stitch
E   Padded satin stitch
F   French knot
G   French knot on stalk
H   Buttonhole stitch
J   Straight stitch
K   Laid stitch tied diagonally
L   Backstitch
M   Bullion stitch
N   Close fly stitch
P   Long and short stitch
Q   Close herringbone
R   Pekinese stitch

over each heavy straight line; make bullion stitches after other embroidery is done in the area.

To work buttonhole stitch on hummingbird in wing area, work stitch in shell shape as indicated in two sections on pattern. For laid work on head, lay stitches lengthwise across in color 15 and tie down with color 22.

On wren wing, work alternate rows of color 5 and color 4.

In upper wing area of remaining bird, make straight stitches at top of divisions in color 4 as indicated, then work buttonhole stitches in lower part with color 18, making ends of stitches blend into straight stitches. On bottom part of wing, alternate rows of color 1, color 16, and color 4. Alternate straight stitches in tail of color 16 and color 4.

On morning glory leaves, work laid stitches across leaves first, then work veins over yarn of laid stitch.

For flowers in upper left of Fall Picture, work buttonhole stitch around each circle with ends of stitches converging at center.

If making complete pictures as shown, add small patches of grass in spaces between motifs, using outline stitch for each blade.

When embroidery is complete, block and mount following directions on pages 280–81.

SIX DOG PORTRAITS

Six handsome show dogs—beagle, German shepherd, boxer, Boston terrier, cocker spaniel and collie—make a charming set of cross-stitch "prints." Worked over Penelope canvas, with the canvas threads drawn out afterward, the dogs were embroidered in natural colors with embroidery floss on linen.

SIZE: 7″ x 9″ each.

EQUIPMENT: Ruler. Pencil. Scissors. Embroidery and sewing needles. Embroidery hoop (optional). Rust-proof thumbtacks. Basting thread. Penelope (cross-stitch) canvas, 7-mesh-to-the-inch, about 7″ x 9″ for each picture.

MATERIALS (for each picture): White or cream linen, 10″ x 12″. Six-strand embroidery floss: one skein of each color indicated on Color Key (less will be needed if making all six dogs). Heavy cardboard. Frame, 7″ x 9″, rabbet size.

DIRECTIONS: Read embroidery directions on page 280 and cross-stitch directions on page 284, referring to section on Penelope canvas. Fold each piece of linen in half horizontally, then vertically, to find center. Mark point with pin. Carefully center canvas over center point of linen and baste. Use full six strands of embroidery floss in needle. Follow chart for each picture, working over canvas and through linen. Each square of chart represents one stitch. Find center point of design on chart and begin working cross-stitches from center, following chart for placement of colors.

When design is completed, remove basting threads and draw out canvas threads, leaving the embroidered cross-stitch on linen. Block embroidery as directed on page 280, and frame.

NOTE: The design may also be worked on counted-thread fabric, without using the Penelope canvas.

BOSTON TERRIER

Light, medium, and dark green, black, navy, white, very dark brown, medium and dark gray.

BEAGLE

Light, medium, and dark green, white, black, gold and very deep gold, navy, medium and dark gray, medium and dark brown.

COCKER SPANIEL

Light medium, and dark green, black, navy, dark gray, medium blue-gray.

COLLIE

Light, medium, and dark green, white, black, very deep gold, medium and very dark brown, toast, medium gray.

GERMAN SHEPHERD

Light, medium, and dark green, black, light and dark beige, deep gold, navy, dark brown, dark toast, dark gray.

BOXER

Light, medium, and dark green, white, deep gold, medium, medium-dark, and very dark brown, medium gray, toast.

COLOR KEY

◼ Black	◢ Deep gold	▨ Medium green
◼ Navy	● Gold	+ Light green
◢ Very dark brown	◺ Dark toast	S Dark beige
▼ Dark brown	○ Toast	− Light beige
◹ Medium-dark brown	▯ Dark gray	◼ Medium blue-gray
◻ Medium brown	▲ Medium gray	• White
▬ Very deep gold	◧ Dark green	

BEAGLE

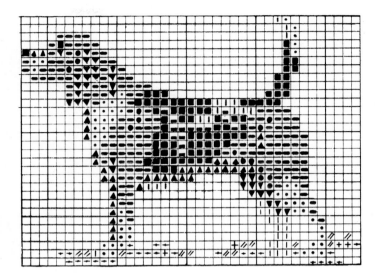

GERMAN SHEPHERD

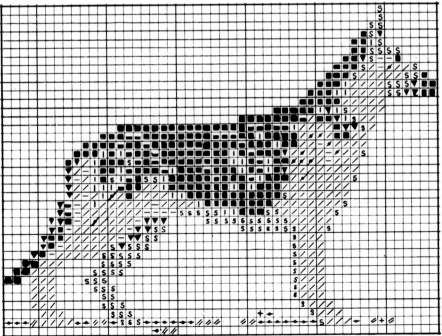

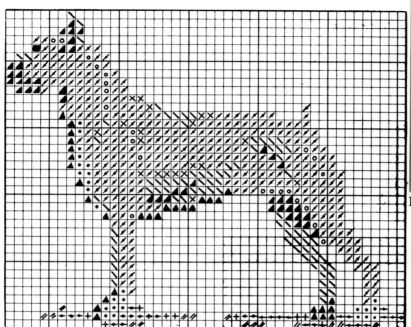

BOXER

BOSTON TERRIER

COLOR KEY

- ■ Black
- ⊟ Navy
- ◣ Very dark brown
- ▼ Dark brown
- ◹ Medium-dark brown
- ⊠ Medium brown
- ⊟ Very deep gold
- ◿ Deep gold
- ⊡ Gold
- ◺ Dark toast

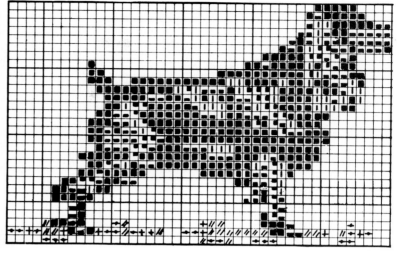

COCKER SPANIEL

COLLIE

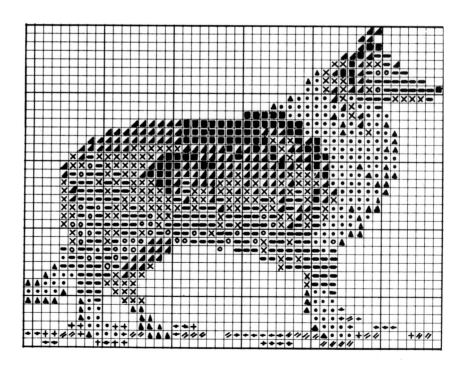

◯	Toast
I	Dark gray
▲	Medium gray
➡	Dark green
⧄	Medium green
+	Light green
S	Dark beige
−	Light beige
▣	Medium blue-gray
•	White

TURTLE PICTURE

A color-clad turtle and winged pals create a delightful picture embroidered in wool, with chain and split stitches predominating. The hanging is mounted on wood and framed with twisted cord.

SIZE: Approximately 12″ x 16″.

EQUIPMENT: Paper for pattern. Soft and hard-lead pencils. Ruler. Tracing paper. Dressmaker's tracing (carbon) paper. Masking tape. Scissors. Large-eyed embroidery needle. Stapler. Straight pins.

MATERIALS: Natural-color linen 17″ x 21″. Yarn, such as knitting worsted: small amounts of bright yellow, golden yellow, orange, shocking pink, soft pink, brown, olive green, pale green, white, dark red, black; medium yellow-green, 19 yards for cord. Canvas stretcher strips, two 12″ and two 16″. Staples. All-purpose glue.

DIRECTIONS: Enlarge pattern by copying on paper ruled in 1″ squares. Trace pattern. Place tracing on right side of fabric with carbon between, making sure there are equal margins all around; tape in place. Go over lines of tracing with hard-lead pencil to transfer design to fabric. Remove tracing, carbon.

Work embroidery, following stitch and color keys. See details for stitches on page 282. Use one strand of yarn in needle throughout, unless otherwise specified. Work the stems that are not marked on pattern in split stitch with olive green yarn; work the leaves that are not marked in lazy daisy stitch with olive green yarn. Work two lines of outline stitch in brown along bottom edge of turtle body. For the lines of both butterfly antennae and ladybug antennae, split brown yarn and use only single ply to work in split stitch. Work the bird beak and feet with small straight stitches, using orange yarn.

When embroidery is finished, assemble canvas stretcher according to instructions, and then stretch embroidered linen over stretcher tautly, being sure threads of fabric are straight; staple fabric securely on back. With medium yellow-green yarn, make twisted cord with four strands, long enough to fit around picture (see instructions on page 287). Glue cord all around picture, using pins to hold it in place until glue dries.

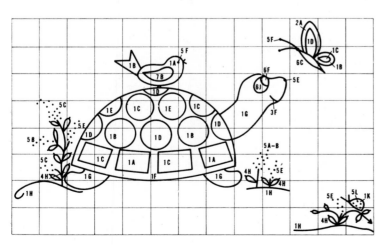

COLOR KEY

A Bright yellow
B Golden yellow
C Orange
D Shocking pink
E Soft pink
F Brown
G Olive green
H Pale green
J White
K Dark red
L Black

STITCH KEY

1 Split stitch
2 Chain stitch
3 Outline stitch
4 Lazy daisy stitch
5 French knot
6 Satin stitch
7 Close fly stitch

"PATCHWORK" CAT

This charming cat design, a collage of color, is embroidered on a pillow in two easy stitches—chain and outline. Combining any desired colors, here's a great project for using up leftover yarns!

SIZE: Approximately 16″ square.

EQUIPMENT: Paper for pattern. Pencil. Ruler. Tracing paper. Dressmaker's tracing (carbon) paper. Scissors. Large embroidery hoop. Large-eyed embroidery needle. Sewing needle. **To Block:** Soft wooden surface. Brown wrapping paper. Square. Rustproof thumbtacks.

MATERIALS: Upholstery fabric, 36″ wide, ½ yard. Sewing thread to match. Medium-weight yarn: black and colors shown, or as desired. Knife-edge foam pillow form, standard 16″ square.

DIRECTIONS: Enlarge pattern by copying on paper ruled in 1″ squares. Trace pattern. Cut upholstery fabric into two 17″ squares. Center tracing on right side of one fabric square with carbon between. Go over all lines of design to transfer to fabric. Place fabric in large embroidery hoop.

Refer to stitch details on page 282, and work embroidery as follows: Embroider color areas (not face) in chain stitch, following contour of each area (see illustration). With black yarn, outline entire cat, tail, back legs, front paws, and make features with outline stitch. Make a blue eye and a green eye in horizontal satin stitch. Fill in mouth with red yarn in chain stitch.

Block embroidery following directions on page 280.

Place the two 17″ pillow squares together, with right sides facing. Sew together with ½″ seams; leave a 13″ opening in center of one side. Turn pillow to right side and insert foam form. Turn raw edges of opening in and sew opening closed.

GENTLE JUNGLE BEASTS

A friendly lion and tiger are each worked with floss and crewel yarn on natural homespun for two delightful animal portraits. The lion is made in three stitches; the tiger is done all in split stitch.

SIZE: 14″ x 11″ each.

EQUIPMENT: Paper for patterns. Tracing paper. Dressmaker's tracing (carbon) paper. Dry ball-point pen. Pencil. Ruler. Large-eyed embroidery needle. Embroidery hoop. Tack hammer. Scissors.

MATERIALS: Beige cotton fabric, 18″ x 15″ for each. Six-strand embroidery floss: bright orange, brown, black, and medium orange (for lion's mane only). Lightweight yarn or crewel wool: gold-color and white. Heavy mount-

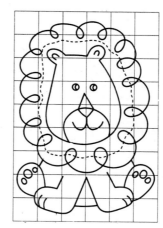

ing cardboard 14″ x 11″ for each. Straight pins. Masking tape.

DIRECTIONS: Enlarge patterns above for lion and tiger by copying on paper ruled in 1″ squares. Trace patterns. Center tracing on right side of fabric with carbon between; go over lines of design with dry ball-point pen to transfer. Use an embroidery hoop to keep fabric taut while working embroidery. Each animal is embroidered entirely in split stitch except for the lion's mane, which is worked in satin stitch secured with backstitch along short dash line of pattern. See stitch details on page 282. Use color illustration and the patterns as guides. Use six strands of floss or one strand of yarn in needle for all embroidery.

Use bright orange floss for outlines. Work rows of split stitch following contour of areas (see illustration), to fill solidly. Use gold-color yarn for heads and bodies; white for mouth areas, outer eyes, and tiger's chest area. Use black floss for lower section of noses, ears, pupils, mouths, paw pads, head markings, body and tail stripes on tiger. Use brown for upper section of noses. Use medium orange for the lion's mane.

When embroidery is complete, mount, following directions on page 281.

LION AND MOUSE PORTRAIT

A fluffy mane gives an added dimension to this friendly embroidered lion. The mane and the mouse's body are stitched primarily in Turkey work, with other easy stitches supplementing.

SIZE: 16″ x 13″.

EQUIPMENT: Embroidery needles. Embroidery scissors. Ruler. Hard- and soft-lead pencils. Paper for pattern. Dark-colored dressmaker's tracing (carbon) paper.

MATERIALS: Yellow linen or homespun-type fabric, 20″ x 17″. Small amounts of knitting worsted or similar weight yarn. Heavy mounting cardboard, 16″ x 13″. Straight pins. Masking tape.

DIRECTIONS: Enlarge pattern by copying on paper ruled in 1″ squares. Using dressmaker's carbon, transfer designs to fabric, leaving margins as shown. Mark over lines with a dark pencil if necessary. Follow color illustration for yarn colors.

To embroider lion, follow letters on pattern and stitch key (see page 282 for stitch details). Work mane in Turkey-work loops (uncut), starting first round outside of face and working around to mane outline.

When embroidery is finished, see Blocking and Mounting directions on pages 280–81.

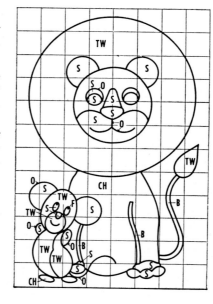

STITCH KEY

O Outline stitch
B Buttonhole stitch
TW Turkey work loops
F French knot
S Satin stitch
CH Chain stitch

HIPPO PICTURE

Yarn embroidery in five basic stitches creates tall river grasses as a setting for a happy, sun-drenched hippo. The felt pieces are glued on a burlap background, then embroidered with knitting worsted.

SIZE: 18″ x 26″.

EQUIPMENT: Paper. Ruler. Pencil. Scissors. Large-eyed needle. Dressmaker's tracing (carbon) paper. Straight pins. Stapler. Canvas stretchers two 22″ and two 30″ (to use as an embroidery frame). Chalk.

MATERIALS: Natural burlap 24″ x 32″. Staples. All-purpose glue. Felt: gold, 6″ x 8″; mustard, 12″ x 20″; medium blue, 6″ x 26″; turquoise, 3″ x 26″; light blue 4″ x 26″. Knitting worsted (see color key). Canvas stretchers two 18″ and two 26″ (for framing).

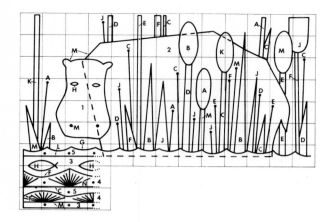

DIRECTIONS: Enlarge pattern by copying on paper ruled in 2″ squares. Wave pattern is to be repeated across. Make a separate pattern for each felt piece, numbers 1-5 (dash lines indicate where pieces are overlapped); letters indicate embroidery.

With ruler and chalk, mark picture area 18″ x 26″ on burlap, leaving equal margins all around. With enlarged pattern over dressmaker's carbon, mark position of felt pieces on burlap. Cut felt pieces for hippo and water; glue onto burlap, overlapping as indicated by dash lines. With pattern and carbon, mark embroidery lines, dots, and embroidered areas, indicated by letters, onto felt and burlap. Stretch burlap over assembled canvas stretchers 22″ x 30″, stapling along sides. Follow color key for yarns, and see stitch details on page 282. Work split stitch and satin stitch with one strand of yarn and all other embroidery with two strands.

Embroider in outline stitch around edge of felt head

and body. Embroider eyes in satin stitch, nostrils in French knots. Embroider along top edges of waves in chain stitch; embroider along side edges and bottom of water in chain stitch with dark green yarn. Outline fish bodies and tails in split stitch, then work over body in satin stitch. Embroider straight stitches in waves. Dots on waves are French knots: top row of knots is bright green, next row turquoise, next row royal blue, and bottom row pale blue.

Embroider single-line reeds in split stitch, with a French knot at top. Embroider tapered grasses and thick stems in vertical lines of long chain stitches to fill areas. Embroider cattails in satin stitch.

Remove embroidery from large stretchers and restretch on 18″ x 26″ canvas stretchers, being sure threads of burlap are straight. Staple burlap on back of stretchers, folding corners.

Whimsical Pictures

APPLE-PICKING TIME

As in the two scenes that follow, appliqué and embroidery here combine in a very easy way. The skin areas only are felt appliqués, eliminating the need to turn edges under. The stitch used is mainly split stitch, but lazy daisy, outline, satin stitch, and French knots are used also. Working the stitches at different angles—as on the apple tree—gives the impression of a third dimension. The faces are embroidered with floss; all other embroidery is done in Persian yarns.

PUMPKIN PATCH
COLOR KEY

1. Light brown
2. Beige
3. Dark gold
4. Pale gold
5. Dark yellow
6. Medium yellow
7. Pale yellow (2)
8. Medium blue
9. Light blue
10. Dark orange (2)
11. Light orange
12. Olive green
13. Light yellow-green
14. Medium gray-green (2)
15. Rose
16. Medium red

STITCH KEY

A. Satin stitch
B. Outline stitch
C. French knot
D. Lazy daisy stitch
E. Straight stitch
F. Split stitch

Heavy lines separating pumpkin sections and pumpkin outlines are worked with a single ply of light brown yarn. The olive green area at feet of girl is worked with one ply of yarn in long horizontal straight stitches; embroider this area before surrounding areas. Work leaves of pumpkins with single ply of yarn in satin stitch. Using one ply of yarn for stems and tendrils of pumpkins, embroider in satin stitch for wider areas, split stitch for single-line areas.

LITTLE KNITTER

Using one strand of light brown floss, outline mouth in outline stitch; fill with pink satin stitch. Using one strand of light brown floss, work nose and jawline in outline stitch. Using two strands of light brown floss, work eyebrows and eyelids in split stitch; make eyelashes in straight stitches.

On dress yoke, work rows of white split stitch across top and bottom and fill with white French knots. For petticoat lace, work on top of medium blue embroidery: use one ply of white yarn and make a French knot at each tiny circle; connect French knots with straight stitches.

Knitting needles are long straight stitches, with a short stitch across ends.

LITTLE KNITTER
COLOR KEY

1 Light blue (2)
2 Medium blue
3 Off-white
4 Light brown
5 Beige
6 Dark brown
7 Fuchsia

STITCH KEY

A Satin stitch
B Outline stitch
C French knot
D Lazy daisy stitch
E Straight stitch
F Split stitch

LITTLE DAVID WALL HANGING

On the following page, Little David serenades his four friends with his harp in a grand-scale wall hanging that is worked in a combination of techniques—appliqué and embroidery with bulky yarn. Curly textured sheep wool is made with French knots; a variety of other stitches fill in the details. Measuring 47" by 55" approximately, the wall hanging is stapled to stained wood stripping. Big yarn tassels add a finishing touch.

SIZE: 47" x 55".

EQUIPMENT: Tracing paper. Paper for patterns. Pencil. Ruler. Scissors. Straight pins. Iron. Sewing and large-eyed needles. Saw. Sandpaper. Hammer. Brush for stain. Piece of cardboard 5" wide. Staple gun.

MATERIALS: Loosely woven upholstery fabric in neutral shade for background: 48" wide, 1½ yards (or equivalent to measure 48" x 56"). Heavy linen fabric: approximately one yard each of the following: off-white, brown, dark gold; approximately one-half yard each of the following: copper, medium green; scrap of yellow. Sewing thread to match fabric colors. Heavy yarns: yellow, yellow-gold, dark gold, brown-gold, brown, black, beige, cream, white, russet, medium blue, dark blue, dark green. Wood stripping, four strips, 58" x 1½" x ½". Brown stain. Staples. Small finishing nails.

DIRECTIONS: To make pattern, trace illustration and also outline of hanging (approximately 9⅝" x 11¼"). See instructions on page 281 (Method 3) for enlarging patterns in following manner: Divide illustration in half and then in quarters (lines marked 1); divide each quarter into halves and in quarters (lines marked 2); then divide each remaining area into halves and quarters (lines marked 3). On large piece of paper, draw rectangle 47" long and 55" wide (the size of finished hanging). Mark off rectangle in halves and quarters with lines just as you did for the picture. Then carefully copy parts of designs into each area.

See directions for appliquéing on page 284. Trace individual parts of design separately for appliqués. Place pattern on fabric as follows. Mark outline of pattern on fabric, then cut piece from fabric ¼" larger all around than pattern to allow for hem. Cut piece for David's body, head (all area to top of hair), arms, legs of off-white linen. Cut David's shirt, rock upon which he sits, and body of lamb at far left of brown linen. Cut two remaining sheep of dark gold linen. Cut harp of copper linen. Cut bird of yellow linen. Cut all leaves of medium green linen. Slash fabric hems almost to edge of pattern outline. Turn hems under and press flat. Carefully place pieces on background cloth. Pin in place, noting where pieces overlap. With matching sewing thread, slip-stitch pieces to background.

Work embroidery (referring to stitch details on page 282) as follows. Make David's hair in couching, with longer stitches of yellow yarn and couching stitches of finer yellow-gold yarn. Outline David's body, face, arms, legs, hands, and also rock seat with brown yarn in outline stitch. With brown yarn, make David's nose in one long straight stitch, nostril in one French knot, mouth in two straight stitches, the largest tacked at center with yarn, eye lines in couching, pupils in horizontal satin stitch. Make spiral lines on rock seat in outline stitch, also with brown yarn. Embroider David's shirt in French knots with dark and yellow-gold yarn to cover completely. With black yarn, outline inner and outer edges of harp in outline stitch, and make lines for harp strings in couching. With yellow-gold yarn, make flower of four lazy daisy stitches at top and bottom centers of harp; make French knot in each flower center and between each of the lazy daisy flower petals. Work curved line on each side of each flower in outline stitch with yellow-gold yarn. Outline face area only of brown lamb at far left with beige yarn. Make eyes of satin stitch with black yarn. Embroider lamb's body in French knots with brown-gold and brown yarn to cover body completely. For leg, make double row of chain stitch with dark gold yarn. Mark off face area of light-colored lamb and fill in face area with yellow-gold yarn in chain stitch, working around from outer edge to center until filled. Make eyes in horizontal satin stitch with brown yarn. Embroider lamb's body in French knots with beige, cream, and white yarn to cover body completely. For each leg, embroider double row of chain stitch with yellow-gold yarn. Mark off face and ear area of last lamb. Outline outer edge of face in outline stitch with dark gold yarn. Fill in ear area in chain stitch with russet yarn. Make eye by working around in chain stitch with black yarn. Embroider body with beige and dark gold yarn in French knots to cover body completely. For each leg, work double row of chain stitch with dark gold yarn. Work buttonhole stitch around each leaf with medium blue yarn. With dark green yarn, embroider stems at left in outline stitch and at right in chain stitch and make French knot between buttonhole stitches on leaves. With dark blue yarn, outline bird and wing in outline stitch; fill in center of wing area in featherstitch; make French knots around outline of wing and make French knot for eye; make tail of three lazy daisy stitches with two French knots. With yellow-gold yarn, fill in beak area with satin stitch; make claws in fly stitch and each leg in double yarn couching.

Turn edges of sides under ½"; press and stitch side hems.

Sand each piece of wood stripping until smooth and free of splinters. Stain each strip and let dry. When dry, staple one strip to top front edge and another to bottom front edge of hanging. Then nail each remaining strip to back of each strip on hanging with edges of hanging between.

To make tassels, wrap yarn around 5" piece of cardboard about 50 times. Tie yarn tightly at one edge of cardboard with about 25" length of separate piece of yarn. Cut through yarn at opposite edge of cardboard. Tightly wrap yarn strands 1½" below knotted end with a 14" piece of yarn; knot. Trim yarn ends evenly. Make tassels of green and gold yarn and hang from top strips as illustrated.

BOY AND GIRL VIGNETTES

A boy, a girl, and their country friends make two charming pictures for a child's room. The embroidery is done in a variety of stitches worked on monk's cloth.

SIZE: 12¾″ x 10¾″, framed.

EQUIPMENT: Paper for patterns. Tracing paper. Pencil. Dressmaker's tracing (carbon) paper. Ruler. Embroidery hoop. Scissors. Regular and large-eyed embroidery needles. Hammer. **For Framing:** Backsaw. Small flat paintbrush. Miter box.

MATERIALS: Beige homespun 16″ x 14″ for each. Six-strand embroidery floss and fine yarn (see the individual directions for all colors). White buttonhole twist or carpet thread. Red-and-white polka dot fabric 16″ x 14″ for each. White iron-on fabric. White sewing thread. Mounting cardboard 12″ x 10″ for each. Straight pins. Masking tape. **For Framing:** Half-round picture molding, ½″ x ½″, 4′ for each. Small wire brads. Yellow enamel paint.

DIRECTIONS: Enlarge patterns by copying on paper ruled in 1″ squares. Trace pattern; center on right side of homespun fabric with carbon between. Go over lines to transfer to fabric.

Read directions for embroidery on page 280 and stitch details on page 282. Place fabric in embroidery hoop. Refer to patterns, illustration, and individual directions. Use six strands of floss and one strand of yarn in needle.

To make mat, cut out center area of polka dot fabric 9″ x 7″. Cut strips of iron-on fabric 1½″ wide to fit around cut-out edges of polka dot fabric; iron onto back of fabric, following directions on package. Center and pin mat over embroidered homespun. With sewing thread, make row of backstitch ³⁄₁₆″ from inner edge and another ¼″ from first all around mat and through homespun. Weave buttonhole twist up and down through every other stitch to form border as illustrated.

To Mount: Stretch fabric over cardboard, following directions on page 281.

To Frame: Cut four pieces of molding to fit around picture, with mitered corners. Nail together. Paint yellow; let dry. Insert picture in frame; use small brads in back of frame to hold picture in place.

GIRL

With brown yarn and backstitch, outline head, ear, neck, hat, brim, sleeve, hand, dress, pinafore, entire doll, shoes, and umbrella bottom. With brown yarn, fill in girl's eye, bird's eye, and shoes in backstitch. With brown yarn, make girl's hair in chain stitch, but make first and last strands in backstitch; make doll's eyes and bird's branch in satin stitch; bird's legs in backstitch. Fill in pinafore with rows of blue yarn couched with buttonhole twist alternating with rows of chain stitch in buttonhole twist. With buttonhole twist, fill in sleeve in diagonal filling stitch. With orange floss, fill in collar in backstitch and make two dots at back in French knots. Fill in dress in trellis and cross-stitch, using 12 strands of orange floss and buttonhole twist. Fill in umbrella bottom, doll's sleeve, and flower at left in backstitch in bright pink yarn. Make doll's mouth in one straight stitch with bright pink yarn. With bright pink yarn, make one row of chain stitch for hat band and straight stitches for streamer. With gold-color floss, make two rows of backstitch within outline of hat crown. Fill in crown in diagonal filling stitch with gold floss and buttonhole twist. Make one row of chain stitch with buttonhole twist across center of hat brim. With yellow floss, fill in hat brim and make doll's hair in backstitch; make bird's beak in straight stitch. Using backstitch, fill in bird's head and wing with pale aqua yarn and body with medium aqua yarn. With green floss, make three tiny lazy daisy stitch leaves on branch and on

ground; make stems and larger leaves, and umbrella handle in satin stitch; make three backstitches in each of the two smaller of these leaves. With yellow floss, outline remaining flower in satin stitch; make cross-stitch in center. Outline center in backstitch with gold floss.

BOY

With brown yarn and backstitch, outline head, ear, hair, overalls, shoes, hand, sleeve, hat crown and brim, rooster's body, head, eye, comb, wattles, all of cat (except whiskers), and vertical lines on houses. With brown yarn, fill in hair with chain stitch; make eyes and nose in backstitch; make doorways in satin stitch. With bright pink yarn, fill in shoes, comb, wattles, and make mouth in backstitch. Make sleeve lines and lines of one roof in bright pink couched with buttonhole twist. Fill in rooster's body with pale aqua yarn, wing and tail lines with medium aqua yarn in backstitch. Use medium aqua yarn for second roof to outline in backstitch; fill in with trellis (without the cross). With bright pink yarn, make tiniest flower in satin stitch and center flower in lazy daisy stitch. Fill in hat crown with gold floss couched with buttonhole twist. Fill in underbrim with gold floss in backstitch. Fill in brim with yellow floss couched with buttonhole twist. Make beak with yellow floss in backstitch. Make hat feather and chimney with orange floss in backstitch. With orange floss, make remaining flower outline in satin stitch. With green floss, make flower stems, lines under houses, neck, sleeve, and pants lines in chain stitch; make flower leaves in satin stitch, make tiny leaves in lazy daisy stitch. Make cross-stitch on overalls with orange floss crossed with gold.

Abstract Pictures

GEOMETRIC SAMPLER

With orange and red predominating, cheerful blocks of embroidery show examples of various stitches and illustrate how the same stitch can be used for different results. Note how the same stitch is used to outline one area and to fill in another; by grouping single stitches you can create a border, or use border stitches to achieve a solid effect. Combinations of stitches, worked one over another, become an exciting motif. A stitch changes in appearance when worked in different types of yarns and flosses. Experiment with your own combinations of stitches, colors, and yarns to create an entirely different effect in a sampler of your own!

SIZE: 16½″ x 12½″, design area.

EQUIPMENT: Sharp, hard pencil. Ruler. Compass. Large and medium embroidery needles. Straight pins. Sewing needle and dark thread. Stapler.

MATERIALS: Even-weave embroidery fabric 24″ x 20″, with the same thread count to the inch vertically and horizontally. Canvas stretchers, two 24″ and two 20″, or frame to fit. Pearl cotton, six-strand embroidery floss, and heavy embroidery cotton; crewel wool; knitting worsted; cotton rug yarn—all in various related colors as desired, or as shown in illustration.

DIRECTIONS: With pins, mark area 16½″ x 12½″, on embroidery fabric; make a line of running stitches to outline this area, using a dark-color thread. This will serve as a guide in marking the embroidery areas. Use a hard, sharp pencil and mark each block on the fabric, following the diagram.

Starting with the vertical strip A, measure in 4¾″ from left-hand side near top and mark the top section of A, following measurements on diagram. Mark each block in successive alphabetical order following measurements. Mark circles lightly with compass. Mark small blocks and circles inside larger blocks as shown.

Stretch fabric over assembled canvas stretchers or other frame and staple in back. Using color illustration as a guide, embroider each block in stitches suggested, or work out your own stitches, referring to stitch details on page 282. To make the stitches in each block work out evenly, count the number of threads horizontally and vertically, and divide equally. On the blocks with center designs, work the center motif first, then proceed outward with different border rows. Work the smaller blocks within blocks first, in satin stitch with a French knot center (unless otherwise indicated); then fill in remainder, and outline blocks if desired.

The smaller circles outside of blocks are all worked in straight stitches, radiating from center with French knots at end of each stitch. The larger circle at top has a satin-stitch center with two straight stitches across and four French knots over them; border is buttonhole stitch; French knots ring the circle.

When embroidery is complete, block (only if necessary) and mount fabric on heavy cardboard, following directions on pages 280–81. Frame as desired.

STITCHES USED: Blocks A: Center is fishbone stitch; sides are fagot filling.

Blocks B: Rows of chain stitch.

Block C: Couching.

Block D: Interlacing stitch with backstitch around outline.

Block E: Roumanian stitch.

Block F: Satin stitch leaf stitch with backstitch around outline; small block is satin stitch.

Block G: Diagonal filling with backstitch around outline.

Block H: Circle is couching with French knot center; background is running stitch; border is couching, straight stitch in clusters, backstitch outline, with cross-stitches in corners.

Block I: Satin-stitch circle with couching outline and straight-stitch triangles; satin-stitch squares; border is rows of chain stitch, couching, coral stitch, threaded running stitch, backstitch.

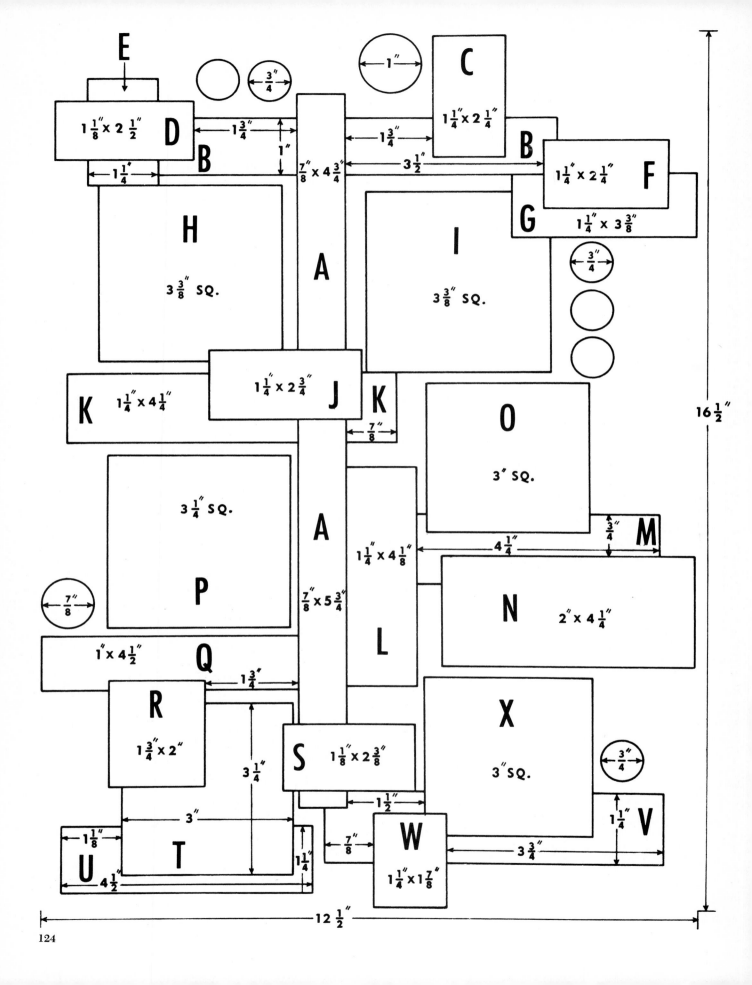

Block J: Triple rows of threaded running stitch with backstitch outline.

Blocks K: Pekinese stitch with backstitch around outline.

Block L: Three rows of satin stitch with outline stitch between and around outside.

Block M: Rows of buttonhole stitch with thread running through.

Block N: Circles are couching with French knot centers; background is running stitch; border is couching and chain stitch.

Block O: Center is straight stitches and French knots, with star filling stitch over middle; wide border from center is backstitch, couching, outline stitch, double lazy daisy stitch, couching, whipped running stitch.

Block P: Center is couching with French knot center and outline stitch outside; middle design is satin stitch, long straight stitches with cross-stitch and French knots; border is backstitch and buttonhole stitch over a heavy thread.

Block Q: Flat stitch with backstitch around the outline.

Block R: Long and short stitch with backstitch outline; small block is satin stitch with backstitch outline and seeding stitch.

Block S: Running stitch with cross-stitch between and whipped running stitch outline.

Block T: Circles are buttonhole stitch with satin-stitch and outline-stitch centers; background is running stitch; outline is couching.

Block U: Diagonal filling with backstitch around outline.

Block V: Backstitch squares with straight stitches within.

Block W: Couching; small block is satin stitch with backstitch outline.

Block X: Center is satin stitch and couching with lazy daisy stitch and straight stitches over center; border is couching, cross-stitches, chain stitch, and couching around outside.

FOUR BOLD ABSTRACT COLLAGES

Let your imagination run free in expressing unlimited designs with embroidery. Four examples show how effectively stitches, colors, yarns, and other materials can be combined to create unusual textures and designs. Follow these general directions for abstract embroidery and then create your very own design!

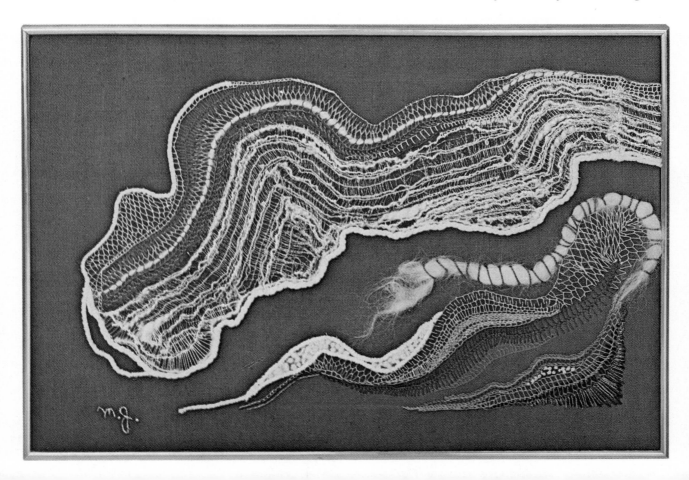

EQUIPMENT: Paper for planning design. Scissors. Straight pins. Needles appropriate to yarns and threads.

MATERIALS: Fabric for background, such as nubby wool, linen, burlap, homespun, or heavy rayon.

Scraps of upholstery fabric for patches in colors to suit scheme. Six-strand embroidery floss. Yarns in a variety of weights and textures from very heavy bulky mohair, straw, and chenille to very fine. String, cord, rope, metallic threads, and anything else that can be used for stitchery. (For lacy effect on yellow and orange picture, we

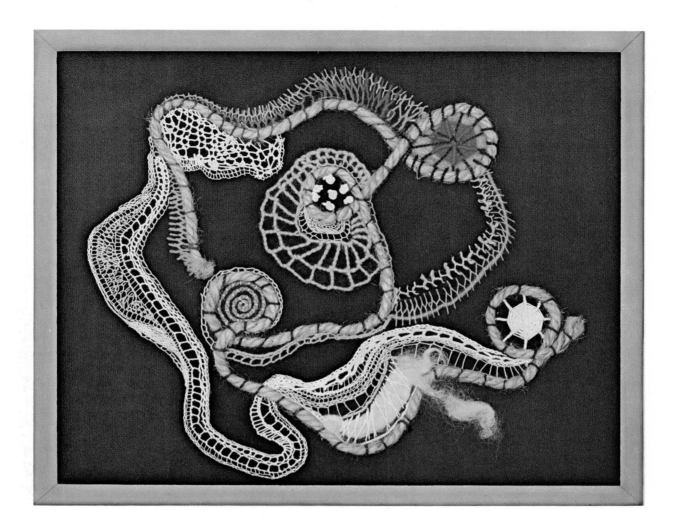

used plastic netting.) Cardboard the size of picture. Straight pins. Masking tape.

DIRECTIONS: Plan the general design and movement of your picture on paper, but do not make pattern. These designs should be imaginative, and it is interesting to create as you work the embroidery. Refer to stitch details on page 282 for embroidery; select any variety you desire. The more stitches and textures you use, the more individual your picture will be. Most of the filled-in areas are Cretan, scale, Roumanian, chain, and Roman chain stitch. Most areas are edged in buttonhole stitch. Heavy yarns can be couched in place with finer yarns.

The pictures with upholstery-fabric patches are worked by overlapping and pinning patches on background fabric, then working embroidery over patches or along out-lines, or both. If upholstery patches have patterns imprinted or embossed, you might embroider over design or fill in all the embossed areas. Loops are of Turkey work, and the shaggy areas are made by cutting loops of Turkey work and trimming.

The pictures without patches are basically made up of curved lines. Rope or heavy yarn is couched in place with fine yarn. Some circles are filled in with spider web stitch, some with French knots made with string. An unusual effect can be obtained by slipping a piece of mohair underneath a section of stitches and then unraveling the ends of the mohair.

For mounting and framing embroidered pictures, see directions on page 281.

11 Embroidery for the Home

Pillows

JEWEL-TONE PILLOWS *Bright geometric designs are embroidered on a felt background with yarn in sparkling colors. All you need are five embroidery stitches to create these pillows on the next two pages.*

SIZE: 14″ x 17″.

EQUIPMENT: Pencil. Ruler. Scissors. Sewing, large-eyed, and tapestry needles. Embroidery frame or canvas stretchers, two 15″ and two 18″. Tailor's chalk. Rustproof thumbtacks.

MATERIALS: Felt in gold, navy blue, or desired color, 36″ wide, ½ yard. Matching sewing thread. Knitting worsted, 1 ounce each of following colors. For gold felt: bright pink, scarlet, tangerine, medium orange, pale yellow, dark gold, wood brown, white. For navy blue felt: bright pink, purple, royal blue, medium blue, turquoise, lime green, white. Kapok or shredded foam rubber for stuffing.

DIRECTIONS: Cut one rectangle out of felt 16″ x 19″ and one 14″ x 17″. With tailor's chalk, mark off areas on larger piece of felt as follows, referring to actual-size diagram on page 136. We have simplified the design in the diagram; you can vary it as you choose. For outer border, mark rectangle 11″ x 14¼″ in center of felt; then mark rectangle 10″ x 13¼″ (½″ smaller). For center area, mark rectangle 5″ x 8¼″; then mark rectangle 4¼″ x 7½″ (⅜″ smaller). Within this center area, mark twelve 1¼″ squares along edges with ⅜″ spaces between squares. Within each square, center and mark a ⅝″ x ⅞″ rectangle. Mark rectangle 1¼″ x 4½″ in exact center. Using diagram as a guide, mark diagonal lines on pillow, starting from midpoint on each side and working toward corners for each row. In center, make two zigzag lines as illustrated.

We give directions for embroidering gold pillow. Colors for blue pillow are given in "Materials." Refer to illustration for variations of color patterns. Place and tack felt in frame or on assembled stretchers.

To make outer border, work sections (as marked on diagram) in satin stitch, alternating eight white and ten yellow stitches along shorter sides; eight tangerine and ten orange on longer sides. Make yellow cross-stitches over white sections; make orange cross-stitches over tangerine sections.

The remaining pattern of border consists of zigzag lines of fly stitch (indicated by solid lines on diagram) alternating with straight stitches in zigzag fashion threaded through loop of fly stitch (indicated on diagram by dash lines), which form triangular and diamond-shaped areas that are to be filled in with straight stitches of varying lengths and colors.

Along each longer side, work fly stitch with yellow yarn. Within each triangular area formed, make one brown straight stitch in center and one pink straight stitch on each side. On shorter sides, do the same with tangerine fly stitch, with pink stitch in center, orange stitches on each side.

Work next zigzag line on all sides of pillow with orange straight stitches, threading them through loops of fly stitch.

From here on, all sides of pillow are worked with the same colors. Within the enclosed diamond-shaped area formed, make double straight stitches with scarlet yarn in center. (Heavy lines on diagram within triangular and diamond-shaped areas always indicate double straight stitches.) On each side of scarlet stitches make one tangerine straight stitch. Within open triangular area, work one gold straight stitch in center and one yellow on each side. Work next zigzag line in fly stitch with tangerine yarn. Within the remaining part of the diamond-shaped area formed, make one orange straight stitch in center, scarlet on each side, and fill in area with white on each side. Make zigzag straight stitch with yellow yarn threaded through loop of tangerine fly stitch. Fill in area formed with double scarlet stitches in center and one pink on each side. Make fly stitch with tangerine yarn again, then fill in area with gold in center and orange on each side. Work last zigzag line with gold yarn threaded through loops of fly stitch. Fill in enclosed area with white straight stitch in center and yellow on each side. Fill in triangular area with yellow straight stitch in center and brown on each side.

For center design, work frame areas in satin stitch with tangerine yarn (lines on diagram indicate which directions the satin stitches are worked within each area). Make tufts in corners of each larger square by working three Turkey work stitches (indicated by dots on diagram) with orange yarn. Cut loops and trim. Work scarlet yarn in satin stitch in small rectangles within larger squares. Make two rows of fly stitch going in opposite directions with yellow yarn. Fill in each of the diamond-shaped areas formed with double scarlet straight stitch and double pink on each side, then fill in area with medium orange straight stitches. Fill in area outside diamond shapes with gold satin stitch.

Take felt out of frame or off stretchers; trim to 14″ x 17″. Place two felt rectangles together, with right sides facing;

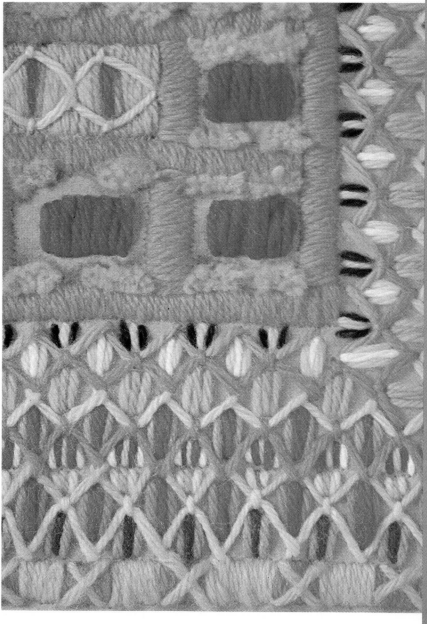

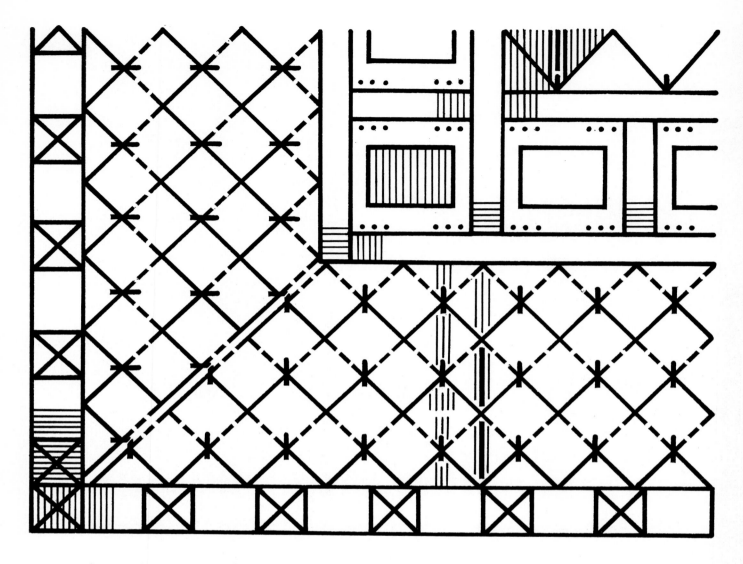

sew together on all sides, close to edges, leaving a 6″ opening in center of one side; turn right side out. Fringe along edges (except along opening) with tangerine yarn; with tapestry needle, pull yarn through felt edge; knot; cut yarn, leaving ends about 2″ long. Work fringe close together. Stuff pillow plumply; sew opening closed. Work fringe as above to cover remainder of edge. Trim fringe ends.

GARDEN PILLOW

Inspired by the colors of an early spring garden, this delicate pillow is filled with flowers, and butterflies. The background is beige cotton fabric, and the satin, straight, stem, and French knot stitches are worked in pearl cotton.

SIZE: 10″ x 16″.

EQUIPMENT: Tracing paper. Pencil. Dressmaker's tracing (carbon) paper. Dry ball-point pen or hard-lead pencil. Masking tape. Ruler. Scissors. Embroidery hoop. Sewing and large-eyed embroidery needles. Straight pins. **For Blocking:** Soft wooden surface. Brown paper. Square. Rustproof thumbtacks. Towel.

MATERIALS: Beige cotton fabric, 11″ x 17″. Pearl cotton No. 5; one ball each of colors listed in color key. Red fabric for backing, 11″ x 17″. Red braid, ½″ wide, 1½ yards. Red and white sewing thread. Muslin for inner pillow, 36″ wide, ⅝ yard. Polyester stuffing.

DIRECTIONS: Read directions for embroidery on page 280. Trace complete pattern. Mark design area with pins in center of beige fabric. With needle and white thread, make running stitches along this outline. Tape edges of fabric to keep them from raveling.

Place tracing in center of outlined area on right side of fabric; place carbon between. Go over design with pen or hard pencil to transfer it to fabric. Remove tracing and carbon. Go over any lines, if necessary, with pencil to sharpen lines.

Place fabric in hoop. To work embroidery, refer to stitch details on page 282, and stitch and color keys on pattern. Make all dots on pattern in French knots. The poppy petal areas are filled in with couching following the contours of the individual petals.

Block, following directions on page 280. Then remove running stitches.

To make pillow, pin embroidered piece and red fabric together with right sides facing. Insert edge of braid between, making all outside edges flush. Stitch together, making ½″ seams; leave open in center of one side for turning. Trim seams. Turn to right side; push out corners.

For inner pillow, cut two pieces of muslin 11½″ x 17½″. Sew together, making ¼″ seams; leave opening in center of one side for turning. Turn to right side. Stuff fully. Slip-stitch closed. Insert into outer pillow. Slip-stitch closed.

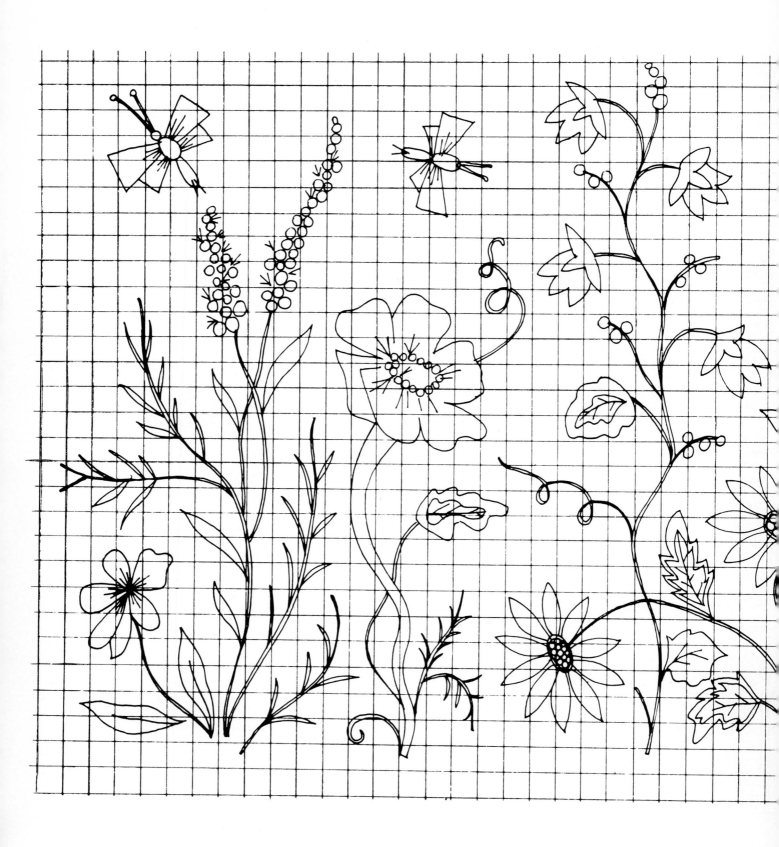

138

STITCH KEY

1 Couching
2 Outline stitch
3 Satin stitch
4 Straight stitch

COLOR KEY

A Very dark green
B Black
C Red
D Medium violet
E Light violet
F Medium light blue
G Light blue
H Aqua
J Turquoise
K Golden orange
L Dark emerald green
M Light emerald green
N Light yellow-green
O Medium yellow-green
P Medium yellow
Q Pale yellow
R Mustard yellow

SPANISH PILLOW

A ring of festive flowers and a brilliant sunburst center are embroidered in fine wool on a background of rich blue felt. The design, Spanish in origin, is worked in five embroidery stitches—satin stitch, outline stitch, split stitch, French knots, and straight stitch. The knitting-worsted fringe, in a bright green, is knotted through the fabric!

SIZE: 16″ diameter without fringe.

EQUIPMENT: Tracing paper. Pencil. Compass. White or yellow dressmaker's tracing (carbon) paper. Dry ball-point pen. White pencil. Large-eyed and sewing needles. Embroidery hoop. Awl. Crochet hook (to use in fringing).

MATERIALS: Medium blue felt, ½ yard (comes 72″ wide, but only two circles each 16″ diameter are re-

STITCH KEY

1 **Satin stitch**
2 **Outline stitch**
3 **Split stitch**
4 **French knot**
5 **Straight stitch**

quired). Fine wool for embroidery, such as crewel wool: deep pink; bright red; bright yellow; dark bright green; nile green; black; white. Bright green knitting worsted. Muslin, 36″ wide, ½ yard. Medium blue and white sewing thread. Polyester fiberfill for stuffing.

DIRECTIONS: Read directions for embroidery on page 280. Trace actual-size pattern; complete quarter-pattern indicated by dash lines. Cut felt into two 16″ diameter circles. Mark center point of one circle. Place felt circle on flat, firm surface. Center pattern on felt circle;

place carbon between. Go over pattern lines carefully with dry ball-point pen, and bear down hard to transfer design to felt. Remove pattern and carbon. Go over lines with a sharp white pencil to keep lines from fading.

Put felt in hoop. Work embroidery, following color illustration and numbers on pattern for stitches. See stitch details on page 282. Note the direction of satin stitches in color illustration. All dots indicate French knots; they are all done in white yarn except for the ones in center; these are yellow.

When embroidery is finished, place two felt circles together, right sides out. Sew together ¼″ from edge, leaving an 8″ opening. For fringing, make holes with awl all around both pillow pieces about ¼″ apart, just inside stitching. Cut knitting worsted into 5″ strands. Insert crochet hook through matching holes of felt pieces, from front to back. Pull through two strands of knitting worsted at mid-point, from back to front, forming loop. Insert yarn ends through loop; pull ends tightly to make knot.

Work fringe in this manner all around pillow, except at opening.

To make inner pillow, cut two circles of muslin, each 18″ in diameter. With wrong sides facing, sew muslin together ½″ from edge, leaving a small opening. Turn right side out. Stuff smoothly and sew opening closed. Insert muslin pillow inside felt pillow. Sew opening of felt pillow closed. Then complete fringe. Trim fringe ends evenly.

Patchwork Pillow

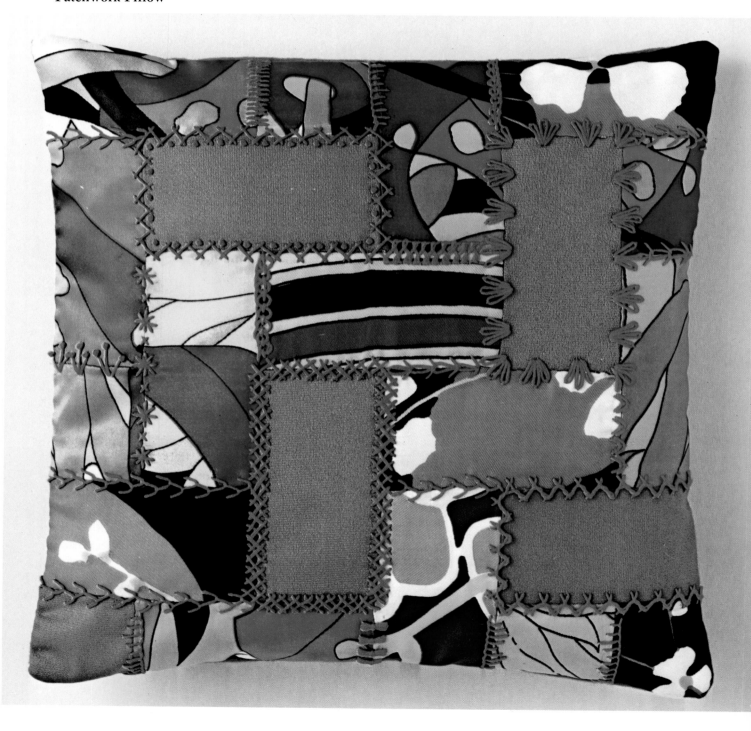

PATCHWORK PILLOW

On the opposite page, a patchwork pillow in fantastic color becomes the background for a sampler of embroidery stitches. Uniform patches in two sizes are sewn together, then the seams are emblazoned with a variety of stitches in a contrasting color.

SIZE: 12″ square.

EQUIPMENT: Pencil. Ruler. Embroidery needle. Stiff cardboard. Scissors. Sewing needle. Steam iron.

MATERIALS: Rayon or silk fabrics in prints and solid color. Unbleached muslin, 12¼″ square. Fabric for pillow back, 12¼″ square. Matching thread. Six-strand embroidery floss, three skeins. Pillow form, knife-edged, 12″ square.

DIRECTIONS: Make two cardboard patterns, 2″ x 2″ and 2″ x 4″. Using patterns, mark each patch piece on wrong side of fabric; cut out, adding ¼″ all around for seam allowance. Arrange pieces, as shown in illustration, to form a 12″ square when seamed. With right sides facing, machine- or hand-stitch pieces together on marked seam lines. Baste patched piece to muslin square. Work decorative stitches over each seam, using six strands of floss in needle and working through both layers of fabric. Steam-press lightly upside down on a padded surface. Remove basting stitches.

With right sides of back and front pillow pieces together, stitch around three sides with ¼″ seams. Turn right side out. Insert pillow form; turn in raw edges; sew.

Starting in upper left hand of illustration, stitches shown are: Roumanian, buttonhole, Pekinese, feather, herringbone with French knots, lazy daisy, interlacing, wheat-ear, straight stitch with French knots, star filling with cross-stitch, double herringbone, threaded herringbone, fagot filling.

PANELED PILLOW AND THREE PINCUSHIONS

Whimsical motifs accent a paneled pillow and three puffy pincushions stitched with the whir of your sewing machine. The flowers on the 10″ by 20″ pillow are appliquéd and detailed with pencil-thin lines. The maxi pincushions, 6 1/2″ square, are "painted" with stitchery and assembled like pillows.

PANELED PILLOW

EQUIPMENT: Paper for pattern. Tracing paper. Pencil. Ruler. Dressmaker's tracing (carbon) paper. Scissors. Straight pins. Straight-stitch sewing machine. Iron. Sewing needle. Dry ball-point pen.

MATERIALS: Tightly woven cotton fabric, 44″ wide, in following colors: orange, ⅓ yard; yellow, ¼ yard; scraps of green. Orange and yellow sewing thread. Fusible bonding web. Unbleached muslin, 45″ wide, ⅓ yard. Shredded foam for stuffing.

DIRECTIONS: Enlarge pattern by copying on paper ruled in 1″ squares. Place tracing paper over pattern and trace entire design carefully. Transfer design to fabric with carbon and dry ball-point pen.

For back of pillow, cut orange fabric 10½″ x 20½″. For front panels, cut 2 pieces orange fabric and 2 pieces yellow fabric each 10½″ x 5½″.

Using patterns, cut appliqués: 2 orange and 2 yellow flowers and centers, 4 sets of green stems and leaves.

Use sewing thread in machine in colors shown for each panel. With presser foot of machine down, work running stitch (about 9 stitches to the inch) horizontally along front panels as shown in illustration.

Place bonding web between appliqué and panel; ad-

here according to directions on package. For stitching on appliqué, keep presser foot down, with machine running slowly; carefully move fabric along the shape of the appliqué, beginning just inside the outer edge, gradually decreasing the size of the shape and moving stitches toward the center (see illustration). Be certain to move fabric slowly to prevent breaking needle. Repeat on all four panels, reversing colors as shown.

Turn under ¼″ on both long sides of one yellow panel and one side of the other yellow panel; place over long edges of orange panels, being sure to reverse direction of flowers; topstitch seams.

Place front and back pieces together with right sides facing. Stitch two long and one short side with ¼″ seams, leaving one short side open. Turn the pillow cover right side out.

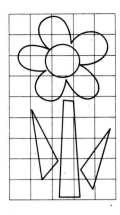

Pattern for Paneled Pillow.

Make inner pillow of muslin, and finish pillow, following directions on page 287.

PILLOW PINCUSHIONS

EQUIPMENT: Paper for pattern. Tracing paper. Pencil. Ruler. Dressmaker's tracing (carbon) paper. Scissors. Straight-stitch sewing machine. Sewing needle. Dry ball-point pen.

MATERIALS: Tightly woven cotton fabric in the following colors, each piece 7″ x 14″: shocking pink, black, purple. Yellow piping, 1 yard. Sewing thread to match fabrics and deep pink, lavender, light blue, turquoise, yellow, orange, white, red, apple green for designs. For inner pillow: unbleached muslin, 36″ wide, ½ yard. Shredded foam for stuffing.

DIRECTIONS: Enlarge patterns by copying on paper ruled in ½″ squares. Complete half-pattern for geometric design indicated by dash line. Place tracing paper over pattern and trace entire design carefully.

For each pincushion, cut two pieces of cotton fabric 7″

square in colors shown in illustration. For front, fold one piece of fabric in half, then fold in half again, pressing lightly at center to make a small cross. Fold paper pattern the same way. Matching crosses, transfer entire design to background fabric with carbon and dry ball-point pen.

Use sewing thread in machine in colors shown for each design. With presser foot of machine down, work running stitch (about 12 stitches to the inch) along pattern lines as shown in illustrations. For mushroom pincushion, make lines of running stitches in various colors across front piece close together for ground area, wider apart for upper background (see illustration). For areas such as spider legs, mushroom stems, leaves, and geometric designs, make close lines of running stitches as shown. To work filled-in areas of spider, flowers, flower centers, insect wings, and mushroom caps, leave presser foot down and, with machine running slowly, carefully move

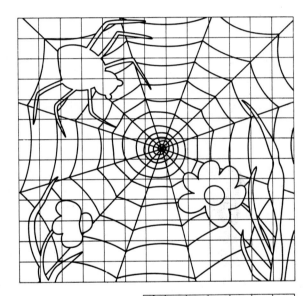

Pattern for Pillow Pincushions.

fabric in all directions (backward, forward, around) until entire area is covered. Be certain to move fabric slowly to prevent breaking needle.

Place front and back pieces together with right sides facing. Stitch around three sides with ¼″ seams. Turn right side out. For mushroom pincushion, baste piping to right side of front piece, with raw edges out; place front and back pieces together and assemble as instructed above.

Make inner pillows of muslin and shredded foam and finish pincushions, following directions on page 287.

BUTTERFLY PILLOWS

Two airy butterfly pillows in sunlit shades of green, yellow, orange, and blue look like one giant butterfly when placed side by side. Worked in tapestry yarns, the stitches are simple—only the outline stitch and the chain stitch are used. The pillows are made of monk's cloth.

SIZE: 10″ square each.

EQUIPMENT: Large sheet of tracing paper. Pencil. Ruler. Tracing wheel. Dressmaker's tracing (carbon) paper. Scissors. Tapestry and sewing needles. Embroidery hoop.

MATERIALS: Monk's cloth (preshrunk and bleached white), 11″ x 44″. White sewing thread. Muslin, ⅔ yard, 36″ wide. Tapestry yarn: medium blue, 1 skein; apple green, 1 skein; medium green, 2 skeins; light orange, 1 skein; gold, 2 skeins; yellow, 2 skeins. Polyester fiberfill for stuffing.

DIRECTIONS: Read directions for embroidery on page 280. Enlarge pattern by copying on paper ruled in 1″ squares. For each pillow, cut a piece of monk's cloth 11″ square. Center pattern on cloth square, allowing ½″ for seams all around, with carbon between. Go over pattern lines with tracing wheel to transfer design to cloth.

Place fabric in hoop. Embroider design with tapestry

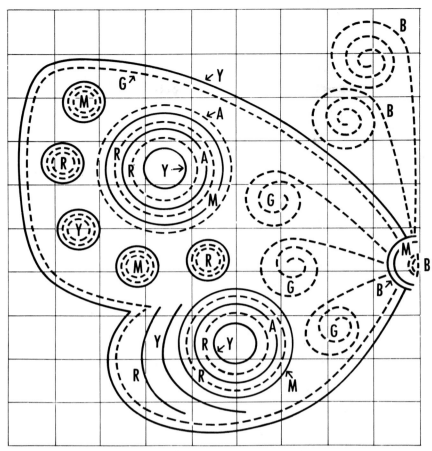

COLOR KEY

B Medium blue
G Gold
R Light orange
Y Yellow
A Apple green
M Medium green

Pattern for Butterfly Pillows to be enlarged on 1″ squares.

yarn, following pattern and color key; short dash lines are outline stitch, solid lines are chain stitch. (See stitch details on page 282.) Embroider two squares, reversing half-butterfly.

Cut back for each pillow from monk's cloth 11″ square.

Place back and front together, right sides facing; sew together ½″ from edge, leaving one side open. Turn to right side.

Make two inner pillows of muslin and insert into embroidered covers, following directions on page 287.

PAISLEY PILLOW

Popular paisley in small and large motifs makes a pillow of graceful elegance. The solid areas of design are filled in with satin stitch; chain, straight, and outline stitches complete the pattern. Embroidery floss in three vivid colors is worked on orange-gold fabric.

SIZE: 13″ square.

EQUIPMENT: Paper for pattern. Pencil. Ruler. Scissors. Embroidery and sewing needles. Dressmaker's tracing (carbon) paper. Tracing paper. Dry ball-point pen. Embroidery hoop. Steam iron.

MATERIALS: Light orange cotton broadcloth, 14″ x 28″. Orange sewing thread. Six-strand embroidery floss, 2 skeins each bright orange, hot pink, and purple. Pillow form, knife edge, 14″ square.

DIRECTIONS: Read directions for embroidery on

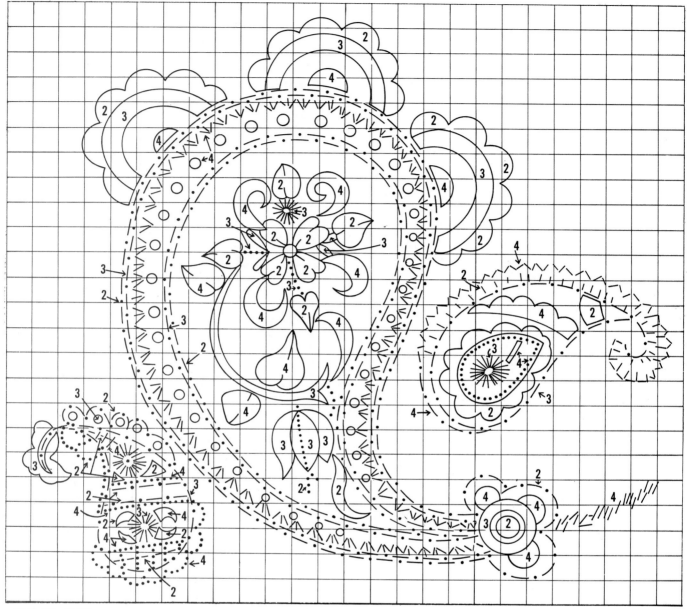

COLOR KEY

2 **Orange**
3 **Pink**
4 **Purple**

Pattern for Paisley Pillow; enlarge on ½″ squares.

page 280. Enlarge paisley design by copying on paper ruled in ½″ squares. In copying the design, make all dot-dash and dotted lines solid lines. Trace pattern. Cut orange fabric in half crosswise. On one piece, transfer design, using dressmaker's carbon and dry ball-point pen.

Place fabric in hoop. Work all embroidery with three strands of six-strand floss in needle. Refer to stitch details on page 282. Following pattern, work all completely outlined areas in satin stitch; work dot-dash lines in chain stitch, making each chain about ³⁄₁₆″ long; work dotted

lines in outline stitch; all short lines are straight stitch. Areas indicated by the number 2 are to be worked in orange floss; number 3 areas are pink; number 4 areas are purple. Work each section of petals and leaves separately in satin stitch. Steam-press lightly upside down on a padded surface; let dry.

With right sides of back and front pillow pieces together, stitch around three sides with ⅜″ seams. Turn right side out. Insert pillow form; turn in raw edges; sew.

Paisley Pillow

SCROLL PILLOWS

These delicate scroll pillows have tone-on-tone embroidery in easy chain stitch for a subtle effect.

SIZES: Square pillow, 13½″ square; round pillow, 14″ diameter.

EQUIPMENT: Paper for patterns. Tracing paper. Pencil. Ruler. Compass. Scissors. Dressmaker's tracing (carbon) paper. Dry ball-point pen. Embroidery and sewing needles. Towel for pressing. Cording foot for sewing machine. Iron.

MATERIALS: Linen-weave rayon or cotton fabric (tightly woven fabric is not suitable), ½ yard for each. Matching sewing thread. Muslin, ½ yard for each. Stuff-ing, such as Dacron, kapok, or shredded foam. Six-strand embroidery floss in darker shade of fabric color. Cable cord, ⅛″ diameter, 1¾ yards for square pillow, 1½ yards for round.

DIRECTIONS: Read directions for embroidery on page 280. Enlarge motif patterns by copying on paper ruled in 1″ squares; complete half-patterns as indicated by dash lines. Cut pillow cover according to individual directions. Following individual directions, draw pillow shape on large piece of tracing paper; arrange four com-

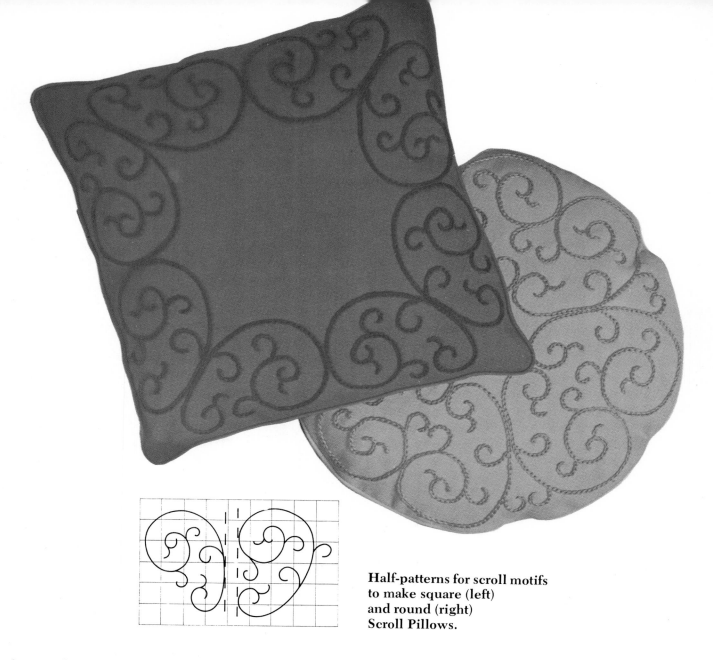

**Half-patterns for scroll motifs
to make square (left)
and round (right)
Scroll Pillows.**

plete motifs around edge for complete design (see illustration). Using dressmaker's carbon and dry ball-point pen, center and transfer design to right side on one piece of fabric (front). Using full six strands of embroidery floss in needle, work design in chain stitch (see page 282 for stitch detail).

Press pillow cover, right side down, using folded towel for padding under embroidered area. To make piping, cut matching fabric strip on the bias, ¾" wide, long enough to fit around pillow. (Piece strip if necessary.) Encase cording in bias strip; stitch close to cord with cording foot.

With right sides of pillow back and front facing, insert piping between, raw edges of all three together. Baste along seam line of piping; stitch with ¼" seams, leaving 10" opening for inserting inner pillow. Trim seam; turn right side out; press. Cut and sew inner pillow of muslin,

using same pattern as for pillow cover and leaving 5" opening for stuffing. Trim seam; turn right side out; press. Stuff softly. Turn in edges and slip-stitch opening in muslin pillow closed. Insert muslin inner pillow into pillow cover. Keeping piping in place, slip-stitch opening in pillow cover closed.

SQUARE PILLOW

Cut two pieces of fabric, each 14" square. Draw 13½" square on tracing paper. Arrange completed motifs at each corner, with sides of each touching; trace.

ROUND PILLOW

Cut two 14¼" diameter circles of fabric. Draw 14"-diameter circle on tracing paper. Arrange four completed motifs around circle, with sides touching; trace.

FINNISH GIRL AND BOY PILLOW

A Finnish girl and boy stalk flying fowl on a field of homespun. Wool and floss are worked in satin, long and short, and outline stitches from actual-size pattern.

SIZE: 14" square.

EQUIPMENT: Paper for pattern. Ruler. Pencil. Scissors. Embroidery needles. White tissue paper.

MATERIALS: Heavy-weight natural-color upholstery, handwoven, or homespun fabric, two pieces 15" square. Six-strand embroidery floss and crewel wool in colors given in the Color Key (all but leaves are worked in crewel wool). Sewing thread to match fabric. Softly stuffed inner pillow, 15" square.

DIRECTIONS: Read directions for embroidery on page 280 and refer to stitch details on page 282. Trace pattern. Transfer design to one piece of background fabric, using "Marking with Running Stitch" method described on page 286. If fabric is very loosely woven, stitch a line close to edge to prevent raveling.

Following color key and numbers in pattern, embroider the following parts in satin stitch: zigzag area in bottom border; small circles and segmented circles; triangles,

squares, and circles in boy and girl; cheeks; squares and triangles on background. Embroider the following parts in long and short stitch: remainder of bottom border; hem of girl's skirt and arms; boy's pants, arms, and hat; gun; birds; leaves (shade the leaves as indicated, making one color blend into other); large circles (use two shades of pink). Embroider hair and remaining lines in outline stitch. Make features navy blue with white satin-stitch eyes and navy blue pupils.

When embroidery is completed, place front and back together with right sides facing; stitch around three sides, allowing ½″ for seams. Turn right side out. Make inner pillow according to directions on page 287, insert in pillow cover, and slip-stitch remaining side of cover closed.

TWO SCANDINAVIAN PILLOWS

For these pillows from Finland, only a few stitches are used to embroider the designs, which are created through a subtle combination of color, line, and texture.

SIZE: 15″ x 19″ each.

EQUIPMENT: Paper for patterns. Ruler. Pencil. Scissors. Embroidery needles. White tissue paper.

MATERIALS: Medium-weight upholstery, handwoven, or homespun fabric, two pieces 16″ x 20″ for each pillow. Embroidery thread, such as linen, six-strand cotton, silk or rayon, fine pearl cotton, or fine wool. Sewing thread to match fabric. Softly stuffed inner pillow, 16″ x 20″, for each.

DIRECTIONS: Read directions for embroidery on page 280 and refer to stitch details on page 282. Enlarge patterns by copying on paper ruled in 1″ squares. For each pillow, transfer design to one piece of background fabric, using "Marking with Running Stitch" method described on page 286 (which is the Finnish technique). If fabric is very loosely woven, stitch a line close to edge to prevent raveling.

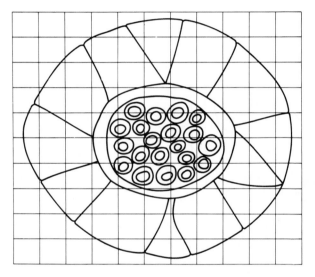

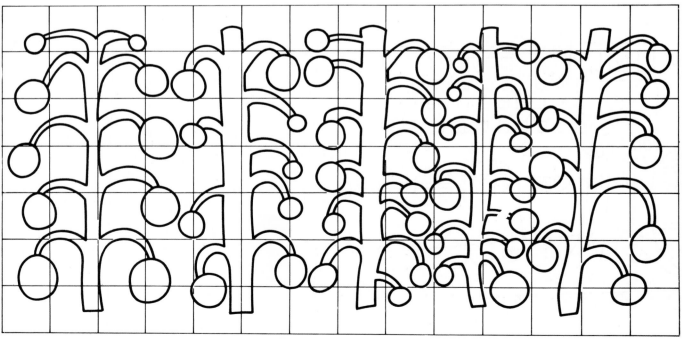

154

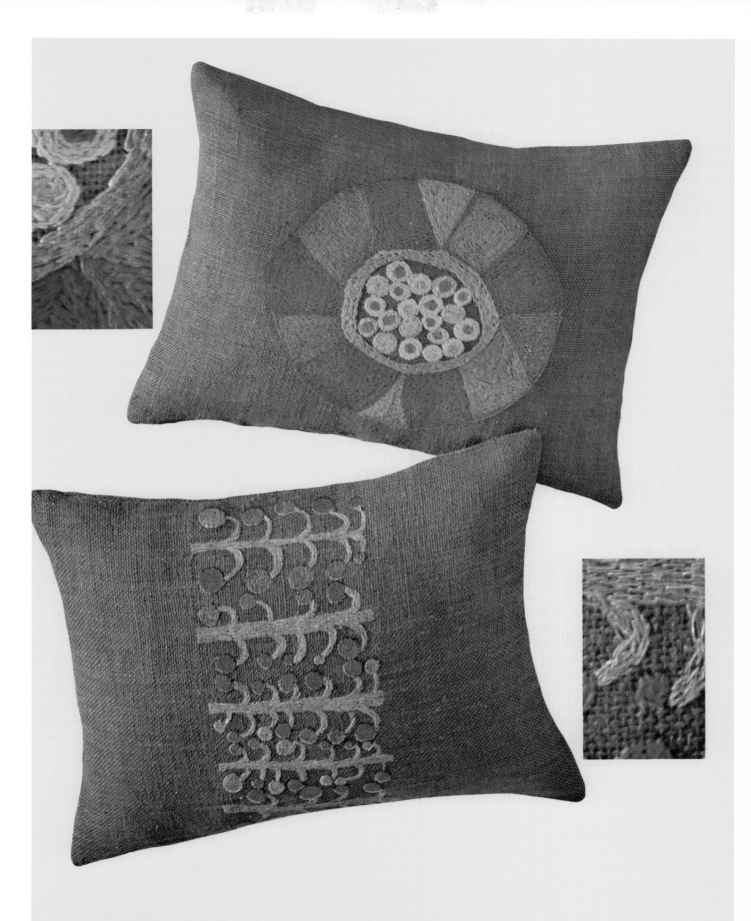

The embroidery is done in outline stitch and long and short stitch. To fill areas solidly with these stitches, work in straight rows or in circular or rectangular lines, close together. To obtain bright, iridescent colors, combine two or three colors or shades of a color, using one, two, or three strands of each color in the needle. Embroider designs following illustrations and individual instructions.

When embroidery is completed, place front and back together with right sides facing; stitch around three sides, allowing ½″ for seams. Turn right side out. Make inner pillow according to directions on page 287, insert in pillow cover, and slip-stitch remaining side of cover closed.

POSY PATCH

Work entirely in outline stitch. Use six strands of embroidery floss in needle. Starting at center of each segment of large outer circle, embroider around and outward in spiral, oblong, or triangular shape, according to shape of segment, using one color for entire segment. Make rows close together and work to outer edge to fill. Work small circles in center in same way, using one color at center and a second color for outer rows. Embroider inner circular band in two colors, working rows to fill areas.

BERRY BRAMBLE

Work the branches in long and short stitch, using two shades. Work berries in outline stitch, starting at center and working around in touching rows to edge, as shown; work berries in solid colors, but use a different type of thread for each berry color for added contrast.

VEGETABLE PILLOWS

Vegetables from a jolly giant's garden make charming toss-about pillows. The white squash, cucumber, carrot, eggplant, and lima bean pod are cut from polished cottons or wools and boldly embroidered with tapestry yarns in simple stitches. The carrot has a shaggy topknot of green wool yarn. The pillows range in size from 16″ to 24″.

EQUIPMENT: Paper for patterns. Tracing paper. Dressmaker's tracing (carbon) paper. Dry ball-point pen. Pencil. Ruler. Scissors. Sewing needle. Large-eyed embroidery needle. Compass.

MATERIALS: Fabrics, sewing thread, and tapestry yarn (see individual directions for colors). Dacron batting for stuffing.

DIRECTIONS: Read directions for embroidery on page 280. Enlarge patterns by copying on paper ruled in 2″ squares; complete half- and quarter-patterns indicated by long dash lines. Trace patterns. Fine lines indicate lines to be embroidered. Cut pieces out of fabric indicated in individual directions, adding ⅜″ all around for seam allowances. When sewing pieces together, make ⅜″ seams. Make pillows following individual directions. Transfer embroidery and design lines to fabric as indicated with dressmaker's carbon and dry ball-point pen. Refer to stitch details given on page 282 when doing all embroidery.

SQUASH

Out of white cotton, cut two complete scalloped shapes and one 12½″-diameter circle. Place the scalloped pieces together with right sides facing. Sew together around edges, leaving two scallops open. Clip into seam at curves. Turn to right side. Fill shape with stuffing. Turn edges of opening in and slip-stitch the opening closed.

Transfer pattern lines to the circle. Cut piece of lining fabric 9″ in diameter; place cotton and lining, centered, together, with wrong sides facing; place a layer of stuffing between; baste the three thicknesses together. Work embroidery as indicated through the three thicknesses. Fill in the center 1″ circle by couching gold-color yarn with yellow yarn around in spiral. Work the lines radiating out from center and lines of 3″ and 8½″ circles with yellow yarn in running stitch. With gold yarn, fill in the spaces between the radiating lines at center with two short straight stitches on each side of a longer straight stitch. Clip into ⅜″ seam allowance of circle and press under. Place circle on top center of scalloped piece; place a thick layer of stuffing between; pin edges in place. With yellow yarn, sew together at edges through all thicknesses with running stitches.

CUCUMBER

Out of green polished cotton, cut two basic pieces. On piece which will be front, transfer lines for embroidery, following pattern. With apple green yarn, embroider the

lines at one end in long and short stitch, the long lines in outline stitch, and the dots in French knots.

Place the two cucumber pieces together, right sides facing; sew together around edges, leaving a 6″ opening at side. Clip into seam at curves. Turn to right side. Stuff fully; turn edges of opening in and slip-stitch opening closed.

CARROT

Cut two pieces out of orange polished cotton. Lightly transfer lines across on right side of one piece. With bright orange yarn, make running stitches across along lines. For carrot top, cut 70 pieces of bright green yarn, each 10½″ long. Place yarn strands together and fold them all in half. Sew strands together across fold. With bright orange yarn, make 5″ long piece of twisted cord, following directions for making twisted cord on page 287.

Place the two orange pieces together, right sides facing; insert and pin yarn carrot top between fabric (across top where indicated by double crosslines on pattern) with folded edge flush with seam. Insert about 4″ of twisted cord at bottom point. Sew together along edges, leaving a 6″ opening at side. Clip into seam at curves. Turn to right side. Stuff carrot. Turn edges of opening in and slip-stitch closed.

EGGPLANT

Cut two main pieces out of purple cotton; cut two stems out of green polished cotton. With right sides of purple

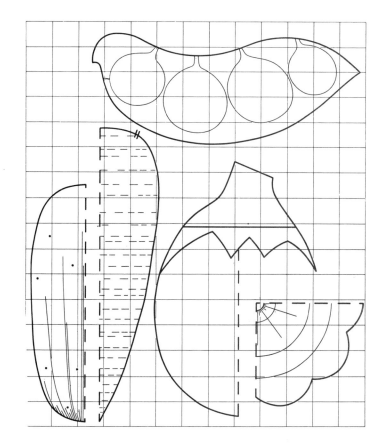

pieces facing, sew together at edges; leave top completely open. Clip into seam at curves and turn to right side. Place the two stem pieces together with right sides facing; sew together around edges, leaving bottom completely open. Clip into seam at curves and turn to right side. Stuff purple piece fully, then stuff stem fully. Place stem over top of eggplant. Turn bottom edges of stem under ¼″ and slip-stitch to purple eggplant.

LIMA BEAN POD

Cut two pieces out of apple green wool. Using pattern, transfer embroidery lines on right side of one wool piece. With right sides facing, sew together along top and ends, leaving bottom open. Turn to right side. First fill entire pod with one layer of stuffing, then fill the bean area with thick pads of stuffing. With olive green yarn, make running stitches through all thicknesses, along lines for embroidery. Turn edges of opening in and slip-stitch closed.

REVERSE-APPLIQUÉ PILLOW

A giant flower, vibrant with color, splashes across this pillow. The design is worked in the fascinating reverse appliqué technique: several fabrics are layered together, and the motifs are cut into the top layer, revealing the colors underneath. The embroidered details add to the interesting texture.

Enlarge pattern on 1″ squares. Areas marked X are cut from orange fabric only.

SIZE: 14″ square.

EQUIPMENT: Pencil. Ruler. Paper for pattern. Tracing paper. Dry ball-point pen. Sewing and embroidery needles. Embroidery scissors. Dressmaker's tracing (carbon) paper. Embroidery hoop. Steam iron.

MATERIALS: Cotton fabric; bright orange, 14¾″ x 29½″; bright pink, 14¾″ square; coordinated print, about 6″ square. Six-strand embroidery floss, one skein each: deep yellow, purple, and deep lavender. Orange sewing thread. Pillow form, 14″ square, knife-edge.

DIRECTIONS: Read directions for embroidery and appliqué on pages 280 and 284. Enlarge flower design by copying on paper ruled in 1″ squares. In copying the pattern, mark all dot-dash lines in solid lines. Trace pattern.

Cut orange fabric in half crosswise. On one orange piece, transfer all solid lines shown on pattern above, buds marked A, and long and short flower stems with leaves, using dressmaker's carbon and dry ball-point pen. Place pink fabric under marked orange fabric, with an oval-shaped piece of print fabric about 4¼″ x 5¼″ between, in flower center area; baste together. Save scraps

of print fabric for bud appliqués. All areas marked X on pattern are to be cut from the orange fabric only. Allowing ⅛″ inside marked lines for turn-under, cut out X areas with embroidery scissors, starting with spiral flower center. Pin spiral strip in place, turn under ⅛″ on all edges and slip-stitch to print fabric. Cut out all other areas marked X, allowing ⅛″ inside lines; turn under ⅛″ and slip-stitch to pink fabric. From scraps of print fabric cut the three buds marked A, adding ⅛″ for turn-under all around. Turn under edges, baste, and slip-stitch to orange. With dressmaker's carbon and dry ball-point pen, transfer remainder of dot-dash lines to pink areas, to print fabric in flower center, and to buds; all dot-dash lines and areas are to be embroidered using three strands of floss in needle. (Refer to stitch details on page 282.) Work areas on flower center and buds in satin stitch with lavender floss. Work triangles in petals around center in satin stitch using purple floss for outer triangles and lavender for center triangles. Embroider flower stems in rows of outline stitch with yellow floss; make larger leaves in yellow satin stitch. Outline stems and larger leaves with purple floss. Make the three smaller leaves on large stem in lavender satin stitch with yellow outline. Inside each flower petal, work chain stitch with yellow floss, and continue chain outside embroidered triangles. Steam piece, wrong side up.

Place front and back pillow pieces together with right sides facing. Stitch around three sides, making ⅜" seams. Turn right side out. Insert pillow form; turn in raw edges; slip-stitch together.

CROSS-STITCH BUTTERFLY PILLOW

This brilliant butterfly is cross-stitched over Penelope (cross-stitch) canvas directly onto the white fabric. When the embroidery is complete, the canvas is drawn out, strand by strand.

SIZE: 14" x 15".

EQUIPMENT: Embroidery needle. Scissors. Sewing thread in pastel color. Penelope (cross-stitch) canvas, 7-mesh-to-the-inch, 14" x 15". Piece of cardboard, 2" wide.

MATERIALS: White linenlike fabric, 15" x 32". White sewing thread. Six-strand embroidery floss: green, 13 skeins; orange, 3 skeins; yellow, 1 skein. Knife-edged pillow form, 15" x 16".

DIRECTIONS: See page 284 for how to cross-stitch and how to work over Penelope canvas. Cut two pieces of white fabric, 15" x 16". On one piece, locate vertical center line (center of 16" edges) and mark with running stitch in pastel thread for placing the butterfly design. Center Penelope canvas over fabric and baste in place.

For the embroidery, use full six strands of floss in the needle.

COLOR KEY

◪ Green
⊟ Orange
⊡ Yellow

CHART FOR BUTTERFLY PILLOW

Follow chart and color key; each square of chart represents one cross-stitch. Start 5″ down from center top and work center top stitch of butterfly head (between antennae) with green floss. Continue center line of crosses down to bottom of body. Following chart, work to right, completing half of body, one antenna, and right wing. Starting at left of center, work left side. When design is completed, remove basting and canvas threads.

Place back and front of pillow together, right sides facing; sew together ½″ from edge, leaving one side open.

Turn to right side. Insert pillow form in embroidered cover. Turn in remaining edges; slip-stitch closed.

With three skeins of green floss, make twisted cord (see page 287). Sew around pillow over seam.

For tassels, use 2″ piece of cardboard and one skein of green floss for each tassel. Wrap floss around cardboard; tie strands together at one edge of cardboard. Cut strands at opposite edge. Wrap another piece of floss around all strands tightly, just below tie. Sew to corners of pillow.

ALPHABET PILLOWS

Alphabets worked in simple stitches give these two pillows a distinctive "sampler" look. The red "brick" mansion with a mansard roof is made of fabric; the quaint "clapboard" house with twin chimneys is worked completely in embroidery.

SIZES: Mansion pillow, 15½" x 12¾"; House pillow, 15" x 12½".

EQUIPMENT: Paper for patterns. Tracing paper. Pencil. Ruler. Dressmaker's tracing (carbon) paper. Scissors. Hard-lead pencil. Straight pins. Sewing and embroidery needles.

MATERIALS: For Mansion Pillow: Heavy unbleached muslin, 13" x 10". Floral prints: 13" x 12" for inner border; ½ yard, 45" wide, for pillow and piping. Assorted fabric scraps for appliqués. Six-strand embroidery floss: 1 skein each yellow-green, emerald green, royal blue, red, cocoa brown. **For House Pillow:** Heavy unbleached muslin,

12½″ x 9½″. Floral prints: 13″ x 12″ for inner border; ½ yard, 45″ wide, for pillow and piping. Six-strand embroidery floss: 1 skein each bright yellow, bright pink, black; 2 skeins each rust and emerald green. **For Both:** Matching sewing threads. Muslin for inner pillows, 1 yard. Fiberfill for stuffing. Cable cord, ¼″ diameter, enough to go around each pillow.

DIRECTIONS: Enlarge patterns by copying on paper ruled in 1″ squares. Dash lines on Mansion's fence indicate where fabric is overlapped.

Mansion: Read directions for appliqué on page 284. Trace pattern for each appliqué piece. Place separate patterns on wrong side of selected fabrics. Using carbon paper and hard-lead pencil, transfer design to fabrics. Cut out pieces, adding ¼″ all around each piece. Fold under ¼″ on each piece; press.

Following pattern, pin appliqués in place on back-

ground. Using matching sewing threads, appliqué pieces to background fabric by taking tiny running stitches spaced about ¼″ apart.

Using dressmaker's carbon, transfer alphabet and corner motifs to muslin above appliquéd scene.

Use full six strands of floss in embroidery needle. Using satin stitch, embroider royal blue stars, red apples, and yellow-green leaves. Using outline stitch, embroider royal blue alphabet, emerald green outlines of leaves and stars, cocoa brown windowpanes and roof slate. Make doorknob in straight stitch.

House: Trace entire pattern. Using dressmaker's carbon and hard-lead pencil, transfer design to unbleached muslin background. Using six strands of floss in needle, embroider as follows: work lines of house and roof in rust outline stitch. Work alphabet with black in outline stitch and satin stitch on wider parts. Work green leaves, bright

yellow flower petals and windows, bright pink flower centers, and rust chimney bricks in satin stitch.

Inner Floral Borders: For each pillow, cut 2½″-wide fabric strips as follows: two same length as sides of muslin piece; two 2″ longer than top and bottom of muslin piece. Fold each strip in half lengthwise and turn in ¼″ on each long edge; press. Insert ¼″ along each side of design piece between turned-in edges of shorter border strips. Slip-stitch border to muslin. Repeat at top and bottom, slipping fabric strips over muslin and side borders; slip-stitch in place.

To Make Pillows: Cut floral fabric for pillowcase: two

pieces each 15″ x 13¼″ for Mansion; two pieces each 15½″ x 13″ for House. Slip-stitch embroidered piece to center of one pillowcase piece.

From remaining floral fabric, cut enough 1″-wide bias strips to fit around outer edge of pillow, seaming strips as necessary for desired length. Place cable cord along lengthwise center of bias strip. Bring raw edges together, and stitch along fabric close to cable cord.

With raw edges out and flush with edges of pillow fabric, baste piping around pillow front. To join ends of piping, cut off excess with ends overlapping ½″. Cut ½″ of cable cord off inside one end and turn fabric in ¼″. Insert other end and slip-stitch together. Stitch piping in place. Place pillow front and back together right sides facing, with piping between. Stitch together, making ¼″ seams. Leave 6″ opening for turning and stuffing. Turn to right side.

Make each inner pillow of muslin and finish pillows, following directions on page 287.

GINGHAM PILLOW TOYS

The irresistible pillow toys shown on the next two pages are made from perky pink, blue, yellow, and green gingham. The sun, fish, caterpillar, and cat all have stuffed gingham bodies gaily decorated with embroidery.

EQUIPMENT: Paper for patterns. Lightweight cardboard. Pencil. Ruler. Scissors. Sewing and embroidery needles. Compass.

MATERIALS: Polyester fiberfill. Checked gingham in shades of yellow, pink, green, and blue. Sewing thread to match. Small pieces of felt in bright yellow, bright pink, turquoise, green, light blue. Six-strand embroidery floss in medium green, pink, red, yellow, and blue; pale yellow and green. Small amount blue yarn. Additional materials given in individual directions.

DIRECTIONS: Enlarge patterns on page 168 by copying on paper ruled in 1″ squares; complete half-patterns as indicated by long dash lines. Place pattern on wrong side of fabric; go around outline with pencil. Leave at least ½″ between pieces. When cutting fabric, allow ¼″ outside marked lines (for seam allowance). Use marked line for stitching line. Do not add ¼″ to felt pieces. Eyes are two 1″ circles of pale blue felt and two ⅝″ circles of turquoise, whipstitched in place with double strand of pale blue sewing thread. Nose is ¾″ circle of pale pink felt. Mouth is outline stitch worked with three strands red floss. Embroider pieces as indicated in individual directions. See stitch details on page 282.

Place fabric pieces together, right sides facing. Stitch together, leaving opening for stuffing. Trim seams, clip at curves, and turn right side out. Stuff so pieces are softly rounded.

CATERPILLAR

Made of four 6″-square sections. Cut a 3½″ square out of each color gingham for each section (four squares of each color). Taking ¼″ seams, stitch each group of squares together to form a multicolored 6½″ square. Stitch the four multicolored squares together to form a 24½″ x 6½″ strip. Sew eyes to end head square. Cut a ½″ circle of pale pink felt for nose; whipstitch in place with three strands red floss. Embroider mouth as directed. Using three strands of pink floss, tack a lace flower to center of each of twelve remaining 3″ squares. Using two strands of medium green floss, embroider around lace flowers with lazy daisy stitches as shown. Cut one 6½″ square of each color gingham for back; stitch together to form 24½″ x 6½″ backing strip. Cut two hat pieces of yellow felt; stitch together along curved top portion, ⅛″ in from edges. Stuff lightly. Cut a ¾″ x 4½″ strip of green felt; stitch to brim of hat through all thicknesses, leaving bottom open. Cut a strip of ½″ wide white lace-flower trim; tack along hat brim.

Cut sixteen feet out of felt, so each 3″ square has two feet matching the fabric color. Referring to illustration, baste feet along one long edge on right side of strip of 3″ squares, with straight edges of feet and raw edges of strip even. Baste hat in same manner to opposite edge of head square. With right sides facing, place remaining gingham strip on top; stitch the two strips together along edges, leaving tail end open. Turn right side out. Beginning at head end, stuff each section and stitch across to form square. Repeat until all sections are stuffed and stitched; slip-stitch tail edge closed. Tuft body sections by pulling blue yarn through at each center and knotting tightly.

SUN

Using compass, draw two 8″ circles on yellow gingham. For sunrays, cut a cardboard triangle pattern 4½″ tall and 2½″ wide at base. Trace three pairs of triangles on blue,

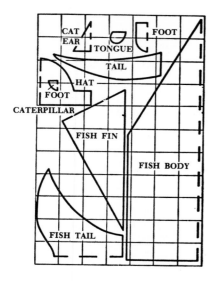

green, and pink gingham; cut out, adding ¼" seam allowance all around. On one 8" circle, sew on eye and nose pieces, using double pink sewing thread for nose. Cheeks are 1¼" circles of bright pink felt stitched with pink sewing thread. Embroider one of each pair of rays as shown with outline stitch and lazy daisy stitches in pale green and yellow floss. Right sides facing, sew each pair of triangles together, leaving base open. Turn right side out and stuff. Baste rays around circumference on right side of one yellow circle, with points facing toward center, and raw edges of rays and circle even. Right sides facing, place second circle on top of first and stitch along seam line, leaving an opening two rays wide; turn right side out. Stuff plumply and slip-stitch the opening closed.

CAT

Cut a 5½" square of each color gingham. Cut a 5½" x 10½" rectangle of pink and one of green gingham. Stitch the two rectangles together along one long edge to form a 10½" square for back. Stitch four squares together to form a 10½" square for front. Embroider yellow, green, and pink squares with lazy daisy stitches and French knots as shown, using six strands blue, pink, and green floss. Cut and stitch eyes and embroider mouth. Cut tongue of bright pink felt; whipstitch with three strands red floss. Whiskers are outline stitch embroidered with six strands blue floss. Stitch white baby rickrack along seam lines of front. Cut two tail pieces of green gingham, adding ¼" seam allowance; stitch together, leaving straight end open. Turn right side out and stuff. Cut one foot each of bright green, turquoise, yellow, and pink felt. Cut two ears of green felt. Referring to illustration, baste ears, tail, and feet along edges on right side of back piece, with raw edges even. Right sides together, place embroidered piece on top of back piece; stitch all around, leaving edge of one square open. Turn right side out; stuff. Slip-stitch opening closed.

FISH

Cut two fins of yellow and two of green gingham from doubled fabric, adding ¼" seam allowance. Stitch each pair together, leaving medium-long sides open. Turn right side out; stuff. Cut two tails of pink gingham; stitch together, leaving straight end open; turn and stuff. Cut two bodies of blue gingham. For scales on one body tack on turquoise lace in a curve; embroider a curved line of outline stitch next to lace with yellow floss. Embroider remainder of scales in yellow and green outline stitch with pink lazy daisies. Referring to illustration, baste tail and fins along edges on right side of one body piece, with raw edges of body and other parts even. Place remaining body piece on top, right sides facing; stitch, leaving bottom edge open from tip of nose halfway to fin (this will be the mouth). Stuff, and slip-stitch opening closed. Sew eyes in place. Nose is a 1¼" bright pink felt triangle stitched with pink thread. Cheek is a 1¼" yellow felt circle stitched with yellow thread. Mouth is outline stitch in red floss and conceals slip-stitched closing.

CRIB SET

A magical tree with heart-shaped leaves gives the sampler look to a ruffled coverlet for baby. The matching pillow repeats a bird motif from the coverlet. The background is simple gingham and the embroidery is cross-stitch.

SIZE: Coverlet, 22½″ x 33″ (without ruffle); pillowcase, 10″ x 12″ (without ruffle).

EQUIPMENT: Scissors. Tape measure. Embroidery and sewing needles. Embroidery hoop (optional).

MATERIALS: Blue-and-white-checked gingham, 7 squares to the inch, 3½ yards. Six-strand embroidery floss (8.7-yard skeins): 1 skein each orange, brown, royal blue; 2 skeins yellow; 4 skeins medium blue; 6 skeins medium green. White sewing thread. Unbleached muslin for inner pillow, 21″ x 12½″. Fiberfill for stuffing.

DIRECTIONS: Cut gingham fabric for coverlet top and lining, each 23″ x 33½″. Cut four strips, each 10½″ x 58″ for coverlet ruffle. Cut two gingham pieces for pillowcase, each 10½″ x 12½ ″; cut ruffle for pillowcase, 4″ x 62″.

COVERLET

Fold gingham for coverlet top in half twice to find center. Use four strands of floss in needle to work cross-stitch. Following directions for working cross-stitch and referring to the paragraph on gingham, page 284, begin em-

COLOR KEY

- Orange
- Brown
- Royal blue
- Yellow
- Medium green
- Medium blue

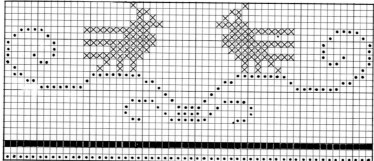

broidering the tree design at center of gingham, starting at center of tree (arrows on chart). Use hoop if desired. Following chart and color key, complete cross-stitch tree and saying.

For cross-stitch border, measure 3″ in from edge of fabric around entire coverlet top. Work solid row of green cross-stitches around entire coverlet. Skip one row of gingham checks; work a second row of solid cross-stitch in yellow within green border.

To assemble ruffle, stitch strips together, end to end, right sides facing, for length approximately 6½ yards long; stitch ends of length together. Fold in half lengthwise and gather double raw edges with running stitches.

Keeping raw edges of ruffle out and flush with raw edges of embroidered piece, baste ruffle to right side of coverlet all around, adjusting gathers evenly. Stitch ruffle in place. Place gingham lining on top of embroidered piece, over ruffle; baste and stitch around with ¼″ seams, leaving a 6″ opening for turning.

Turn coverlet right side out and slip-stitch opening closed.

PILLOWCASE

Starting ¾″ up from one 12½″ edge of gingham piece, work border as shown on chart, extending cross-stitch rows to within ¼″ from fabric edges (seam allowance). Work remainder of design as charted.

Fold strip for ruffle in half lengthwise. Using running stitch, gather strip for ruffled edge.

With right sides together and making ¼″ seams, stitch pillow front and back together around three sides, leaving open at bordered end. Having raw edges even and right sides together, stitch ruffle around pillowcase opening.

To make inner pillow, cut two pieces of muslin each 10½″ x 12½″. Stitch muslin pieces together, making ¼″ seams. Leave a 4″ opening for turning. Turn case to right side; stuff firmly with fiberfill. Turn in raw edges and slip-stitch opening closed.

Table Settings and Dining Accessories

POMEGRANATE CLOTH

This graceful pomegranate repeat motif, reminiscent of the Blue Onion pattern, is machine embroidered in the three traditional shades of blue. This pattern can be embroidered on any size linen cloth.

SIZE: 70″ square.

EQUIPMENT: Large piece of tracing paper for pattern. Pencil. Ruler. Sewing machine with zigzag setting. Needle. Dressmaker's tracing (carbon) paper. Dry ball-point pen. Embroidery hoop, 7″ diameter.

MATERIALS: Off-white linen fabric, 72″ wide, 2 yards. Off-white sewing thread (for hem). **For Embroidery:** Mercerized sewing thread, size 50 (600-yard spools): royal blue (A), three spools; pale aqua (B), one spool; deep aqua (C), three spools.

DIRECTIONS: Press fabric; make sure that fabric is cut along straight grain and ends are straight. To make mitered corner: On two adjacent sides that form corner to be mitered, fold and press 1″ hem to right side of fabric. Pull point of corner up so it stands at right angles to rest of fabric; refold hem, leaving corner pulled up. Fold corner to right and left, creating a diagonal crease. Stitch together along crease. Cut off corner ¼″ from stitching. Turn mitered corner to wrong side. Repeat on all corners. Fold and press ¼″ of hem to wrong side along all edges. Refold hems to wrong side along original 1″ hem line; topstitch all around, ⅛″ from inside folded edge.

Enlarge pattern by copying on paper ruled in 1″ squares. Place pattern on right side of fabric with carbon paper in between. Make sure all arrows are 2½″ from edge of fabric that is parallel to arrow. Transfer design to fabric with dry ball-point pen. Pattern as given is for lower right corner; transfer design to this area first. Then flip pattern over to wrong side, matching portion of corner motif and adjacent motif, and transfer design to right-hand side above lower right corner. Transfer design to remaining corners in same manner. Transfer entire design before beginning to embroider, as the process of embroidering will pull and distort the fabric somewhat and will make exact positioning difficult.

See threads listed in "Materials" and pattern for color key, and refer to illustration. Colors for all motifs are the same. Set machine for close zigzag stitch to embroider all lines except shaded areas, seeds, and buds. Embroider lines A on pattern in royal blue with stitch width set at #3. Embroider lines B in pale aqua and lines C in deep aqua with stitch set at #4.

For remainder of design, set machine for free-motion embroidery (check your book, as setting varies from machine to machine), set stitch width at #5, and remove presser foot. Place fabric in embroidery hoop with motif to be embroidered in center; work in short back-and-forth motion. Use deep aqua shaded to pale aqua to fill shaded areas. Work the three lines of buds in pale aqua (outer line), deep aqua (middle line), and royal blue. Work seed outlines in royal blue.

174

STRAWBERRY CIRCLE

Sweet strawberries scattered on a field of crisp white organdy are machine appliquéd with a zigzag stitch. The delicate blossoms and stems are hand-embroidered with embroidery floss.

SIZE: 60″ diameter.

EQUIPMENT: Pencil. Ruler. Yardstick. Scissors. String. Straight pins. Paper for patterns. Tracing paper. Dressmaker's tracing (carbon) paper. Sewing machine with zigzag attachment. Embroidery hoop. Needle. Scissors.

MATERIALS: Organdy (at least 36″ wide): 3½ yards white, ½ yard each of green and red. Mercerized cotton sewing thread (not polyester): white, green, and red. Six-strand embroidery floss: white, bright yellow, and medium green.

DIRECTIONS: From white organdy, cut two 36″ x 63″ pieces. Sew together along 63″ edges with ½″ seam, using close zigzag stitch. Mark a 60″-diameter circle on fabric (finished size) as follows: Tie a long length of string to a pencil. Find the exact center of fabric and pin other end of string to center, leaving 30″ of string between pencil and center. Swing pencil around lightly to mark cloth area. With pencil and yardstick, lightly mark 60″-long line directly across center seam line. Mark lines, horizontally and vertically, parallel to lines in center, making them 10″ apart (see diagram for one-half of tablecloth; repeat on other half).

Enlarge patterns for strawberries by copying on paper ruled in 1″ squares. Heavy lines indicate cutting lines; fine lines indicate hand-embroidery lines. Trace motifs separately. Referring to diagram and using dressmaker's tracing paper, transfer motifs to right side of one-half of fabric. Reverse arrangement for other half of cloth. Using patterns, trace leaves on green and strawberries on red organdy; cut out each ¼″ larger all around than pattern. Pin leaves and strawberries in place on cloth. With match-

ing thread and close zigzag stitch, sew each piece in place along traced outlines; trim away excess ¼". If necessary, use a pencil to define lines to be embroidered.

Refer to stitch details on page 282 and use three strands of floss in needle. With green floss, work stems and leaf veins in outline stitch; work strawberry petals in lazy daisy stitch. In satin stitch, work flower petals in white and flower centers in yellow. When embroidery is finished, use white thread to work close zigzag stitch along horizontal and vertical marked lines. Do not stitch

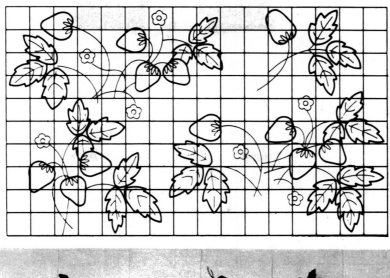

over any motifs. Open out seam allowances of center seam; press. Zigzag stitch over seam; trim seam allowances.

Mark scallops evenly along outer edge of marked circle (see diagram). With green thread, satin stitch (very closely worked zigzag stitch) on machine along scallop outline, making a border ⅜″ wide. Trim fabric beyond stitching. Starch, then press completed tablecloth.

FLOWER-RING CLOTH

An exquisite garland of white flowers borders a tablecloth in a crisp white-on-blue color scheme. The repeat pattern is worked in four embroidery stitches with pearl cotton on a purchased tablecloth.

EQUIPMENT: Paper for patterns. Tracing paper. Ruler. Dressmaker's tracing (carbon) paper (white or yellow). Soft- and hard-lead pencils. White pencil. Embroidery needle.

MATERIALS: Circular tablecloth of cotton, linen, or similar closely woven fabric. (We used cloth 68″ in diameter; to adjust design to any diameter, see directions below.) Pearl cotton, size 8, ten 95-yard spools, white.

DIRECTIONS: Read directions for embroidery on page 280. Enlarge pattern by copying on paper ruled in ½″ squares. Trace pattern (double motif) from bottom up to dash line. A portion of next motif, which is a repeat of the first, is given above dash line to show how design is continued (refer to illustration).

To make pattern for size of cloth being used, trace outline of one-quarter of the cloth on paper. Place traced

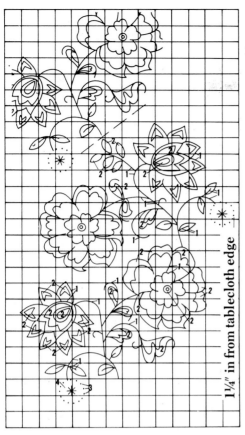

1¼″ in from tablecloth edge

double motif near edge of paper quarter-circle, with small ring of dots 1¼″ from hemmed edge (see pattern). Mark area double motif will cover. Continue placing and marking double motif around quarter-circle in same manner to determine how many repeats will be necessary to complete one-quarter of the cloth. If necessary, adjust spacing by leaving more or less space between motifs. Trace all details of each double motif as fitted onto paper quarter-circle. Place pattern on fabric cloth with edges flush and carbon between. Using hard-lead pencil, transfer motifs for one quarter to cloth. Position pattern on second quarter of cloth; transfer design as for first. Repeat for third and fourth quarters. Remove pattern and carbon. If necessary, go over lines of design with white pencil to sharpen or correct.

Using one strand of white cotton in needle, and referring to numbers on pattern, Stitch Key, and stitch details on page 282, embroider design around cloth as shown in illustration.

STITCH KEY

1 **Outline stitch**
2 **Satin stitch**
3 **French knot**
4 **Star filling stitch**

"BLUE ONION" SET

The charming place mat and matching napkin on page 181 are embroidered in two tones of blue cotton floss on crisp white linen. Seven basic stitches are all you need to work this handsome pattern!

SIZES: Place mat, 14″ x 19½″; napkin, 13¾″ square.

EQUIPMENT: Pencil. Ruler. Tracing paper. Dressmaker's tracing (carbon) paper. Dry ball-point pen. Straight pins. Embroidery needle. Embroidery hoop. Sewing needle. Zigzag sewing machine for hemstitched hem.

MATERIALS: White linen or linenlike fabric, 15¾″ x 21¼″ for place mat, 15″ square for napkin. Six-strand embroidery floss, one skein each royal blue and pale aqua. White sewing thread.

DIRECTIONS: Read directions for embroidery on page 280. Trace actual-size embroidery patterns. For place mat, using dressmaker's carbon and dry ball-point pen, transfer main design to left side of fabric 1¾″ in from side and 2½″ up from bottom edge. Trace small design in lower right corner 2¼″ in from side and 3″ up from bottom

edge. For napkin, trace small design in one corner of 15″ square. Center design about 2½″ in from adjacent sides, turning axis of design diagonally across corner (see illustration).

Place fabric in hoop. Using three strands of floss in needle and following stitch details on page 282, embroider design. Use pale aqua to embroider all fine lines and areas outlined in fine lines. Use royal blue for all heavy lines and areas outlined in heavy lines. Numbers on pattern indicate stitches (see Stitch Key). All dots are French knots; use six strands of floss in needle for heavy dots and three strands for small dots. Lines in pointed ends of large leaves indicate direction of satin stitch. Small flowers are filled in with herringbone stitch.

When embroidery is completed, prepare for hemstitching by pulling out two threads of fabric, 1½″ from place-

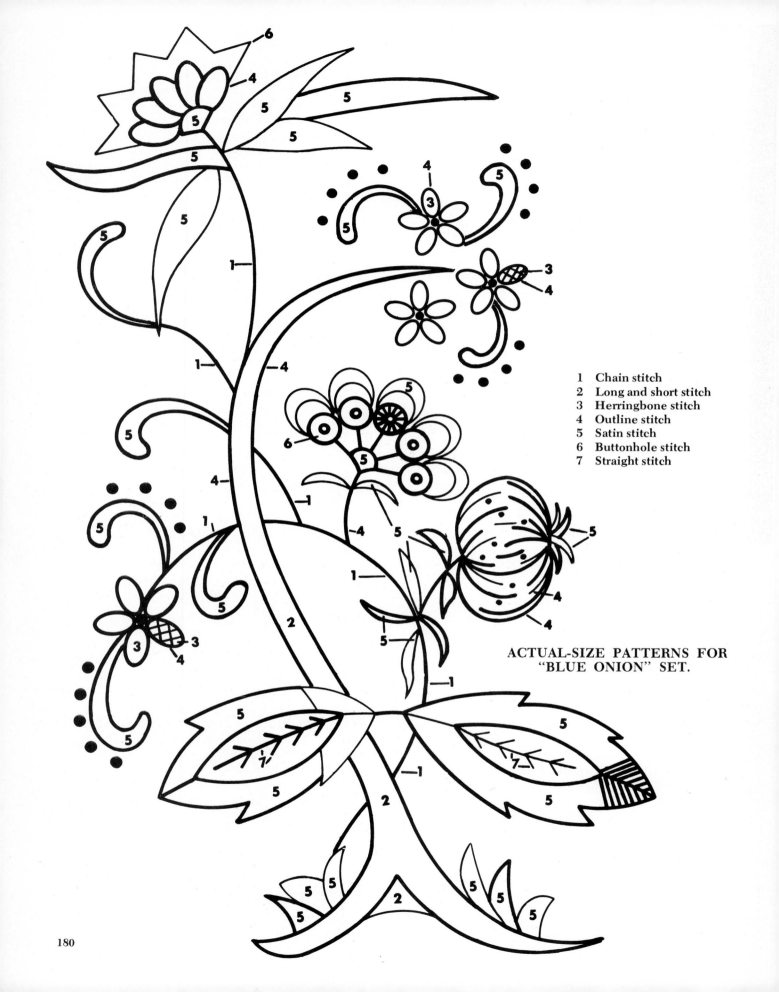

1 Chain stitch
2 Long and short stitch
3 Herringbone stitch
4 Outline stitch
5 Satin stitch
6 Buttonhole stitch
7 Straight stitch

ACTUAL-SIZE PATTERNS FOR
"BLUE ONION" SET.

mat edges and 1¼″ from napkin edges. To miter corners, fold fabric ⅞″ all around to back for place mat, ¾″ for napkin. Pull up fabric at corners so remainder of hem lies flat; flatten and crease mitered fabric to both sides. Stitch adjacent sides of hem together along crease lines at each corner, from tip of corner to outer corners of creases. Refold hem to front; turn under ¼″ and baste hem in place. For machine-hemstitched finish, use blind-stitch disk in machine; stitch on top of hem at inner edge, through hem and pulled-thread line. Steam-press.

TEA COZY SET

This delightful and unusual twosome is worked in simple, quick-to-do straight stitch, which creates a bold design of stars, diagonals, and borders.

SIZES: Tea Cozy, 10″ x 13″; Place Mat, about 14″ x 19″.

EQUIPMENT: Scissors. Ruler. Sewing and embroidery needles. Straight pins. Tailor's chalk.

MATERIALS: Even-weave linen, with 27 threads to the inch: for Tea Cozy, 14″ x 34″; for Place Mat, 15″ x 20″. Sewing thread to match. Six-strand embroidery floss, 2 skeins in desired color. **For Cozy:** Cotton batting 10″ x 26″ and 2½″ x 23″. Unbleached muslin for lining, 36″ wide, ¾ yard.

DIRECTIONS: Read directions for embroidery on page 280. **Tea Cozy:** Cut two pieces of linen 11″ x 14″ for front and back, and a boxing strip 3″ x 34″. Use four strands of the six-strand floss in needle and work all stitches over four threads of the linen; for stars, work each stitch over four threads from the outside to center. On piece of linen for front, measure up 1½″ from one long edge and mark a line across with tailor's chalk. Fold in half crosswise to find center of the line; begin embroidery at center mark. Following chart from arrow at center point, start work from center to left, then from center to

right, to be sure first panel is centered on fabric. Each grid of chart represents a thread of linen. Fill in the border at the right side of chart; only the four corners are left blank. Work star pattern alternately with diagonal pattern. Repeat chart, excluding bottom border, four times. Then repeat star pattern to match bottom and work border across top. Work panel two more times to the left of the first panel and two times to the right. Embroider linen piece for the back of cozy the same. With right sides facing, baste boxing strip around top and sides of front piece; stitch boxing and front together with ½″ seams. With right sides facing, stitch back piece to other edge of boxing with ½″ seams.

For lining, cut two pieces of muslin 11″ x 14″, two pieces 10½″ x 13½″. Cut a muslin boxing strip 3″ x 34″ and one 2½″ x 33½″. Cut two pieces of batting 10″ x 13″ and boxing strip 2″ x 33″. Baste batting pieces to the smaller muslin pieces, leaving even margins of muslin all around. With muslin sides facing, sew boxing around top and sides of both smaller pieces as for embroidered cozy. Sew

CHART FOR TEA COZY SET

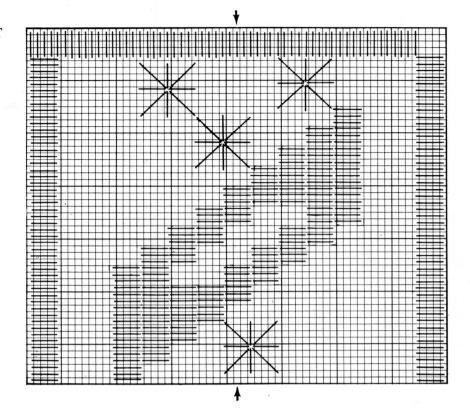

larger muslin pieces and boxing strip together in same manner; turn right side out. Insert batting-muslin piece inside plain muslin. Turn in lower edges of plain muslin piece ½″ and slip-stitch to batting-muslin piece all around. Insert complete padded lining into cozy cover. Turn in bottom edges of cozy fabric ½″ and slip-stitch to lining all around. Tack lining and cover together through top corners. For loop, cut a strip of linen fabric 1½″ x 2½″ long. Fold under ¼″ on all edges and press. Fold strip in half lengthwise and slip-stitch long edges together. Fold strip in half crosswise and sew ends together and to top center of tea cozy.

PLACE MAT

On 15″ x 20″ piece of linen, measure and mark with tailor's chalk a line 1″ in from each short side and ⅝″ in from adjacent longer sides. Embroider in same manner as for tea cozy. Embroider one panel across right edge of mat, having border on marked line. Repeat chart, excluding bottom border, six times, then work stars and top border as for cozy. On the left side, work the chart in reverse. Continue border along long sides.

For hems, fold fabric to wrong side 10 threads from end borders and 5 threads from long borders; press. Turn in edges on all sides and slip-stitch hem to wrong side.

SERVIETTE AND BREAKFAST SETS

Thread-count stitchery adds dazzle and charm to these unique place settings. The Serviette Set has a square doily and a matching place mat with a pocket to hold the napkin, making it perfect for indoor or outdoor dining. The Breakfast Set includes a pretty and practical napkin holder, a matching place mat, and a delightful egg cozy!

SERVIETTE SET

SIZE: Place mat, 13″ x 19″; doily, 7¼″ square.
EQUIPMENT: Scissors. Sewing and embroidery needles. Ruler. Straight pins. Pencil. Tailor's chalk. Masking tape.

MATERIALS: Even-weave yellow linen with 20

threads to the inch, 14½″ x 23¼″ for place mat, 8″ square for doily. Six-strand embroidery floss: one skein each of aqua, lilac, and red. Yellow sewing thread.

DIRECTIONS:

PLACE MAT

Overcast raw edges of 14½″ x 23¼″ linen to keep from raveling. Measure 7¾″ from left along both edges and with tailor's chalk mark a line across linen. Measure 4¼″ in from left end and mark another line across (see diagram). This area is to be folded over for pocket. Embroidery around edges of this area is to be worked on wrong side of linen so that when pocket is folded to right side, embroidery will be on top.

Read directions for cross-stitch on page 284. To work cross-stitch, use three strands of aqua floss in needle and work crosses over two threads of linen (each X on chart is to be worked over two horizontal and two vertical threads of linen). To embroider large dots, use four strands of floss in needle and work in satin stitch, taking stitches between threads of linen and on top of threads to make solid dots (see chart at right and also embroidery stitch details on page 282). Alternate colors of dots in red and lilac. Mark ¾″ around each side for hems. Start embroidery two threads in from hem lines.

Starting at 7¾″ mark, embroider zigzag cross-stitch border and 18 large dots, following outer border of chart B to right and working right corner as indicated on chart. Embroider zigzag cross-stitch and 15 large dots down right

side; repeat corner at bottom. Embroider bottom border same as for top border.

Turn mat to wrong side and embroider border around the 4¼″ pocket area, starting two threads in from hem lines and following chart A. Slash into hem allowance at 4¼″ line at top and bottom. Turn edges on hem line to right side of mat for pocket area. Fold ¼″ in on all edges and slip-stitch hem. Make hem around remainder of mat, turning allowance over to wrong side. Fold pocket over to front of mat. Slip-stitch together along top and bottom

SERVIETTE SET

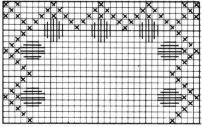

CHART A

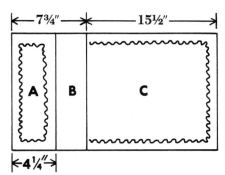

CHART B

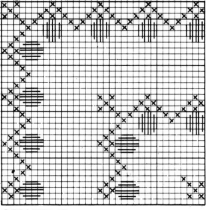

PLACE MAT DIAGRAM

edges. Slip-stitch long edge of pocket to mat, leaving a 6″ opening for napkin 1½″ from top.

DOILY

Mark ¾″ hem line all around 8″ square linen. Starting two threads in from hem line, embroider border and inner square following chart B; work seven large dots along each side between corners. Turn hems to wrong side and slip-stitch as for mat.

BREAKFAST SET

SIZE: Place mat, about 13¼″ x 17¼″.

EQUIPMENT: Scissors. Embroidery needle. Tape measure. Tracing paper. Pencil.

MATERIAL: Even-weave cream or white linen fabric

with 27 threads to the inch: 14″ x 18″ for place mat; 5″ x 10″ for egg cozy; 5″ x 19″ for napkin holder. Sewing thread to match linen. Six-strand embroidery floss, one skein each orange and yellow. **For Egg Cozy:** Cotton flannel or batting and thin lining fabric, each 5″ x 10″. **For Napkin Holder:** Cardboard box approximately 6½″ long, 2½″ wide, and at least 3½″ high. All-purpose glue.

DIRECTIONS:

MAT

Cut linen 14″ x 18″. Measure 1¼″ in from all edges and pull a thread out at this point on each side (this is hemming line). For embroidery, use two strands of six-strand floss in needle, and work in cross-stitch (see directions on page 284). Following chart and illustration, working from left to right and starting ¼″ in from pulled threads, repeat cross-stitch pattern at each end of mat.

To make mitered corners for hems, fold two adjacent sides over to right side of mat ¾″ in from edges. Pull up corner and stitch diagonally across corner. Repeat for each corner. Turn hem to wrong side; turn in ¼″ on all edges; baste hem. Hemstitch by hand or by machine over edges and through pulled-thread lines.

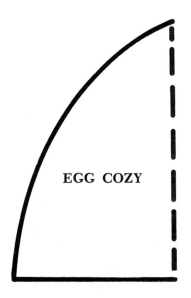

EGG COZY

CHART FOR BREAKFAST SET

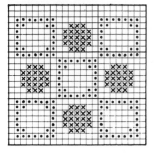

EGG COZY

Trace the actual-size pattern, completing the half-pattern, indicated by long dash line. Using pattern, cut two pieces of linen and two of lining fabric. Mark an outline ¼" in from cut line for seams. Cut two pieces of flannel or batting, following seam size.

Work cross-stitch pattern as for mat, repeating chart to fill entire area within seam lines on both linen pieces.

With right sides facing, stitch the two linen pieces together on seam lines around curved sides. Turn to right side. Using six strands of floss in needle, embroider a row of chain stitches across top of cozy, following the seam line. Stitch a flannel piece to wrong side of each lining piece. With right sides of lining pieces facing, stitch together around curved sides. Insert lining in linen cover. Turn in bottom edges of linen cover and lining and slipstitch all around.

NAPKIN HOLDER

If box is higher than 3½", cut down each side evenly to this measurement. Cut a strip of linen 5" wide and 19" long (or length to fit around box plus 1"). Measure 1¼" in from each long edge and pull a thread from linen at these points. Starting ¼" down from top pulled thread and ½" from one end, work cross-stitch pattern, repeating chart for design along length of linen strip to within ½" of opposite end.

For top and bottom hems, fold ¾" on each long edge over to back. Turn in ¼" at edge and baste. Hemstitch by hand or machine over edge and through pulled-thread line. Fold strip in half crosswise, right sides facing. Stitch ends together with ½" seams (measure piece to fit snugly over box first). Slip linen cover over box; glue top and bottom edges of cover all around to box.

STRAWBERRY SET

This bright, fresh table setting is embroidered entirely on a zigzag sewing machine! The mat is 11-1/2" by 17-1/4"; the napkin, 9" by 9-3/4".

EQUIPMENT: Paper for patterns. Pencil. Ruler. Tracing paper. Tape measure. Straight pins. Scissors. Dressmaker's tracing (carbon) paper. Dry ball-point pen. Sewing machine with zigzag setting. Embroidery hoop with side screw, 8" diameter. Steam iron and two terry-cloth towels for pressing.

MATERIALS: Sturdy cotton fabric, 45" wide, ½ yard beige for each place mat-napkin set (or ½ yard will do for two place mats). Lightweight interlining material, 36" wide, ½ yard, for each place mat only. Scraps of fabric for practice. White sewing thread. Machine embroidery thread (amounts vary, but a place mat-napkin set can be done with less than one spool each): bright red, dark red, black, white, bright yellow, light green, medium green, pale yellow, and medium brown.

DIRECTIONS: Enlarge patterns by copying on paper ruled in 1" squares; complete half-pattern of place mat only; do not complete border design as this would reverse

it: continue border design all around. Trace place mat pattern onto tracing paper. Draw a rectangle 9″ high x 9¾″ wide on tracing paper; trace napkin strawberry (in center of place mat pattern) onto lower left corner, matching lines of pattern with ruled lines. Using dressmaker's carbon and dry ball-point pen, trace both designs onto right side of fabric, allowing at least 2½″ border around each. You need not trace seed marks on strawberries nor fine lines (which indicate shading) onto fabric. Do not cut fabric around patterns. Pin interlining material to fabric underneath design area of place mat; machine-stitch together outside the place mat edge.

To do the machine embroidery, place fabric in embroidery hoop, using the larger ring on the wrong side of the fabric, the smaller ring on top, on the right side (opposite the way it is used in hand embroidery). Keep fabric taut but not distorted. Practice the technique on scraps first.

Prepare sewing machine for embroidery according to individual instruction booklet. Set zigzag dial to wide (4 or 5) on stitch dial unless instructed otherwise. Remove presser foot; lower feed dog; loosen top tension slightly. Use white sewing thread in the bobbin; thread machine according to instructions that follow. To do fill-in embroidery, turn the hoop so that the design section is worked on its side rather than face front. As you zigzag stitch, move hoop from side to side following the traced design shape and filling in the outlined areas. The side motion will help you to follow the outlines. To shade the embroidery, change the thread color, then zigzag over the fill-in embroidery. The fine lines indicate the general shading areas, but being exact is not crucial.

Begin embroidery by fill-in stitching strawberries using bright red threads. Shade berries with dark red. Then use black thread and the small zigzag setting to make small bartacks to resemble the seeds. You need not move the hoop at all while making bartacks.

Next embroider the flowers: do the petals in white, then the centers in bright yellow. Stitch around the outer edges of the petals using bright yellow and a setting of "0" or fine.

Stitch strawberry caps using medium green; stitch stems with light green. For the leaves, fill-in the full leaf outline using light green. Then use medium green to shade around the outer edges and the interior area where indicated by fine lines. On the leaf edges that form the border (at sides of place mat and on the napkin), use small zigzag setting to stitch over those lines.

For the basket-edge border, work fill-in embroidery with pale yellow thread, but you must turn the hoop to have the stitches follow the basket outline. For the fine

lines, set machine at "0" or fine and use brown thread. For the interior basket outline, use brown thread and small zigzag setting where possible; otherwise use "0" or fine setting. For the place mat and napkin outline, use small zigzag setting and brown thread.

When all embroidery is complete, trim away fabric close to outer stitching. To finish edges, raise feed dog, replace presser foot, set zigzag wider and stitch around slowly while moving fabric to follow outer edges. On wrong side of place mat, trim away excess interlining in center area, cutting close to embroidery. Place embroidery face down between two terry towels and steam-press on wrong side.

THREE BORDERED LUNCHEON SETS

Strawberry, red daisy, and scroll motifs dart lightly across the linen edges of checked place mats. Matching napkins, with fabrics reversed, have one corner embroidered to match the place mat motif. Only five embroidery stitches are needed to make these charming, inviting table settings.

SIZE: Place mats, 16″ x 20″; napkins, 17″ square.
EQUIPMENT: Soft- and hard-lead pencils. Ruler. Paper for patterns. Tracing paper. Dressmaker's tracing (carbon) paper. Scissors. Straight pins. Sewing and embroidery needles. Steam iron.
MATERIALS: Red-and-white-checked gingham, 44″ wide, ⅝ yard for two place mats and two napkins. (**Note:**

The place mats and napkins shown were made of gingham with checks not readily available. Gingham comes with ⅛″, ¼″, and 1″ checks. If you use our amounts, and ¼″ checked gingham, you will get the same size place mat and napkin; however, the checks will appear somewhat different.) White linen or linenlike fabric, 44″–45″ wide, 1 yard. Red and white sewing thread. Six-strand embroi-

dery floss, 8.8-yard skeins (see amounts and colors in individual directions).

DIRECTIONS: Trace actual-size patterns. Enlarge pattern given on squares by copying on paper ruled in ½″ squares; trace patterns.

Place Mat: For each, cut four border strips of white fabric each 3″ wide: two 20½″ long, two 16½″ long. Use the four strips to make a border following instructions "To Make Mitered Corners," below. Place longer strips at top and bottom, shorter strips at sides.

To Transfer Design: Following illustration or pattern, mark placement of motifs along border. Using dressmaker's carbon between tracing of pattern and right side of fabric border, transfer motifs to border with hard-lead pencil. Remove paper. Go over design lines if necessary to make design clearer.

To Embroider: Read directions for embroidery on page 280 and refer to stitch details on page 282. Use colors and number of strands of floss and stitches indicated in individual directions. Work stitches carefully to keep the border shape from becoming distorted. When all embroidery is finished, steam-press.

To Finish Place Mat: Cut piece of checked gingham 16½″ x 20½″; press ¼″ to right side all around. Place border over right side of checked fabric, with edges flush. Pin and baste in place. Topstitch along inner and outer edges of border ⅟₁₆″ in from each edge. Remove all basting stitches.

Napkin: For each, cut piece of white fabric 17½″ square; press ¼″ to right side all around; baste. Trace and transfer motif to upper right-hand corner of fabric. Embroider as for place mat. Steam-press.

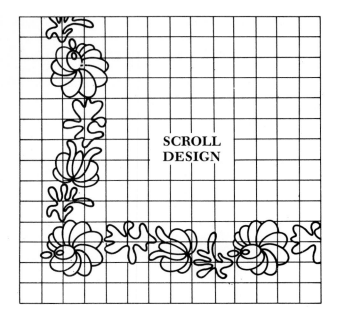

SCROLL
DESIGN

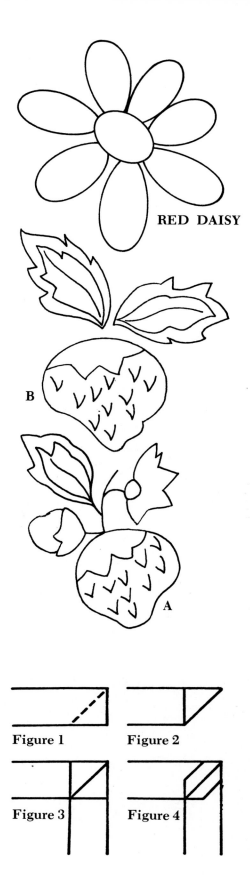

RED DAISY

B

A

For border, cut four pieces of checked gingham, each 1½″ wide and 17½″ long. Miter corners and assemble following instructions "To Make Mitered Corners." Steampress border. Pin and baste border to napkin, then topstitch as for place mat.

STRAWBERRY SET

You will need approximately two skeins red, one skein each of dark green, white, and yellow for one place mat and one napkin. Use two strands of floss in needle. Follow illustration for colors. Use motif A for place mat and motif B for napkin. Fill in strawberries, hulls, and white flower petals with split stitch, following contours. Fill in outer area of each leaf and each yellow flower center with satin stitch. For vein in each leaf center, use a very narrow satin stitch on a diagonal. Embroider the short stems in outline stitch. Embroider the marks on strawberries in fly stitch.

RED DAISY SET

You will need six skeins of red floss for one place mat and one napkin. Use three strands of floss in needle. Outline centers and fill in petals, following contours, with chain stitch.

SCROLL SET

You will need four red and two pink skeins for one place mat and one napkin.

After enlarging and tracing design, complete design by continuing along entire border. Transfer design to fabric.

Using four strands of floss in needle, work embroidery entirely in outline stitch. Refer to illustration for colors.

Figure 1   **Figure 2**

Figure 3   **Figure 4**

To Make Mitered Corners: Place two strips together, one on top of the other, right sides facing. Fold end up so that end is flush with top edge (see Figs. 1 and 2 opposite); press. Unfold and stitch along fold ¼" in from each edge. Open out strips (see Fig. 3). Trim seam; press open (see Fig. 4). Repeat with two remaining strips. Then miter the corners of each pair of strips together to form a "frame" or border of fabric. Press ¼" of both inner and outer edges to wrong side for hem; baste. Finish, following individual instructions.

CROSS-STITCH "CREATURE" MATS AND RINGS

Cross-stitch creatures parade around the edges of easy-to-make place mats. Add just one motif to center the napkin ring that completes the set.

EQUIPMENT: Needle. Ruler. Scissors. Iron. Tailor's chalk.

MATERIALS: Even-weave linen, 27 threads to the inch, in color desired, 13¾" x 22¼" for each mat; about 3" x 6" for each napkin holder. Six-strand embroidery floss in color desired; contrasting color for eyes and other details. Sewing thread to match linen. Small matchbox for each napkin holder. All-purpose glue.

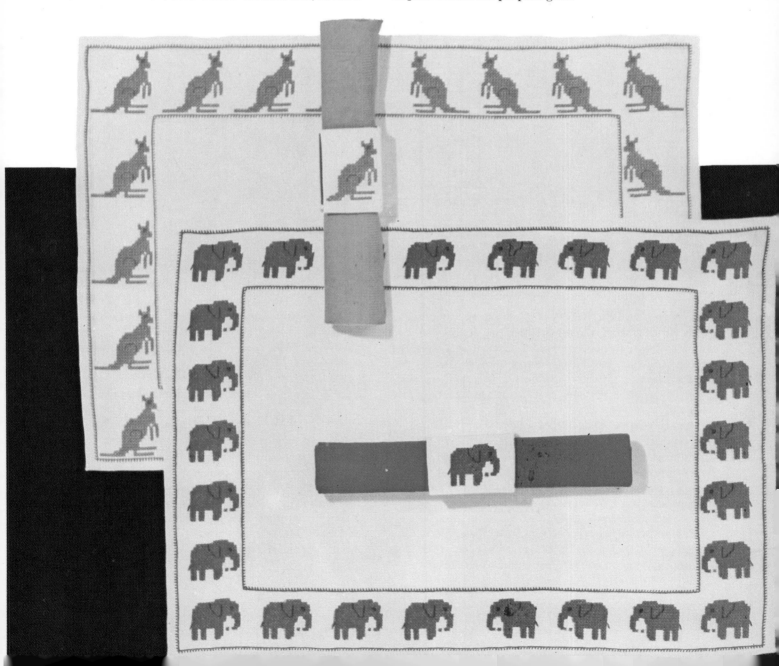

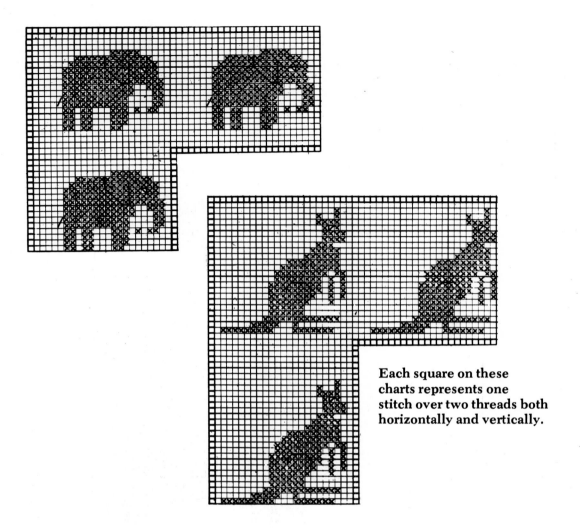

Each square on these charts represents one stitch over two threads both horizontally and vertically.

DIRECTIONS:

PLACE MATS

See page 282 for details of embroidery stitches and page 284 for working cross-stitch on linen. Use two strands of floss in needle to work cross-stitch. Use three strands to work buttonhole stitch borders. Work each stitch over two threads of linen (each square on chart represents one stitch over two threads horizontally and vertically).

For each mat, cut fabric 13¾" x 22¼" (this is enough for largest mat). Measure in 1¼" from edges and with tailor's chalk mark a line across each side. Starting at upper left, work buttonhole stitch along marked line for a few inches across top and down left side. Following chart for desired design, start working motifs across top and down side in cross-stitch. For both designs reverse directions of animals after passing center of longer sides (see illustration). Finish cross-stitch motifs, making number across top, bottom and sides as shown in illustration. Work eyes in cross-

stitch in contrasting color of floss. Using three strands of floss in needle, work ear and leg definitions on elephant and kangaroo in backstitch; work elephant tail in straight stitch. Continue buttonhole stitch border outside motifs around all sides. Trim fabric around all sides to 1¼" if necessary. Work second row of buttonhole stitch around inside of cross-stitch motifs.

For hems, turn under ¼" around all sides and press. Fold ½" to wrong side and slip-stitch hem; press.

NAPKIN RINGS

Remove matches and inner box from match box, using outside frame only. Cut a piece of linen large enough to fit around frame plus ⅜" all around. Place linen around frame with ends overlapping on bottom side; mark outline of top side. Remove linen and embroider motif, centering in outlined area. Turn under ⅜" around one end and both longer sides; press. Glue embroidered piece around frame with turned-under end overlapping raw end.

FLOWER-CENTER TABLE SET

The chain stitch and the satin stitch are all you need to make this luscious, bright tablecloth and napkin set. The brightly colored flower motifs are worked in six-strand embroidery floss on blue cotton fabric, bordered with blue-and-white gingham.

EQUIPMENT: Paper for pattern. Hard- and soft-lead pencils. Ruler. Scissors. Tracing paper. White or yellow dressmaker's tracing (carbon) paper. Straight pins. Embroidery hoop. Sewing and embroidery needles. Steam iron.

MATERIALS: Blue-and-white gingham, 44″ wide, with 1″-wide checks, enough to fit your table, plus desired overhang at each side; ½ yard for four napkin borders. Blue cotton or linenlike fabric, 36″ wide, 1½ yards for cloth insert and four napkins. Blue and white sewing thread. Six-strand embroidery floss: 2 skeins each of bright red and bright green; 1 skein each bright pink, pale pink, bright yellow, gold, and russet.

DIRECTIONS: To Prepare Fabric: Cut piece of blue fabric 17½″ x 23½″ for cloth center; press and baste ¼″ edge to wrong side all around. For each napkin, cut 17½″ square out of blue fabric; press and baste ¼″ edge to right side all around each.

To Transfer Design: Enlarge both embroidery motifs by copying on paper ruled in 1″ squares. Trace designs. Place larger design on center of blue fabric rectangle with dressmaker's carbon between. With hard-lead pencil, go over lines of design to transfer to fabric. Transfer smaller design near one corner of each napkin, allowing about 1½″ for margin and border (see illustration).

To Embroider: See directions for embroidery on page 280. Place fabric in hoop. Use three strands of floss in needle. Refer to embroidery stitch details shown on page 282. Embroider the entire design, except for larger flower centers, in chain stitch along outlines (including the lines radiating out from center). The round centers of larger flowers are completely filled in with satin stitch. See illustration for colors, or use desired colors. When you finish the embroidery, steam-press fabric.

Tablecloth: If checked fabric needed for width of table and overhang is more than 44″, sew two pieces together

lengthwise, matching checks; trim seam to ¼"; press seam open. Pin embroidered rectangle on center of tablecloth and baste to cloth. With blue sewing thread, topstitch all around, ¹⁄₁₆" in from blue fabric edge. Remove basting stitches. Make ¼" hem on all edges of checked cloth; press.

Napkin: For each, cut four strips of checked gingham,

each 1¾" wide, 17½" long. (**Note:** When cutting checked fabric, be sure you have the same pattern for each piece, with a 1"-check in the center of each side.) Miter corners and assemble fabric border following instructions on page 191. Pin and baste border over blue fabric; topstitch ¹⁄₁₆" in along inner and outer edges. Remove basting stitches.

DRAWNWORK PLACE MAT

The stitches on the burlap mat at right are made in the drawn-thread technique, in which open spaces are created by pulling the fabric threads together with satin stitch.

SIZE: 14" x 20" (fringe included).

EQUIPMENT: Scissors. Ruler. Tapestry and sewing needles.

MATERIALS: For four mats: Natural-color burlap, 1¼ yards. Mercerized knitting and crochet cotton yarn, 1 ball natural. Basting thread.

DIRECTIONS: On burlap, mark four pieces, each 14" x 20", allowing a margin all around each.

All stitching is done between threads. Cut strands of cotton yarn in 20" lengths and work with single strand.

To start, bring needle to front, leaving 1½" end of thread on back and work stitching over end; or leave 3" excess when starting and later, with needle, darn excess through stitches on back so no ends are free; clip ends.

To end, weave strand in and out of stitches on back for 2"; clip ends.

Avoid long jumps across back of mat by ending off, or weave needle through stitches on back to next area to be worked.

Stitching will be worked horizontally across short ends of mat starting at top end. Each graph line is one thread. Follow chart and work from right to left, beginning and ending rows 1" plus 8 threads in from marked sides. Begin with satin-stitch bars. Refer to embroidery stitch details on page 282. Each satin-stitch bar will cover 2 threads vertically and will be one thread apart as indicated on chart. Work the two rows across from right to left. Work next line of pyramid stitching as indicated, but working as buttonhole stitch on uneven ends of stitches; repeat high and low pyramids across. Work next two rows of stitching in satin-stitch bar. For square eyelet stitch, work in satin stitch but cover threads indicated on chart and always bring needle up through center space. Square eyelets are separated by two rows of satin-stitch bars as indicated on chart; repeat eyelets and bars until you have reached the left (approximately 12 eyelets), allowing 1" plus 8 threads from edge and making sure to end in two vertical rows of satin-stitch bars. There may be a difference in size due to

thickness of burlap threads. To finish band, repeat from star (* on pattern) in reverse.

Thread-trace mat from ends of band along long sides to opposite end of mat with long basting stitches. Work opposite end of mat same as first end. Cut out mat allowing 1″ plus 8 threads beyond embroidery.

Squared Edging: Beginning at right corner on long edge of mat, count 4 threads from sides of stitching and 4 threads from last satin bar stitched row; work from right to left. Following stitching details A through D, repeat across, ending same distance from edge on opposite end. For outer row of squared edging, count up 4 threads from first row of edging and fray all excess across. Follow diagrams E and F and, working from right to left, repeat across to end of mat making sure step F is pulled more tightly to keep frayed ends bound more tightly. Work edging sequence around entire mat as shown in illustration.

Trim fringe evenly all around. Make four mats.

STITCH DESIGN   SQUARE EDGING

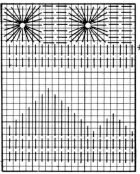
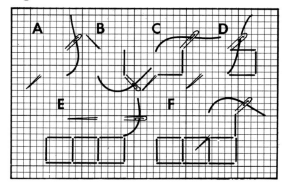

TEA COZIES

Both the blue tea cozy and the red tea cozy bring an old favorite item up to date with exuberant, contemporary designs. The blue tea cozy combines the boldness of freely embroidered pattern with the subtle juxtaposition of varying shades of the same color for a stunning effect. The red tea cozy has the iridescence of color produced when two related shades are combined.

SIZE: 12½″ x 14″.

EQUIPMENT: Paper for patterns. Tracing paper. White tissue paper. Ruler. Pencil. Scissors. Embroidery needles.

MATERIALS: Medium-weight upholstery, hand-woven, or homespun fabric, 36″ wide, ½ yard for each. Embroidery thread, such as linen, six-strand cotton, silk or rayon, fine pearl cotton, or fine wool. Sewing thread to match fabric. Cotton fabric for lining cozy. For quilting, thin fabric and cotton batting.

DIRECTIONS: Read directions for embroidery on page 280 and refer to stitch details on page 282. Enlarge pattern for blue cozy by copying on paper ruled in 1″ squares. Trace actual-size pattern for red cozy. To transfer designs to background fabric, use the "Marking with Running Stitch" method described on page 286.

To obtain bright, iridescent colors, combine two or three colors, or shades of a color, using one, two, or three strands of each color in the needle. Embroider designs following color illustrations and individual instructions.

To Assemble Tea Cozy: Cut one piece of fabric 15″ wide and 27″ long. Fold in half crosswise to mark center; embroider design on front half. Fold in half crosswise again with right sides facing and stitch sides together with ½″ seams. Turn right side out. For padding, cut two pieces of cotton batting, one piece of lining fabric, and a piece of thin fabric, each 14½″ x 26″. Place the two layers of batting on wrong side of lining, with thin fabric on top of batting. Stitch through all four thicknesses in lines about 2″ apart, along the entire length, to quilt. Fold padding in half crosswise with lining sides together, stitch side seams. Insert padding in cozy cover; turn in bottom edges, slip-stitch together.

BLUE COZY

Use fabric with wide stripe, as illustrated, or join light and dark fabric. Combine three strands of two colors or two shades of a color in needle for solid inner part of circles. Work in outline stitch, starting at center and working around and outward in touching rows to fill. Work separated circular lines in black, using six strands of floss or two strands of pearl cotton in needle.

RED COZY

Use a loosely woven red fabric. Embroider with four strands of embroidery floss in needle. Extend the vertical dash lines at bottom of design to bottom edge of background fabric. Embroider this bottom area in vertical lines of running stitch, blending orange, burnt orange, rust, light brown, and a bit of light pink here and there. Embroider in running stitch across inside of circles marked 7 in a slightly brighter red than background red. Remainder of embroidery is chain stitch. Follow color key and numbers on pattern. Colors 2, 3, 4, 5, and 6 on the

BLUE COZY

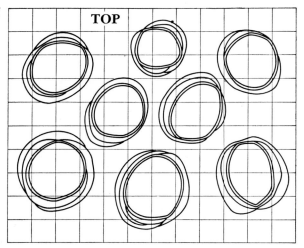

TOP

RED COZY

COLOR KEY

1 Medium brown
2 Golden brown
3 Brown-green
4 Yellow-green
5 Bright green
6 Blue-green
7 Red

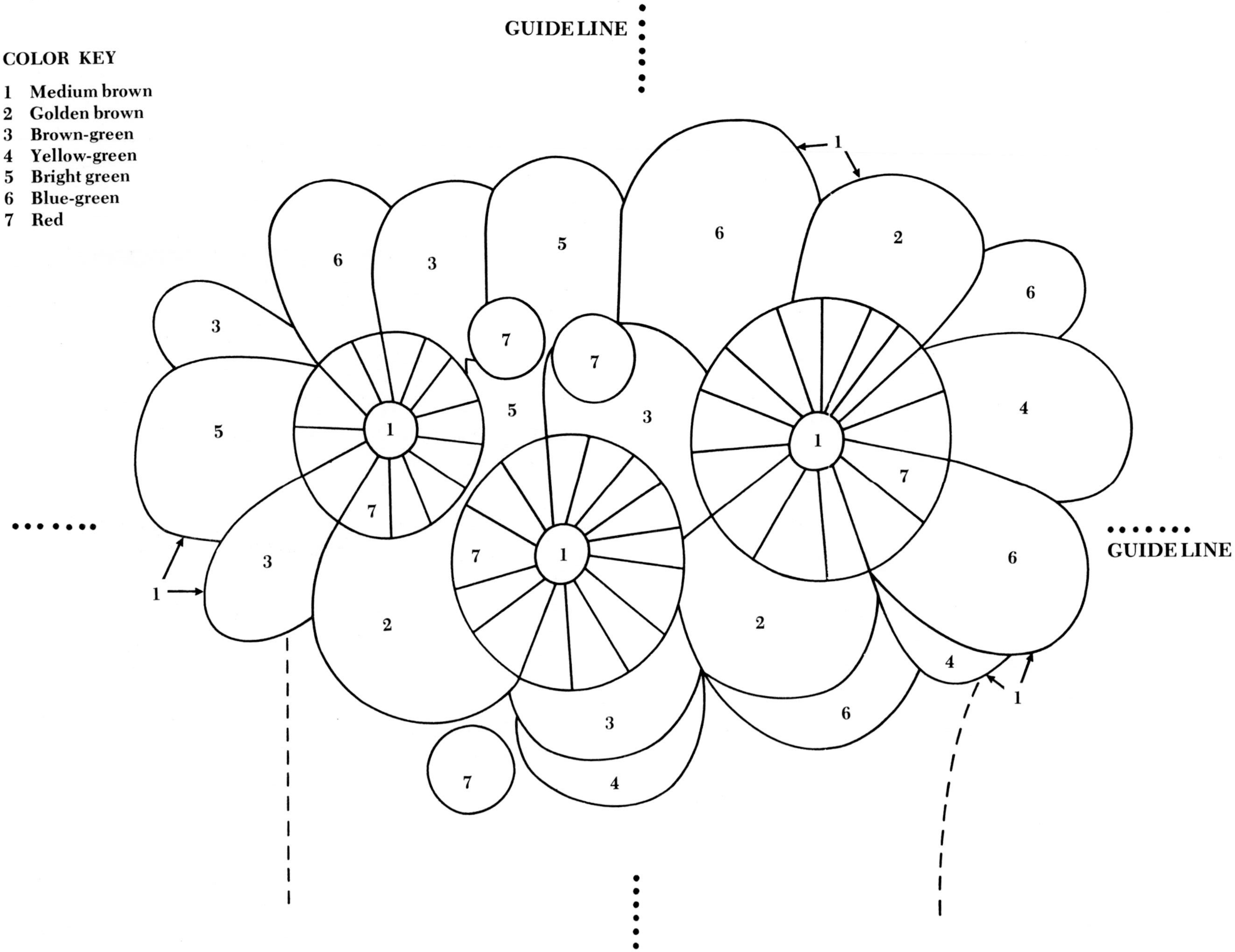

198

color key are made by combining one or two strands of a few shades of embroidery floss in the needle. Embroider the outlines of areas first with one row of chain stitch in medium brown. Fill in areas with curved rows of chain stitch to fill. For color 2, combine golden yellow and tan

floss in needle. For color 3, combine light green, golden yellow, and tan. For color 4, combine light green and golden yellow. For color 5, combine light green, medium green, and golden yellow. For color 6, combine blue and medium green.

POTHOLDER DUO

Potholders lovely enough to come out of the kitchen and into the most elegant of dining rooms have flowers of lazy daisies and French knots in outline-stitch squares; the buttonhole stitch edges a central cross-stitch motif worked on a checked background.

SIZE: 7″ square each.

EQUIPMENT: Scissors. Ruler. Pencil. Embroidery and sewing needles.

MATERIALS: Cotton or linen fabric, white or natural, about 9″ x 18″ for each. Batting, flannel, or other soft material for padding, 8″ x 24″. White sewing thread. Plastic ring, ⅞″ diameter, for each. Knitting and crochet cotton: for Flower Squares, bright pink, yellow, and dark green;

for Cross-Stitch Squares, bright pink and golden yellow. Indelible ink.

DIRECTIONS: Read directions for embroidery on page 280. For each potholder, cut two pieces of cotton or linen fabric for front and back 7½″ square. Cut three pieces of padding fabric 7″ square. Mark lines and embroider designs on front piece with one strand of knitting and crochet cotton in needle, following individual directions below and stitch details on page 282. Turn in ¼″ all around front and back pieces and baste. With padding between front and back, right sides out, slip-stitch together all around. Work buttonhole stitch all around plastic ring closely and sew ring to one corner.

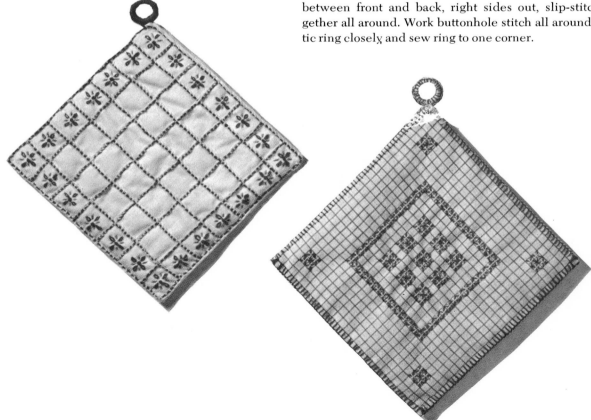

FLOWER SQUARES

Use plain fabric. Mark a 7″ square on front piece with ruler and pencil. Then mark off this square in 1″ squares. With bright pink thread, embroider all lines in outline stitch. With yellow thread, work over each outline in buttonhole stitch. In all outside squares, work a French knot at center and four lazy daisy petals around center with bright pink; embroider a straight stitch in dark green between each lazy daisy stitch. Buttonhole ring in bright pink.

CROSS-STITCH SQUARES

Use fabric with ¼″ checks (or mark fabric in ¼″ squares with indelible ink). With sewing thread, mark a square in basting stitches 2″ in from each side, making a square of 14 checks on each side. With bright pink thread, embroider cross-stitch from corner to corner of line of checks, inside the basted outline. Two checks inside this square, work nine squares of four checks each, with one check space between each square. Four squares in from each corner of fabric, make a cross-stitch square of four checks. With golden yellow thread, work an upright cross-stitch over each cross-stitch previously made. Turn in ¼″ all around fabric and work buttonhole stitch around edge in bright pink over one row of checks, making three stitches in each check. Run golden yellow thread in and out of buttonhole stitches all around edge. Buttonhole ring with pink and yellow.

Sewing Accessories

SONGBIRD SET

A needlebook and a matching pincushion display exquisite songbirds crewel-embroidered in a variety of stitches and subtle coloration.

EQUIPMENT: Tracing paper. Dressmaker's tracing (carbon) paper. Pencil. Dry ball-point pen. Ruler. Sewing and crewel needles. Scissors.

MATERIALS: White linenlike fabric, less than ¼ yard for both (two pieces 6¾" x 4½" for needlebook; two pieces 4" x 4¾" for pincushion). Crewel wool, one yard or less of the following: dark blue (A), medium blue (B), pale blue (C), dark brown (D), russet (E), tan (F), green, red, white (G), black; for needlebook only, yellow. Bright blue cotton piping, 1 yard for both. Blue and white sewing thread Dacron or cotton stuffing for pincushion. Piece of pale blue felt 5½" x 3½" for needlebook.

DIRECTIONS: Read directions for embroidery on page 280.

NEEDLEBOOK

Finished size: 6¼" x 4". Cut two pieces of fabric each 6¾" x 4½". Trace actual-size pattern; center design on right half of one piece of fabric and, using dressmaker's carbon and dry ball-point pen, transfer to right side of fabric. Following letters for colors listed above and on patterns, and referring to embroidery stitch details on

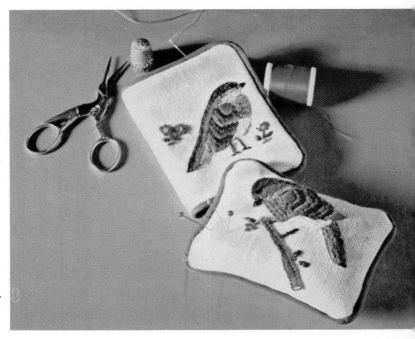

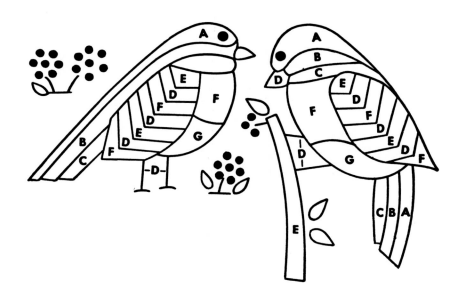

page 282, embroider design using single strand of yarn throughout. Fill blue areas with rows of outline stitch following contours of areas. Work upper part of breast in rows of chain stitch. Work lower chest in long and short stitch. Work all wing sections in satin stitch. Work legs and feet in outline stitch. Work beak in straight stitch. For eye, make French knot with black yarn. Using green, work leaves in satin stitch. Using red for petals and yellow for centers, work flowers in French knots. Using tan, work flower stems in outline stitch and lines under stems in straight stitch.

To assemble, place the two pieces of white fabric together with right sides facing; place piping between, with raw edges out; baste. Stitch all around ¼" from edge, rounding off corners; leave 2" opening in center of one long side. Clip into curves at corners. Turn to right side. Turn edges of opening in ¼" and slip-stitch closed. Center and pin piece of felt on side which is not embroidered. With white thread, stitch along crosswise center of felt and through all thicknesses of fabric. With scissors, round felt corners.

PINCUSHION

Finished size is 3½" x 4¼". Cut two pieces of fabric each 4" x 4¾". Trace actual-size pattern and transfer to right side of one piece of fabric; embroider as for needlebook. Work branch in buttonhole stitch along one long side, then back again on opposite side.

Assemble with piping as for needlebook. Stuff fully before stitching opening closed.

FELT NEEDLE CASES

A butterfly, a turtle, a fish, and a bird have true-to-life details worked in easy stitches with embroidery floss. A piece of flannel is sewn between felt pieces for needles.

EQUIPMENT: Scissors. Pinking shears. Ruler. Pencil. Paper for patterns. Tracing paper. Dressmaker's tracing (carbon) paper. Dry ball-point pen. Embroidery needle.

MATERIALS: Felt (small amounts for each; see individual instructions for colors, or use desired colors). White flannel. Six-strand embroidery floss (see individual directions for colors).

DIRECTIONS: Enlarge patterns by copying on paper ruled in 1″ squares. Complete Butterfly half-pattern indicated by long dash line. Cut pieces out of felt, as indicated in individual directions. Trace embroidery designs. With carbon and dry ball-point pen, transfer designs to appropriate felt pieces. With pinking shears, cut inner pieces out of flannel slightly smaller than felt pieces, as indicated in individual directions.

Read directions for embroidery on page 280. See stitch details on page 282. Embroider felt pieces with three strands of floss in needle. Large dots are French knots, short dash lines are done in backstitch or outline stitch; eyes and bird beak are straight stitch; turtle shell is buttonhole stitch; feathers and scales are fly stitch. Assemble needle case with flannel between, matching X's for each. Stitch all pieces together between X's with backstitch (except for Bird), using two strands of floss to match felt.

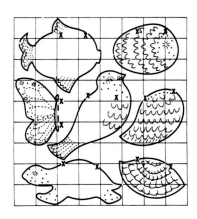

FISH

Cut one entire body and two oval pieces (one will be back without embroidery) of yellow felt. Cut two oval pieces of flannel smaller than pattern. Use pale orange floss for embroidery. Place embroidered oval piece on front of body with flannel between; place one oval piece under body with flannel between. Stitch together.

TURTLE

Cut body out of dark green felt. Cut shell out of dark gold felt. Cut flannel, smaller than shell pattern. Embroider French knots with pale green floss. Embroider shell in medium green floss. Embroider eye brown. Assemble.

BIRD

Cut body and wing of medium blue felt. Use pale yellow floss for beak. Use red floss for feathers on body. Use white floss for feathers on wing, French knots on body, and backstitch on tail. Assemble bird with flannel between; secure pieces together by making French knots between X's on wing with white floss, working through all three thicknesses.

BUTTERFLY

Cut two double wings of lavender felt; cut one smaller of flannel. Cut body of black felt. Embroider only one pair of wings. Work lines in outline stitch with black floss. Work French knots on wings with white floss. Work straight-stitch star flowers with blue floss. Assemble wings with flannel between; stitch together down center twice. Place body on top center; make French knots on body with blue floss through three thicknesses.

YARN PINCUSHIONS

Five unusual textured mini "pillow" pincushions are embroidered in yarns that are thick and thin, shiny and dull. Some of the stitches used on an open-weave fabric background are the outline stitch, chain stitch, satin stitch, and French knot. Turkey work loops make a fringe for one pillow and the center for a small round cushion, 4″ in diameter.

EQUIPMENT: Paper for patterns. Pencil. Ruler. Tracing paper. Dressmaker's tracing (carbon) paper. Dry ball-point pen. Scissors. Large-eyed and sewing needles. Small embroidery hoop (optional). Crochet hook size G.

MATERIALS: Coarse or loosely woven fabric, such as coarse linen, butcher linen, hopsacking, burlap. Yarn in harmonizing colors and varying textures, such as knitting worsted, fingering yarn, mohair, crewel wool. Foam rubber 2″ thick. Sewing thread.

DIRECTIONS: Read directions for embroidery on

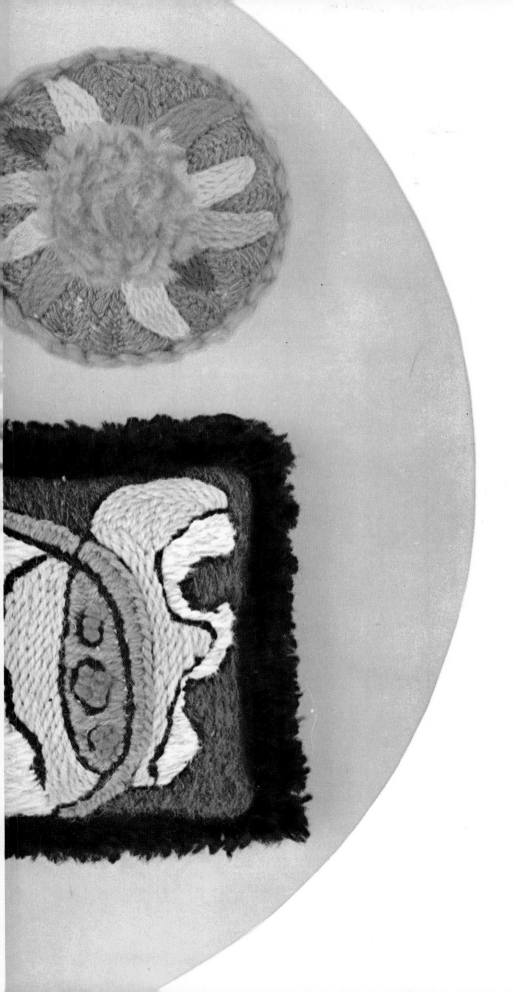

page 280. Enlarge patterns by copying on paper ruled in 1″ squares; complete quarter-pattern indicated by dash lines. Trace patterns. Place patterns on fabric with carbon between and go over lines of tracing with dry ball-point pen to transfer outlines and design lines of each pincushion to fabric.

Place fabric in hoop if desired. If not using hoop, be careful to avoid pulling fabric out of shape by making stitches too tight. Referring to illustration for colors (or using your own color combinations), embroider each pincushion. Refer to stitch details on page 282 and choose your own stitches. You can use outline stitch to outline each section if desired. For filling in areas, you can use rows of outline stitch worked closely together, or use satin stitch, chain stitch, French knots, featherstitch, or any other stitch desired. For tufted center or area, or fringed edging (see largest pincushion), make Turkey work loops, then cut through loops and trim to desired length.

When embroidery is finished, cut out embroidered piece, leaving ½″ all around for seam allowance; cut second piece the same size for back. With right sides facing, sew seams all around, leaving one side open for inserting foam rubber. Turn to right side; push corners out neatly. Cut foam rubber the size of pincushion. Pinch top and bottom edges of foam together and sew them together; this will round off outside edges and top. Insert foam rubber into pincushion. Turn raw edges of opening in and sew closed.

For edging, crochet a chain a little longer than the perimeter or circumference of pincushion; if you wish to make a loop for hanging, add 6″ to length. Tack chain around seam of pincushion; form loop at one corner or just overlap ends and sew securely.

Patterns for Yarn Pincushions to be enlarged on 1″ squares.

SPRIGGED SEWING SET

Muslin pincushion and needlebook are embroidered with sprigs of dainty flowers and finished with small ribbon bows. Needlebook encloses felt pages.

SIZES: Pincushion: about 5″ diameter; needlebook: 4½″ x 2¾″.

EQUIPMENT: Tracing paper. Pencil. Blue dressmaker's tracing (carbon) paper. Embroidery hoop, needle, and scissors. Regular scissors. Ruler. Pins. Pinking shears.

MATERIALS: Unbleached muslin, 8″ x 18″ for pincushion; 8″ x 6″ for needlebook. Off-white sewing thread. Six-strand embroidery floss, one skein each of the following: yellow, rose pink, green, deep purple, medium purple, lavender, pale blue. Pale green satin ribbon, ⅜″ wide, 1 yard. Stiff white cardboard. Small amount

of white felt. All-purpose glue. Absorbent cotton for stuffing.

DIRECTIONS: Read directions for embroidery on page 280. Trace patterns for pincushion and needlebook; complete half-pattern for pincushion indicated by dash line. To complete pattern for needlebook, flop pattern (matching center) for right side of design; do not repeat center.

With dressmaker's tracing carbon, transfer design to fabric as indicated in individual directions. Place fabric in embroidery hoop. Referring to stitch details on page 282, work all flowers, flower centers, and leaves in satin stitch,

206

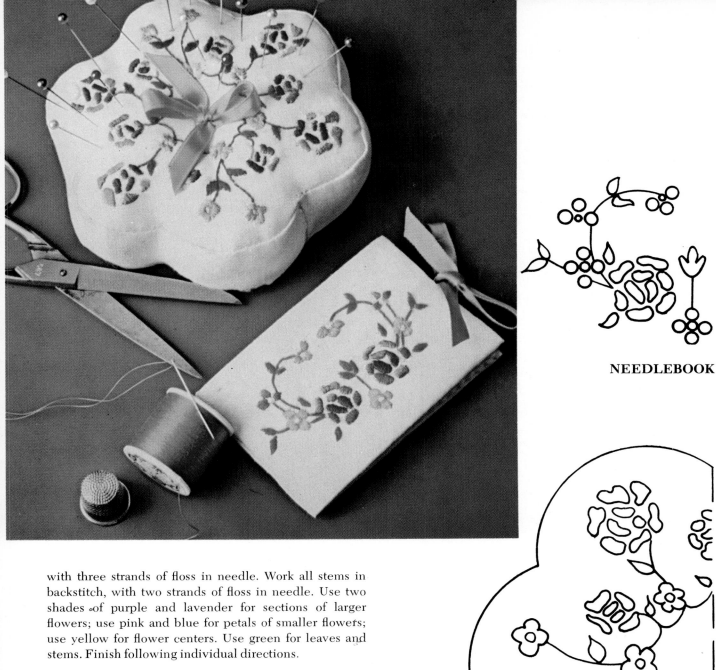

NEEDLEBOOK

with three strands of floss in needle. Work all stems in backstitch, with two strands of floss in needle. Use two shades of purple and lavender for sections of larger flowers; use pink and blue for petals of smaller flowers; use yellow for flower centers. Use green for leaves and stems. Finish following individual directions.

PINCUSHION

Using pattern, mark and cut two scalloped pieces of muslin, adding ¼″ all around for seam allowances; cut one scalloped piece of cardboard same size as pattern. Work embroidery design on one piece of muslin.

To assemble, cut strip of muslin 2″ x 17″. With right sides facing, and making ¼″ seams, pin one long edge of strip to edges of embroidered piece; sew all around. Repeat with other scalloped muslin piece at remaining long edge of strip, leaving a 6″ opening at point where narrow ends of strip meet. Clip into seam allowances all around. Turn to right side. Insert cardboard, making sure it is flat against bottom piece of muslin. Stuff fully with absorbent cotton. Turn edges of openings in and slip-stitch closed.

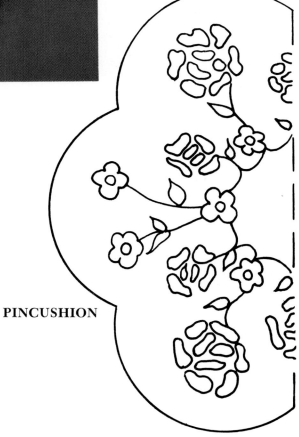

PINCUSHION

Cut 10″ length of ribbon. Knot one end of length of full six strands of floss in a needle; insert needle into center bottom of pincushion and out through center top. Catch center of ribbon, and insert needle back into pincushion (just 1/16″ away); bring needle out through bottom; knot. Tie bow.

NEEDLEBOOK

Cut pieces of muslin each 6¼″ x 4¾″. Mark off 1″ margin on each. Transfer and work embroidery on one marked-off area.

To assemble: With right sides facing, place muslin pieces together; sew across one end on marked line 2¾″. Cut two pieces of cardboard 4¼″ x 2¾″. Place each on wrong side of muslin within marked area. Fold 1″ margins, mitering corners, to wrong side, and glue to cardboard. Using pinking shears, cut two white felt needle pages 4½″ x 2¼″. Cut two pieces of cardboard 3¾″ x 2¼″. Cut two pieces of ribbon 6″ long. Glue ¾″ of one end of one felt page to one end of cardboard; fold felt over to other side of cardboard. Catching in ½″ of ribbon at center of outside end, glue cardboard side to one wrong side of book, with felt page attached at center. Repeat at other side of book with second piece of ribbon.

WRIST PINCUSHIONS

Wrist pincushions, novel and practical, keep pins handy when you sew. These gay, original designs are made of appliquéd-and-embroidered felt circles.

SIZE: 2⅝″ diameter each.

EQUIPMENT: Tracing paper. Pencil. Ruler. Compass. Scissors. Paper punch. Embroidery needle. Straight pins.

MATERIALS: Felt: two 2⅝″ diameter circles for each: large and small scraps in colors shown, or as desired. Six-strand embroidery floss in colors desired. Black elastic, ¼″ wide, 7″ for each. Sewing thread: black, and to match pincushion colors. Cotton batting.

DIRECTIONS: Trace designs; complete half-patterns indicated by long dash lines. Heavier lines on patterns

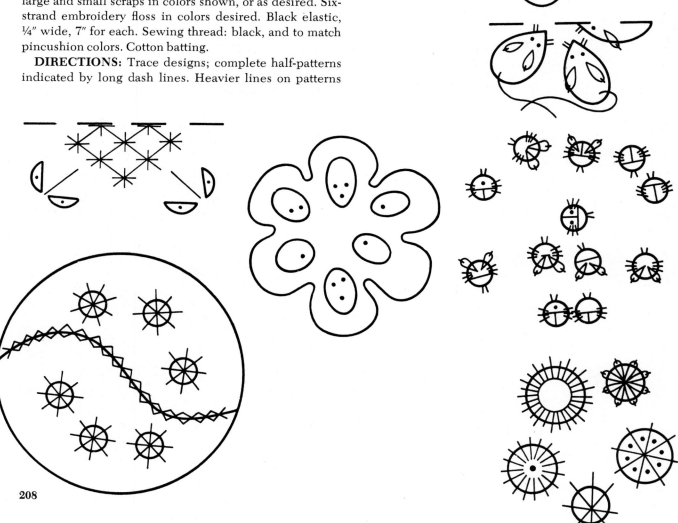

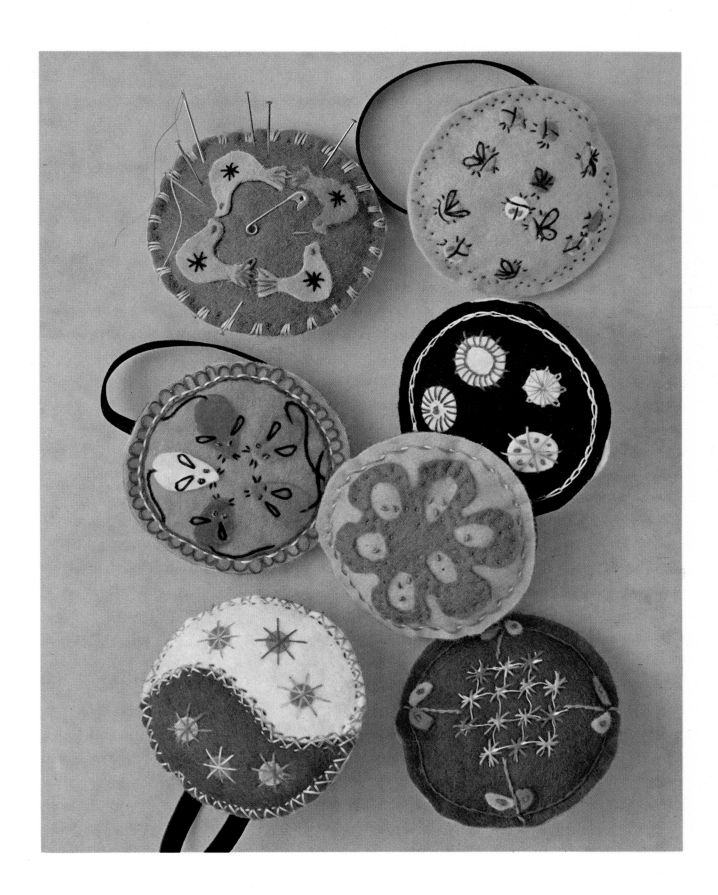

209

are felt pieces; finer lines are embroidery. Follow color illustration for colors of felt and embroidery, or use your own color schemes. See stitch details on page 282. For each pincushion, cut two 2⅝"-diameter circles of felt. Cut motifs of felt and pin to one felt circle for top; secure with embroidery stitches, using two strands of floss in needle. Punch out felt circles for bug bodies and star centers. Embroider over edges of circles and other pieces to secure to pincushion top. Dots on patterns are French knots, crossed lines are single or double cross-stitch, straight lines are straight stitch, loops are lazy daisy stitch; mouse tails are outline stitch, trellis design is laid horizontal and vertical threads with double crosses over intersections.

Cut 7" piece of black elastic, sew ends together to form a ring, then whip securely across bottom circle. Sew top and bottom circles together with small running stitches close to edge with matching thread, leaving an opening for stuffing; do not break off thread, but leave long. Stuff circle fully and continue stitching to sew opening closed. Embroider over stitching line, using chain stitch, buttonhole stitch, outline stitch threaded or looped with another color, or cross-stitch.

Special Decorative Accents

DENIM ALBUM COVER

Graceful cross-stitched letters from an antique sampler plus curvy flowers make this album cover a unique and personal treasure. Scattered cross-stitches give a "dotted swiss" effect to the denim background; entire design is worked over Penelope canvas.

SIZE: 13" x 14" shown.

EQUIPMENT: Pencil. Ruler. Scissors. Sewing and embroidery needles. Basting thread. Embroidery hoop (optional). Penelope (cross-stitch) canvas, 10-mesh-to-the inch, same size as album cover. Tweezers. **For Blocking:** Brown paper. Soft wooden surface. Square. Hammer. Rustproof thumbtacks.

MATERIALS: Photo album, approximately 13" x 14", with removable covers. (**Note:** Covers attached with screws are recommended; if covers are tied, you will need grommets for the eyelets.) Blue denim fabric (see "Directions" for estimating amounts for your album). Six-strand embroidery floss (8.7-yard skeins): 1 skein each purple, red-orange, light green, dark green; 3 skeins pink. All-purpose glue.

DIRECTIONS: Remove screws or ties from album

COLOR KEY

⊠ **Pink**

◩ **Dark green**

◪ **Purple**

◉ **Light green**

▤ **Red-orange**

cover. Measure front and back covers. Adding 2″ to width and doubling height, cut out denim for each cover. (**Note:** If album pages have a separate binding, cut fabric same measurement as width, ½″ longer at top and bottom.)

Using basting thread, outline size of album front on denim, having equal amounts of fabric at top and bottom,

½″ at center binding, 1½″ at outer edge. Center canvas within cover outline. Baste canvas to fabric.

Follow the directions on page 284 for working cross-stitch over Penelope canvas. Using four strands of floss in needle, follow chart and color key to work design. Add or subtract pink background crosses to enlarge or reduce design area to fit your album. When embroidery is finished, remove basting threads and use tweezers to remove Penelope canvas.

Block embroidered piece following directions on page 280.

To cover album, center back album cover on wrong side of corresponding denim. Bring excess at top and bottom to center of inside cover; glue firmly. Mitering corners and trimming at fold, bring fabric at outer edge to inside cover; glue in place. Turn excess fabric at center binding to inside cover; glue firmly in place. Repeat for front cover, being sure embroidery is positioned as desired. For binding on pages, glue fabric on original binding from edge to edge; turn ½″ at top and bottom to inside and glue firmly in place.

Using point of scissors, pierce fabric to accommodate screws. Use grommets to reinforce holes if necessary. Reassemble album.

NOSTALGIC BOUQUET ALBUM COVER

Rainbow-colored flowers are embroidered with Persian or tapestry yarns in six basic stitches—chain, outline, lazy daisy, satin, and straight stitches and French knots. The soft pink fabric gives the flowers a subtle, Victorian quality—perfect for covering an album or to frame a picture!

DESIGN SIZE: 8″ x 7¾″.

EQUIPMENT: Tracing paper. Pencil. Dressmaker's tracing (carbon) paper. Dry ball-point pen or hard-lead pencil. Ruler. Scissors. Straight pins. Sewing needle. Masking tape. Embroidery hoop. Large-eyed embroidery needle. **For Blocking:** Soft wooden surface. Brown paper. Square. Rustproof thumbtacks. Towel.

MATERIALS: Coarsely woven fabric, such as heavy linen or rayon, 36″ wide, about 1 yard. Sewing thread. Any type of medium-weight yarns, such as Persian, tapestry, acrylic, in desired colors (a variety of leftover yarns from other projects would create interesting and different textures and would be very suitable; we used four shades of green; three shades each of orange, red, and mauve; two shades each of pink and light blue; yellow, gold, white, purple, and violet). Two pieces of heavy cardboard, each the size of book to be covered (9″ x 11″ for phone book). Two pieces of thin foam the same size as cardboard. White all-purpose glue.

DIRECTIONS: Design is perfect for phone book cover, generally 9″ x 11″, or album 9″ x 12″. Cut piece of fabric the size of book cover plus about 5″ extra on all sides. Mark outline of design area in center of fabric with pins. With needle and thread, make running stitches along this outline. Tape edges of fabric to keep them from raveling.

Trace complete pattern. Place tracing in center of outline on right side of fabric; place carbon between. Go over design with dry ball-point pen or hard pencil to transfer it to fabric. Remove tracing and carbon. Go over any lines, if necessary, with pencil to sharpen lines.

Read directions for embroidery on page 280. Place fabric in hoop. To work embroidery, refer to embroidery stitch details on page 282 and stitch key on pattern, and also to color illustration for shading. Embroider the roses (smallest circular flowers) with rows of chain stitch as shown in Fig. 1, using a different shade of yarn in the center area of each but continuing the same circular chain stitch. Work the stems in outline stitch and continue into the leaves, filling leaves solidly in outline stitch as shown in Fig. 2. Embroider the large circular flowers with concentric rows of lazy daisy stitch as shown in Fig. 3. Fill the centers of these flowers with French knots. Work petaled flowers in lazy daisy stitch, remaining solid areas in satin stitch, and single lines in straight stitch.

When embroidery is finished, block, following directions on page 280. Remove running stitches.

To make book cover, glue foam onto one surface of each piece of cardboard; let dry. Place foam surface of one cardboard piece down on wrong side of fabric, centering it over embroidered area. Pull fabric edges over to other side and glue securely. For back cover, repeat with plain fabric, cardboard, and foam the same size as front cover. For inside covers, cut two more pieces of fabric the size of covers; press and glue edges under 1″. Cut a strip of fabric 5″ x 16″; fold raw lengthwise edges to center on one side; press and glue. Make another inside cover in same manner. To make loops, cut piece of fabric about ¾″ x 4″. With right sides facing, fold in half lengthwise; stitch together along length only, ¼″ in from raw edges. Turn to right side and fold in half; tack ends together. Make three more loops in same manner for two pairs of back loops. Sew two loops to wrong side of each inside cover along one side for back edge of book, placing them about 2½″ from top and bottom. Place the 16″ folded strips across right side of inside covers 2½″ in from edges opposite loops. Fold 2″ ends of strips to wrong side of inside covers and stitch across ends to secure. Glue inside covers on center of wrong side of outer covers with ends of each strip and loop ends between. Be sure pieces are glued securely; weight down until dry. Slip book covers through fabric cover strips. Tie loops together with yarn.

Figure 1

Figure 2

Figure 3

STITCH KEY

1 Outline stitch
2 Lazy daisy stitch
3 Satin stitch
4 Straight stitch
5 Chain stitch
6 French knot

NOSTALGIA FRAMES

These turn-of-the-century embroideries, worked with silk floss on linen, make perfect frames for a cherished photograph or a tiny mirror.

SIZE: 13⅜" x 11⅜" framed; 12" x 10" mounted.

EQUIPMENT: Paper for patterns. Soft- and hard-lead pencils. Ruler. Tracing paper. Dressmaker's tracing (carbon) paper. Scissors. Sewing thread. Embroidery and sewing needles. Embroidery hoop or frame. **For Blocking:** Soft wooden surface. Brown wrapping paper. Rustproof thumbtacks. Square. Tack hammer. **For Framing:** Single-edged razor blade. Miter box. Backsaw.

MATERIALS: For each: Tightly woven natural-color (dark) embroidery fabric such as linen or Egyptian cotton, 14" x 14". Pearl cotton size 5 or six-strand embroidery floss: for Berry Design: one skein each dark red (A),

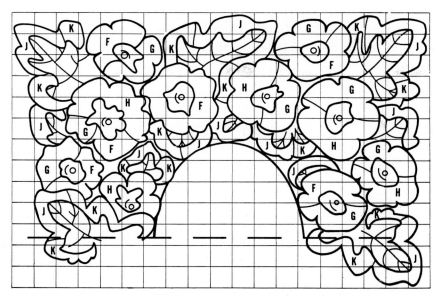

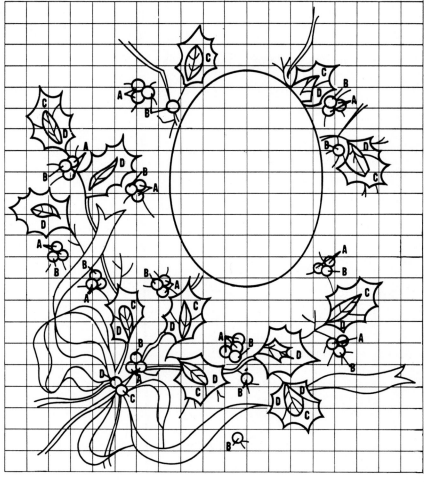

light red (B), light yellow-green (C), dark yellow-green (D); for Flower Design: one skein each pale pink (F), light rose (G), medium rose (H), pale green-gold (J), dark green-gold (K). Waterproof felt-tipped ink markers, for Berry Design only, dark and medium green. **For Framing:** Thick cardboard 12″ x 10″. Masking tape. Straight pins. Wormy chestnut picture-frame molding (rabbeted), 1″ wide, 4½ feet for each (or ready-made frame for 12″ x

10″ picture). Small wire brads or finishing nails. All-purpose glue.

DIRECTIONS: Read directions for embroidery on page 280. Enlarge each pattern by copying on paper ruled in ½″ squares. Trace each pattern. For flower design, trace top half, swing pattern around, matching center leaves, then complete lower half of design. Place fabric right side up on flat surface; center traced pattern on fabric with carbon between; tape to hold securely. Go over tracing with hard pencil to transfer design to fabric. Remove tracing and carbon. With sharp pencil, go over design lines as necessary. Leave oval area marked, but do not cut out until fabric has been mounted. With needle and thread, following threads of the linen and taking small running stitches, mark guidelines 12″ x 10″ around the embroidery area, with design centered.

To embroider, refer to stitch details on page 282 and follow letters on chart for colors (keyed with colors in "Materials").

BERRY DESIGN

Before working embroidery, color in bow area with medium green ink, leaf center areas with dark green ink. Make all berries in satin stitch; fill in bow knot circles with satin stitch. Make all solid sections of leaves in long and short stitch. Make all fine lines in outline stitch. For bow outline, use pale green; for all leaf stems and veins, use dark green unless otherwise indicated.

FLOWER DESIGN

Make all solid sections of leaves and flowers in long and short stitches, making the inner edges very irregular. Make all fine lines in outline stitch. For leaf veins use dark green-gold; use medium rose for lines around flower centers. Using light shade for light flowers and darker shade for dark flowers, make dot in each flower center in French knot.

When embroidery is finished, block and mount, following directions on pages 280-81.

Cut oval out of fabric 1″ inside marked lines; clip into edge all around almost to marked line; mark oval area on board; cut out with razor blade. Turn clipped edges over edges of oval to back of board and tape securely all around on back. Tape picture in oval.

To Frame: Measure and mark molding to fit each side of mounted embroidery; cut pieces with mitered corners. Glue frame pieces together, fitting mitered corners well; glue and nail corners.

Fit embroidery in frame; hold in place with brads hammered in on wrong side.

SILK DESK SET

Green-and-pink paisleys, embroidered on white silk, make an exquisite five-piece desk set. First cover each piece with magenta silk, then glue on the decorative paisley trim. The potpourri of embroidery stitches is worked with six-strand cotton floss.

SIZES: Blotter 13½″ x 22″; trinket box 4¾″ x 6″; address book about 7¾″ x 5¾″.

EQUIPMENT: Paper for patterns. Tracing paper. Pencil. Ruler. Scissors. Utility knife (for cutting boards). Steel straight edge. Dressmaker's tracing (carbon) paper. Tracing wheel or dry ball-point pen. Embroidery and sewing needles. Embroidery hoop. Steam iron. Small flat paintbrush for spreading glue. Tape.

MATERIALS: Medium- and light-weight cardboard. Tightly woven fabric, such as medium-weight silk or a fine cotton, in a light color and a contrasting dark color (we used silk in off-white and deep pink). Cotton organdy. Six-strand embroidery floss: 6 skeins bright pink (color A), 8 skeins bright green (color B). All-purpose white glue. For padding: Cotton batting, polyester fiberfill, or absorbent cotton. Small amount of felt (optional). **For Box:** Octagonal wooden craft box 4¾″ x 6″ x 3⅜″. **For Blotter:** Heavy-weight cardboard; blotter paper, about 13″ x 20″. **For Pencil Holder:** Cylindrical container, about 4½″ high. **For Address Book:** Book measuring about 7¾″ x 5¾″.

DIRECTIONS: Read directions for embroidery on page 280. Enlarge paisley patterns by copying on paper ruled in ½″ squares. Trace patterns. All embroidery is done on the light fabric. Center pattern on right side of the piece of fabric to be embroidered; using dressmaker's tracing paper and tracing wheel, transfer the heavy outlines. Fine lines are guidelines for the height of the longest of the short and long stitches, and should be marked by basting. Baste a piece of organdy to wrong side of fabric; insert in embroidery hoop, and embroider, following individual directions for color; see stitch details on page 282. Areas marked #1 are worked in featherstitch, #2 is seeding stitch, #3 is French knots, #4 is ermine filling stitch, and #5 is a repeat of six short and long stitches worked as follows: Work one long stitch from

marked line to basting. Make three graduated stitches, each one slightly shorter than the last and all starting at marked line. Then make two graduated stitches, each one slightly longer than the last. Repeat the six stitches, beginning with the longest. The innermost heavy line is chain stitch, and the outermost one is outline stitch. Place finished embroidery face down on padded ironing board; steam wrinkles and puckers out gently.

Except for pencil holder, mount embroidered panels as follows: Cut medium-weight cardboard to size indicated in individual directions. Spread and flatten the padding material into a thin layer slightly larger than the cardboard. Dot surface of cardboard with glue near each corner, and place on top of padding; press down lightly. When dry, trim padding to the same size as cardboard. Making sure embroidery remains centered, mark outline of cardboard on wrong side of fabric. Cut fabric ½" outside outline. Place cardboard on wrong side of fabric,

padding side down. Pull up fabric margins over to back of cardboard; tape in place temporarily. Check to see that embroidery is centered. Then untape and glue one side at a time, pleating corners as necessary. Let dry.

Cover the object with the dark fabric as directed; let dry. Apply glue to underside of mounted panel, and place on top of object. Weight down with a book, and let dry. Glue felt to bottom of box and pencil holder, if desired.

BLOTTER

From heavy cardboard, cut one 13½" x 22" piece for main part, two 13½" x 4" pieces for the sides. To cover main part, cut 15" x 23½" piece of dark fabric; center cardboard on fabric. Turn fabric margins to back and glue in place; let dry. For each side piece, cut 6" x 15½" piece of fabric. Center cardboard on top; turn fabric margin to back along one long side only; glue in place. With finished long edge toward center, place side on end of main part; make sure top, bottom, and remaining side edges are even. Turn fabric margins of three sides back to underside of main piece; glue in place. For embroidery, cut two 17″ x 8″ pieces of light fabric. Enlarge and transfer the long pattern as directed above. Transfer the design as given to one fabric piece; embroider areas 1, 2, and 5 of top motif in color A; work the two heavy lines in color B. Reverse the colors for the second motif. Repeat color sequence for the third and fourth motifs. For second side, flop pattern and reverse the entire color sequence of the first side. Cut medium-weight cardboard 3½″ x 13″; finish as directed above and glue to side pieces of blotter. Insert paper cut to fit.

BOX

Cover box top and bottom with dark fabric as follows: Cut two 21½″-long strips, one 6½″ wide for bottom, and one 3½″ wide for top. With brush, apply thin layer of glue all around outside of bottom section. Beginning at what will be center back, wrap 6½″- wide strip around outside, with ¾″ of fabric extending beyond bottom edge; fold overlapping end under ½″ at center back. Apply glue to bottom and fold excess fabric under, pleating as necessary for a smooth surface. Apply glue to rim, insides, and ½″ around inside bottom. Press fabric to inside. Cut a 4″ x 5¼″ piece of matching fabric; fold under ¼″ all around. Apply glue to inside bottom of box and place fabric on glue. Repeat with box top, with ¾″ extending at top instead of bottom.

For embroidery, cut light fabric 8½″ x 10″. Enlarge and transfer the pattern as directed above. (**Note:** The dash line on pattern is for cutting cardboard; do not transfer to fabric. The outside heavy line and inner fine line are for short and long straight-stitch embroidery.) Work areas 1, 2, and 5 of one motif in color A; work the two heavy lines in color B. Reverse the colors for second motif. Work border in color B. Following dash line of pattern, cut cardboard. Finish as directed.

BOOK

To cover book: Measure height and width of front and back covers together while book is closed (book measures wider when closed, because of flexible binding at center). Mark this size on wrong side of dark fabric. Cut out fabric 1″ larger all around. Place open book on fabric, face up; turn fabric margins along marked outline of short edges to inside covers; glue in place. Close book to make sure you have allowed enough play. Open book, and turn remaining fabric margins to inside covers; if necessary, trim fabric at center binding to fit. Glue in place; let dry. Cut two light-weight cardboard pieces ⅛″ smaller all around than inside cover. Cut a piece of light fabric ½″ larger all around than cardboard; glue to cardboard as before. Glue covered cardboard to inside covers.

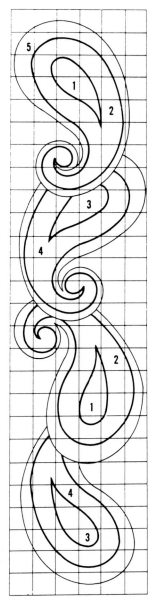

For embroidery, cut fabric about 2″ larger all around than outside front cover. Transfer the paisley pattern for box in reverse; omit lines for border, and reverse the colors when embroidering. Work the border to fit the size and shape of book. Cut medium-weight cardboard ¼″ smaller all around than front cover; finish as directed.

PENCIL CUP

To cover container: Add about 3″ to height of container and 1″ to circumference; cut dark fabric this size. Apply glue to outside of container; wrap fabric around with ½″ extending at bottom; fold the overlapping end under ½″. Apply glue to bottom, and fold excess fabric under. Apply glue to inside of container; neatly fold the excess fabric at top to inside of cup.

Add 4″ to circumference and to height of container; cut fabric to be embroidered this size. Transfer any single motif with areas 3 and 4, and embroider as directed. Add border of short and long straight stitches on long sides. Add ½″ to circumference of container, and subtract ¼″ from container's height; cut light-weight cardboard this size. Center cardboard on wrong side of embroidery, and mark outline. Cut embroidered fabric 2″ longer on two long sides and one short end. Glue, as above, omitting padding. Glue to container, overlapping ends at back. Hold in place with string or rubber band as glue dries.

BABY'S ALBUM

Nothing could be more perfect for a baby album than this strutting stork, embroidered on fabric cut to fit the cover of a loose-leaf photo album.

SIZE: 10½″ x 9″.

EQUIPMENT: Tracing paper. Dressmaker's tracing (carbon) paper (any color that will reproduce on fabric used). Pencil. Dry ball-point pen. Ruler. Scissors. Sewing and large-eyed embroidery needles. Embroidery hoop. Straight pins.

MATERIALS: Heavy linen or cotton fabric, 36″ wide, ⅝ yard. Baby rickrack, 1 yard. Sewing thread to match

ACTUAL-SIZE PATTERN
FOR BABY'S ALBUM.

fabric and rickrack. Fine embroidery yarn, such as crewel wool: one skein white and small amounts of yellow, bright orange, pale green, beige, brown, medium blue, pink. Loose-leaf photo album 10½" x 9" (with fold-back covers).

DIRECTIONS: Trace the actual-size pattern. Cut piece of fabric 10" x 8½". Pin rickrack on right side of fabric ½" in from edges around all four sides; stitch on rickrack with matching thread. With carbon paper between, place pattern on right side of fabric within rickrack border. Go over lines of design with dry ballpoint pen to transfer to fabric.

Place fabric in hoop. Embroider as follows, referring to stitch details on page 282. Using white yarn, embroider the head, neck, and lower section of body solidly in Turkey work loops, making lines of loops follow contour of body. Cut all loops for feathery effect. Embroider chain stitch across body along upper edge of loops. Fill in the top back area in vertical satin stitch. Make loops for tail in outline stitch. Using yellow yarn, embroider the upper line across body back (over satin stitches) in chain stitch. With orange yarn, embroider the beak in satin stitch and the legs and feet in outline stitch. Embroider flower petals on stork's head in satin stitch with yellow yarn. Embroider the flower center in French knots with orange yarn. Embroider the stork's eye in satin stitch with blue yarn. Embroider the baby's blanket in rows of split stitch with green yarn. Embroider baby's head, foot, and hand in split stitch with beige yarn. Embroider hair in tiny Turkey work loops with brown yarn. Embroider flowers on blanket in lazy daisy stitch with yellow yarn. Embroi-

der eyes in French knots with blue yarn; embroider mouth in satin stitch with pink yarn. Embroider petals of flowers in baby's hand in lazy daisy stitch with blue yarn; make French knots in center with yellow yarn.

When embroidery is finished, make fringe around edges of fabric by pulling out threads up to stitched rickrack.

To make cover, cut two pieces of fabric, each 18" x 11¾". With right sides facing, stitch two 11¾" ends together, making ½" seam. Turn in ⅛" at each of the remaining 11¾" ends. Place fabric down flat, right side up; fold each end toward center seam, until piece measures 19" between folds. Fold each end back 1"; pin. Sew straight across at top and bottom just up to edges of end fold on each side, making ½" seams. Turn the center edge at top and bottom to wrong side and hem. Turn cover right side out. Bend back and front album covers to left side and insert in cloth cover. With dabs of glue near corners, secure embroidered piece of fabric on front of cover.

BOOK PETALS

Fresh nosegay bookmarks are embroidered on muslin, then fused to a backing. The finished pieces are edged in machine satin stitch and trimmed to a pretty shape.

EQUIPMENT: Tracing paper. Blue dressmaker's tracing (carbon) paper. Pencil. Dry ball-point pen. Small embroidery hoop. Embroidery needle and scissors. Regular scissors. Ruler. Iron. Sewing machine with zigzag attachment.

MATERIALS: Unbleached muslin or off-white tightly woven cotton fabric, ⅜ yard for all. Six-strand embroidery floss, 1 skein of each color (see Color Key). Mercerized sewing thread (colors in individual directions). Fusible web, 18″ wide, ⅜ yard for all.

DIRECTIONS: Read directions for embroidery on page 280. Cut pieces of fabric the size indicated in individual directions. Trace designs and complete half-pattern D by flopping pattern at center stem. Complete quarter-pattern for border of B indicated by long dash lines. Transfer design to fabric with carbon and dry ball-point pen. If necessary, go over lines of design with pencil to sharpen. Transfer motif C three times vertically, leaving ½″ space between each motif.

Place fabric in hoop. With three strands of floss in needle, work embroidery following Color Key and Stitch Key; refer to stitch details on page 282. Use satin stitch wherever no stitch indication is given.

To finish, cut second piece of fabric and two pieces of fusible web same size as embroidered piece. With iron, fuse fabric together with two pieces of fusible web between. Stitch around edges using satin stitch on machine as indicated in individual directions. Trim off fabric just outside satin stitching.

Design A: Use fabric 8″ x 5½″. With orange thread in machine, satin-stitch along outer line of pattern; trim beyond this line. For tassel, cut 30 strands of yellow floss 5″ long. Make hole at dot on tip and pull strands through hole to halfway point. Knot strands together close to tip.

Design B: Use fabric 9″ x 6″. With aqua thread in machine, satin-stitch along both inner and outer border lines; trim to outer line.

Design C: Use fabric 10″ x 4½″; mark area 2¼″ x 8″ for finished size. Transfer design to center of this area. With olive green thread in machine, satin-stitch along marked outline; then make lines of stitching ⅜″ inside first line, continuing to side, top, and bottom edges. Trim to outer line.

Design D: Use fabric 9″ x 4″. Mark area 7″ x 2″ for finished size. Transfer design in center of this area. Make all the leaves in satin stitch. With golden brown thread in machine, satin-stitch along marked outline; trim to this outline for rectangular shape.

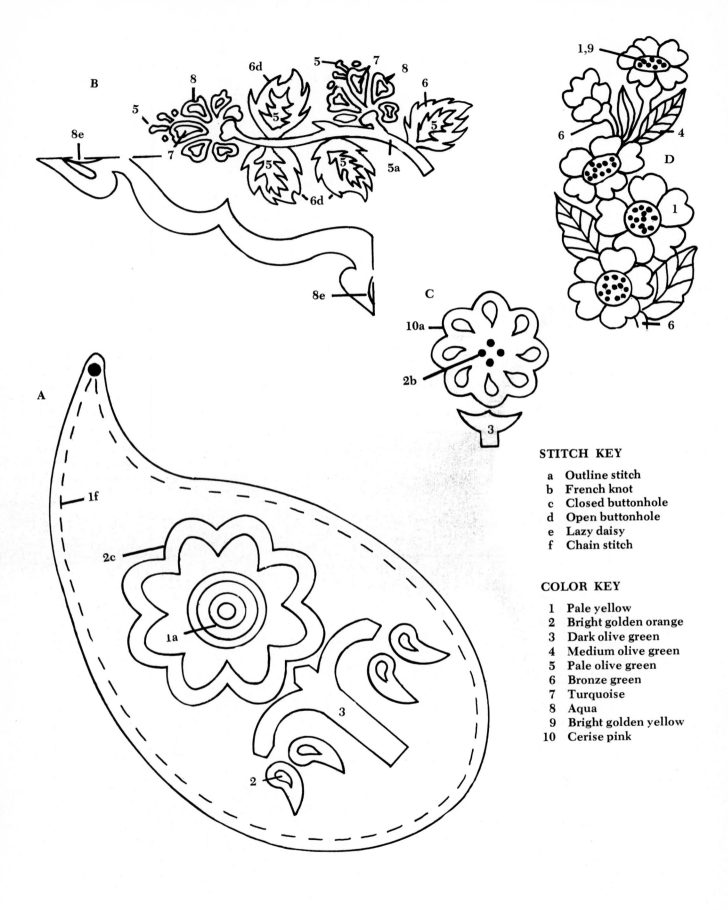

B

8e

5

8

8

6d

5

5

7

7

8

6

5

5a

6d

5

5

1,9

6

4

D

1

6

C

10a

2b

3

A

1f

2c

1a

3

2

STITCH KEY

a Outline stitch
b French knot
c Closed buttonhole
d Open buttonhole
e Lazy daisy
f Chain stitch

COLOR KEY

1 Pale yellow
2 Bright golden orange
3 Dark olive green
4 Medium olive green
5 Pale olive green
6 Bronze green
7 Turquoise
8 Aqua
9 Bright golden yellow
10 Cerise pink

VALANCE PANELS

Make a pretty valance by laying yarn in place and machine-stitching it to fabric, as shown at top. Or work the same design in sewing thread with a zigzag stitch as shown at bottom, for a Jacobean touch.

FINISHED SIZE: 43½" x 11".

EQUIPMENT: Hand-sewing needles. Zipper foot. Dressmaker's tracing (carbon) paper. Dry ball-point pen. Tracing paper. Pencil. Straight pins. Scissors. Staple gun and staples.

MATERIALS: To Make Valance Panel: Fabric: Tightly woven beige linen or hopsacking, 12½" x 44½". Plywood for backing, ¼" thick, 10½" x 43". Olive green cotton bias binding tape, 2" wide, 3 yds. Cording, ½" diameter, 3 yds. **For Yarn Stitchery:** Small amounts of assorted yarns in various weights, such as knitting worsted, sport yarn, fingering yarn, and medium and heavy rug yarn in colors indicated on Color Key. **For Zigzag Machine Embroidery:** #50 machine-embroidery or mercerized sewing thread, two small spools for each shade of green, one spool for each of the other colors indicated on Color Key.

DIRECTIONS: Enlarge same design to use for zigzag machine embroidery or yarn stitchery (below) by copying on paper ruled in 1" squares. Transfer design to fabric, using dressmaker's carbon and dry ball-point pen. Numbers on the pattern indicate color of thread or yarn; letters indicate stitch for yarn stitchery only. Pattern is accurate design for zigzag machine embroidery; shapes of leaves and petals are to be adapted for yarn stitchery following letters on pattern and corresponding stitch details.

Stitch stems and leaves first, then flower petals; centers and base are stitched last.

To Mount for Valance: To make cording for trim, fold 2" bias tape in half lengthwise, with wrong sides facing and cord centered between. Using zipper foot, stitch close to cord. Pin and baste cording to right side of embroidered fabric, having all raw edges even and cording facing inward. Use zipper foot to stitch together very close to cord, inside first stitching line.

To attach to plywood, stretch fabric over edges around perimeter of board; fold back ½" raw edges of cording and fabric; staple to plywood.

If a longer valance panel is desired, reverse design and continue, using longer piece of fabric and plywood.

ZIGZAG EMBROIDERY

EQUIPMENT: Sewing machine with zigzag setting. Embroidery hoop with side screw, 8" diameter.

MATERIALS: White sewing thread. #50 machine-embroidery or mercerized sewing thread. Scraps of fabric for practice.

DIRECTIONS: Prepare machine for embroidery according to individual sewing machine instruction booklet. Set zigzag dial to wide (4 or 5) on stitch dial. Remove presser foot; lower feed dog. Use white thread in bobbin.

Before working on actual fabric, practice on scraps of fabric.

Trace design on fabric. Place larger ring of embroidery hoop on table; place fabric, right side up, with design in center, over embroidery hoop. Push smaller ring of hoop into larger ring, creating a well. (The position of the embroidery hoop for machine embroidery is the opposite of that for hand embroidery.) Slide hoop under the needle; lower the presser bar. Bring bobbin thread up through fabric; holding both thread ends, position needle to start stitching. Almost the entire design is worked with fill-in stitching.

Fill-In Embroidery: Turn the hoop so that the design, or part being worked, is on its side rather than facing you. Move hoop from side to side as needle is zigzagging; guide fabric in hoop to follow shape of design, filling in entire area or outlining as required. The side-to-side motion will make the needle swing the way the pattern lines are drawn.

For Shading: For leaves, start at the base of a leaf; let the needle zigzag to the points. The hoops will have to rotate slightly around the point. Fill in about one third of the leaf, leaving a jagged inner edge. Change thread color and fill in another third of the way, blending into the jagged edge of the first color. Change thread again, and blend into the second color to finish the leaf. Shading of flower petals is done in same manner.

For accent lines, such as veins of leaves and petals, narrow the zigzag stitch and work in the same manner, making a fine line. A row of stitching may be added on the tip of leaves.

Continue to move hoop from section to section, turning hoop so stitching follows direction of leaves, petals, and stems, until entire design is embroidered.

YARN STITCHERY

EQUIPMENT: Straight-stitch (or zigzag) sewing machine. #11 sewing machine needles. Tweezers.

MATERIALS: Fine nylon thread. Any color sewing thread. Scraps of firm fabric and yarn for practice. Dressmaker's tracing (carbon) paper.

DIRECTIONS: It is not necessary to use an embroidery hoop to work yarn stitchery. The yarn is laid on the fabric following the design (use tweezers to guide yarn). As the fabric is moved to form the desired stitch, the up-and-down movement of the nylon-threaded needle secures the yarn to the fabric. The yarn appears suspended

Valances from: **Yarn Stitchery on the Sewing Machine** by Verna Holt

VALANCE PANEL

1 Dark green
2 Yellow-green
3 Pale green
4 Dark blue
5 Light blue
6 Maroon
7 Salmon
8 Terra-cotta
9 Rust
10 Toast
11 Beige
12 Lavender
13 Light purple
14 Dark purple
15 Bright orange
16 Apricot
17 Yellow
18 Pink
19 Rose
20 Dark rose
21 Dark gold
22 Brown
23 Red
24 Strawberry

on the fabric, since the top nylon thread cannot be seen and the bobbin thread does not show.

Before working on actual fabric, practice on scraps of fabric.

Remove presser foot from machine; lower feed dog (teeth) or cover with plate; turn stitch dial to "0" or fine; loosen top tension to 1½–2; use bobbin tension as for regular sewing; thread needle with invisible nylon thread; use any color sewing thread in bobbin.

Trace design on fabric. Put the fabric under the needle; lower presser bar.

See stitch description and details. When stitching one layer of yarn on top of another, let the threaded needle catch the yarn lightly at several points. If stitched down too heavily, the three-dimensional effect may be lost and the needle may break.

STITCH DESCRIPTION AND DETAILS

A. Outline or Running Stitch: Used for stems, straight lines, or curves. Attach one end of yarn at beginning point of design. Using tweezers to guide yarn, stitch lightly along yarn, following design outline.

Aa. Outline Filling: Continue making rows in same manner as outline stitch, but move inward toward center, following contour.

Aa

B. Lazy Daisy Continuous Loops: Used for petals and centers. With a long strand, stitch end of yarn at base of petal (1); loop yarn clockwise to form petal; attach yarn again at base. Make succeeding loops the same way (2). (When yarn is looped the same way for each loop, flower will lie smoothly.) Repeat until you have made a multiple-loop flower; cut off excess yarn.

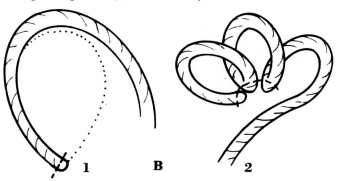

C. Satin Stitch (Filled-In Stitch): Used for leaves. Sew one end of yarn at the left-hand side of the leaf near the base (1); move fabric until the needle is on the opposite side (right) of the leaf. Bring the yarn over to the needle; stitch down. Move fabric again so needle is at left-hand side. Bring yarn back to left-hand side; stitch down. Make sure yarn rows lie close together. Repeat, following design shape (2), until leaf is filled in.

To make a vein on leaf, stitch along center point to base with nylon thread.

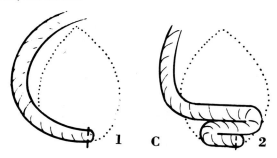

D. Single Lazy Daisies: Used for petals. With tweezers, hold down one end of yarn at the base of one flower petal. Stitch across end to secure (1). With threaded needle only, stitch down center of the petal to point; leave needle in fabric; bring yarn around needle. Holding yarn down with tweezers, stitch across yarn at point of petal (1). With threaded needle only, stitch back to base; bring yarn down to base; stitch across to secure. Without cutting yarn, go to next petal (2); repeat until flower is completed.

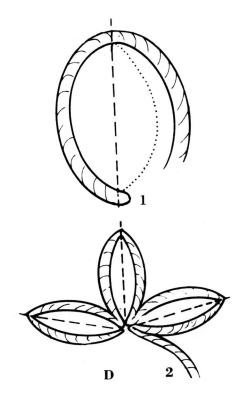

E. French Knot: Used for flower centers and berries, these are actually small loops. With tweezers, hold down one end of yarn; sew across to secure. Use tweezers to hold up a small loop; sew across yarn again. Without cutting yarn, make another loop and stitch again. Repeat until area is filled with small loops placed side by side; cut excess yarn.

Make one French knot for each berry.

F. Loop Variation: For each loop, cut several strands of yarn into 5″ lengths; fold in half together; secure ends to beginning point, forming a loop 2½″ long (1). With threaded needle only, stitch along center toward looped end. With tweezers, hold looped end; stitch across loops ½″ from looped end (2).

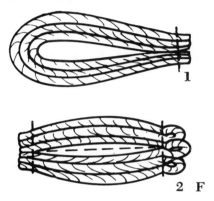

G. Spiral Filling: Start at center of flower; stitch down one end of yarn (1). Lay yarn around in a spiral; stitch lightly over yarn here and there (2).

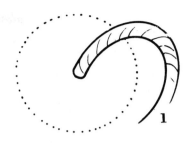

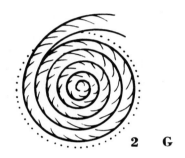

EMBROIDERED SCREEN

Big, bright floral motifs are emblazoned on a screen for on-the-spot elegance. Each motif is 13″ wide and is made with craft yarn couched on fabric, using a conventional sewing machine.

FINISHED SIZE: 45″ x 8′.

EQUIPMENT: Saw. Pencil. Ruler. Hammer. Screwdriver. Yardstick. Scissors. Staple gun and staples. Paper for patterns. Tracing paper. Dressmaker's tracing (carbon) paper. Dry ball-point pen. Straight-stitch (or zigzag) sewing machine. #11 sewing needles. Tweezers.

MATERIALS: Stock lumber for frame: 1″ x 2″, six pieces, each 8′ long; nine pieces, each 11½″ long. Pressed board, three pieces, each 8′ x 15″. Double-action screen hinges with screws, six. 3″ finishing nails. Fabric: Tightly woven homespun cotton, three pieces, each 102″ long x 21″ wide. Acrylic rug yarn, 70-yard skeins, one skein each of colors indicated on Color Key. Fine nylon thread, size 10-15. Any color sewing thread.

DIRECTIONS: Enlarge pattern by copying on paper ruled in 1″ squares. Trace enlarged design six times lengthwise, spacing motifs approximately 4½″ apart and reversing design for every other one, as pictured. Transfer design to fabric, using dressmaker's carbon and dry ball-point pen.

Work design with yarn stitchery (see page 225), following special directions and letters on pattern.

FOLDING SCREEN: Screen is made of three 8′ x 15″ panels attached with hinges. To make frame for each panel, nail three 11½″-long 1″ x 2″ pieces of lumber between two 96″-long pieces: one flush with top edges, one flush with bottom edges, and one across center. For front, nail a piece of pressed board to each frame.

To attach embroidery to frame, stretch fabric over edges around perimeter of board: staple to frame all around. Attach hinges.

FOLDING SCREEN

COLOR KEY

1 Olive green
2 Pale green
3 Royal blue
4 Navy blue
5 Light blue
6 Persimmon
7 Orange
8 Bright yellow
9 Gold
10 Dark green

FOLK ART PILLOWS AND AFGHAN

This bright, lovely set is decorated with traditional distelfink birds and flower sprays. The afghan and pillows are worked in single crochet. The three afghan panels are embroidered and then sewn together. The motifs are worked over paper patterns in satin, chain, and outline stitches.

FOLK ART PILLOWS

SIZE: 15″ diameter, plus edging.

MATERIALS: Yarn of knitting-worsted weight: 8 ozs. white; 1 oz. each of scarlet, marine blue, light orange, emerald green, claret mix (dark red); few yards of black. Crochet hook size H. Large-eyed embroidery needles. White crepe paper, 15″ square. Pencil. Round pillow form, 15″ diameter.

GAUGE: 7 sc = 2″; 4 rnds = 1″.

CROCHET ABBREVIATIONS: sc—single crochet; rnd(s)—round(s); ch—chain; sl st—slip stitch; beg—beginning; inc—increase; st(s)—stitch(es); sk—skip; lp—loop.

PILLOW (make 2 pieces): Beg at center, with white, ch 3. Sl st in first ch to form ring.

Rnd 1: 6 sc in ring. Do not join rnds; mark end of each rnd.

Rnd 2: 2 sc in each sc around—12 sc.

Rnd 3: * Sc in next sc, 2 sc in next sc, repeat from * around—18 sc.

Rnd 4: * Sc in each of 2 sc, 2 sc in next sc, repeat from * around —24 sc.

Rnd 5: * Sc in each of 3 sc, 2 sc in next sc, repeat from * around —30 sc.

Continue to inc 6 sc each rnd until piece measures 15″ in diameter. End off. Be sure second piece has same number of sts in last rnd as first piece.

To Enlarge Designs: Enlarge desired pillow design to actual size by copying on crepe paper ruled in 1″ squares.

To Embroider: Baste crepe paper design on right side of one crocheted piece, centering design. Working through paper and crochet, following Color Key, embroider birds, flowers, and leaves in satin stitch; stems, birds' legs, and heart outline in outline stitch. See page 282 for stitch details.

Cut away crepe paper when embroidery is finished.

FINISHING: Hold pieces for top and back of pillow with wrong sides facing. With white, sc pieces together, inserting pillow form before seam is closed. Sl st in first sc, ch 1. Work 1 more rnd of white, 2 rnds of scarlet and 2 rnds of blue, joining each rnd and increasing in every 20th sc to keep work flat. Steam-press edging.

COLOR KEY

S	Scarlet
MB	Marine blue
O	Light orange
G	Emerald green
CM	Claret mix
B	Black
W	White

PILLOW MOTIF

PILLOW MOTIF

234

PILLOW MOTIF

COLOR KEY

S	Scarlet
MB	Marine blue
O	Light orange
G	Emerald green
CM	Claret mix
B	Black
W	White

FOLK ART AFGHAN

SIZE: 66″ x 46″, plus edgings.

MATERIALS: Yarn of knitting-worsted weight: 48 ozs. white; 2 ozs. each of marine blue, scarlet, light orange, yellow, emerald green, and claret mix (dark red); small amount of black. Crochet hook size H. Large-eyed embroidery needles. One package white crepe paper. Yard-stick. Pencil.

GAUGE: 7 sc = 2″; 4 rows = 1″.

AFGHAN: Center Panel: With white, ch 75.

Row 1: Sc in 2nd ch from hook and in each ch across— 74 sc. Ch 1, turn. Check gauge; piece should be 21″ wide.

Row 2: Sc in each sc across. Ch 1, turn each row. Repeat row 2 until piece is 66″ long. End off.

Side Panel (make 2): With white, ch 43. work as for center panel on 42 sc. Check gauge; piece should be 12″ wide. Make side panels same length as center panel.

Note: Embroider panels before joining them.

To Enlarge Designs: Enlarge designs to actual size by copying on pieces of crepe paper ruled in 1″ squares as follows: three 17″ square pieces for the three bird motifs; one 66″ x 12″ piece for side panel border. (One half of design is given, from corner to center. Copy design on one half of paper's length, then repeat design in reverse for other half of side panel border.) Make another piece the same for other side panel. Finally, rule up one 24″ x 12″ piece for center panel border. Make another piece the same for other end of center panel.

To Embroider: Baste designs in place on afghan panels. Working through paper and crochet, following Color Key, embroider birds, flowers, and leaves in satin stitch, stems and birds' legs in outline stitch, heart containing flowers in chain stitch. See page 282 for stitch details.

In placing three bird motifs on center panel, be sure to leave space at top and bottom of center panel for border. Leave borders for top and bottom of center panel until after afghan is put together; then, fit in designs to coincide with side borders.

Finishing: Cut away crepe paper when embroidery is finished.

Join panels by backstitching them together on wrong side, using a narrow seam. Steam-press seams flat. Finish embroidery on top and bottom borders of center panel.

Edging: From right side, join white at beginning of

AFGHAN BIRD MOTIF

right side edge. Working along side edge, sc evenly across edge to top of afghan, sc in first sc on top edge.

Row 1: Working across top edge, * ch 9, sk 5 sc, sc in next sc, repeat from * across, end sc in last st on top edge. Ch 9, turn.

Row 2: Sl st in center ch of first ch-9 lp, * ch 9, sl st in center ch of next ch-9 lp, repeat from * across, end ch 9, sl st in sc at beg of row 1. Turn.

Row 3: Sl st in each ch to center of first ch-9 lp, * ch 9, sl st in center ch of next ch-9 lp, repeat from * across. Ch 9, turn.

Row 4: Sl st in center ch of first ch-9 lp, * ch 9, sl st in center ch of next ch-9 lp, repeat from * across, end ch 9, sl st in top sl st at beg of row 3. Turn.

Row 5: Sl st in each ch to center of first ch-9 lp, * ch 9, sl st in center ch of next ch-9 lp, repeat from * across. End off.

Work other side edge and bottom edging the same.

COLOR KEY

S	Scarlet
MB	Mariné blue
O	Light orange
G	Emerald green
CM	Claret mix
B	Black
W	White
Y	Yellow

AFGHAN BIRD MOTIF

AFGHAN BIRD MOTIF

SIDE PANEL BORDER

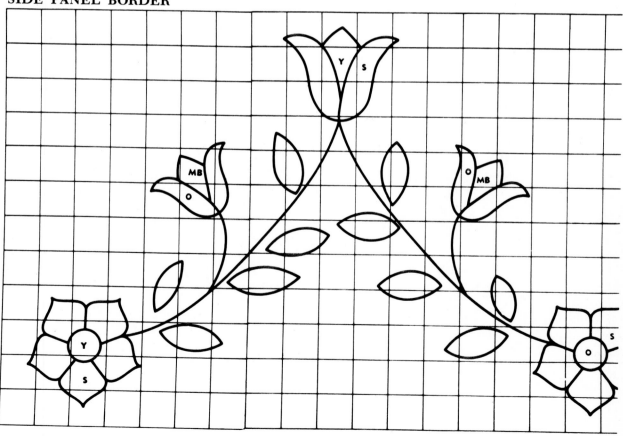

III Clothing and Accessories

Popular Fashions

EMBROIDERED BEACH SET

Vivid flowers follow the plunge on a one-piece swimsuit and repeat on white duck sandal tops. The stitches are simple—satin, scroll, and French knots; the pattern is worked in embroidery floss.

EQUIPMENT: Paper for patterns. Tracing paper. Dressmaker's tracing (carbon) paper. Pencil. Dry ball-point pen. Ruler. Scissors. Straight pins. Embroidery needle. Embroidery hoop. Hammer. Screwdriver. Nail.

MATERIALS: Pattern for one-piece bathing suit similar to the one shown. Fabric and thread as specified on pattern. Lightweight woven polyester interfacing, ¼ yard white. Six-strand embroidery floss; 2 skeins light olive green; 1 skein each: celery green, medium yellow, light orange, deep orange, red-orange, dark purple, light purple, dark blue, light blue. White cotton broadcloth, 20″ wide and at least 10″ long for clog straps. One pair exercise sandals in your size. White upholstery tacks, 16.

SWIMSUIT

Lay pattern on fabric and lining according to directions in pattern. Mark suit pieces, but cut out only back suit, straps, and lining; do not cut out front. From interfacing, cut two bosom pieces on bias; baste on underside of bosom pieces of suit. Place leftover piece of interfacing on bias under embroidery area of lower suit front.

Enlarge patterns by copying on paper ruled in ½″ squares; complete half-pattern B as indicated by dash line. Trace embroidery designs onto paper. Using dressmaker's tracing paper and dry ball-point pen, transfer designs to suit front. Embroidery design A is for top

Pattern for making the Fringed Shawl.

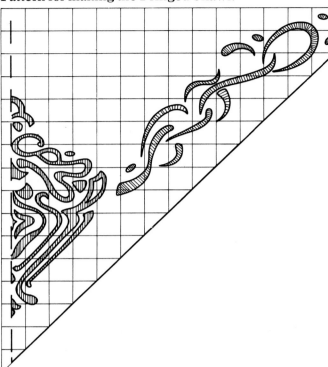

board from corner along one stitched edge of shawl; using blue pencil, make ten equally spaced marks. Thread doubled length of braid, loop end first, through yarn needle. Insert needle at first blue mark about ¼" in from the edge. Bring needle through to underside and remove it from the braid. Pull two braid ends through braid loop; pull tightly. Continue fringing in marked 3" area; then continue marking and fringing until both side edges are complete.

Press if necessary.

CARNATION SET

Decorate a purchased knit-skirt-plus-shawl ensemble with these giant pink carnations in easy satin-stitch yarn for a dramatic, individualized outfit.

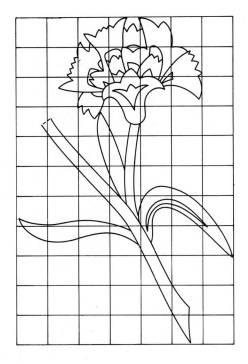

EQUIPMENT: Paper for patterns. Pencil. Ruler. Scissors. Sewing and large-eyed embroidery needles. Sewing thread. White crepe paper or tissue paper.

MATERIALS: Store-bought, plain knit skirt and fringed shawl. Acrylic sport yarn, 2-oz. balls: 1 ball each of green and rose (or two shades of rose).

DIRECTIONS: Enlarge patterns on paper ruled in 1" squares. Referring to individual directions, place crepe paper or tissue paper over design, leaving about a 1" margin on all sides; trace design on paper. Baste paper design on right side of knitting. Working through paper and knitting, embroider flower, leaves, and stem in satin stitch, using outline stitch on narrow portions (see page 282 for stitch details). Cut away paper when embroidery is finished.

SHAWL

Cut crepe paper or tissue paper to measure 17" x 11". Trace large flower design. Center paper design at widest part of shawl, stem in line with center point.

SKIRT

Cut crepe paper or tissue paper to measure 24" x 11". Trace large flower design omitting lower right leaf. Place same paper over design for small flower and continue tracing stem and small flower. Baste paper design on right side of front of skirt.

RUFFLED SHAWL

Influenced by Old Mexico, here's an exuberant shawl with swirly bands of quilted motifs which stitch up fast with pearl cotton. A crisp ruffle flirts with the edges of this cozy muslin shawl, which measures 55" at the top, not including the luscious ruffle.

EQUIPMENT: Hard- and soft-lead pencils. Yardstick. Tracing paper (pieced to size 30" x 58"). Paper for pattern. Red or blue dressmaker's tracing (carbon) paper. Scissors. Straight pins. Regular sewing needle and large-eyed embroidery needle. Sewing machine with ruffler attachment.

MATERIALS: Unbleached muslin, 44"/45" wide, 4¼ yards. Lightweight cotton batting. Yellow basting thread. Pearl cotton, size 3, wine red, two skeins.

DIRECTIONS: Wash muslin to preshrink it and to completely remove sizing. Press well with pressing cloth while damp.

Place fabric on smooth, flat surface. Referring to Diag. 1

and using soft-lead pencil, measure and mark on fabric three triangles each with a 58″ base and a 30″ perpendicular; then mark four bias strips each 8½″ wide. Cut out each piece.

Set aside one triangle for backing and bias strips for ruffle until quilting is finished. Piece tracing paper to size 30″ x 58″ for quilting-design pattern. On tracing paper, mark triangular outline of finished shawl with a 56″ base and a perpendicular 28″ high. Mark line down exact center of triangle. Starting from each side of triangle and referring to Diag. 2, mark off four diagonal areas 3″ wide with 2″-wide areas between, forming seven triangles within outline. The 3″-wide areas are for design.

Enlarge pattern by copying on paper ruled in 1″ squares. Referring to Diag. 2, place pattern under marked tracing paper, centering design in triangle points of 3″ areas. With soft-lead pencil, trace entire pattern. Working from center point toward base (top edge) of triangle, repeat Right Side "S" of design along right side of each 3″ area; then repeat Left Side "S" in same manner along left side of each 3″ area.

Place muslin triangle for shawl front on flat surface. With pin, mark center of base; using soft-lead pencil, mark finished size of shawl on muslin (56″ base, with a 28″ perpendicular). Center and pin traced pattern to muslin, matching outlines and center points. With carbon paper and hard-lead pencil, transfer complete traced design to muslin (do not transfer triangular area guidelines). Remove pattern. Baste along outline of finished shawl on muslin.

For interlining, cut batting same size as muslin. If batting seems too thick, thin it by carefully pulling layers apart and using only half the thickness.

With marked side facing up, place shawl front on muslin lining triangle, with batting between. Pin all layers together. Baste diagonally through all thicknesses along inner and outer edges of each design area.

To embroider (and quilt) design, thread large-eyed needle with single strand of pearl cotton. Make small knot at end of thread and insert needle from lining to front. Take two or three little running stitches through all thicknesses on front (see stitch details, page 282). Pull thread up tightly to pucker fabric slightly. Do not pull needle through to lining side except to end thread. Make stitches about 3/16″ long, with ⅛″ space between each stitch. After a few stitches, you should be able to gauge your stitches evenly. End all threads on lining side with a small knot. Embroider entire design, working from center (right angle) of each 3″ area to outer edge.

When design is finished, remove basting threads and trim edges to ½″ for seam allowance. Trim third muslin triangle for backing to same size as quilted triangle.

To make ruffle, sew the four bias strips together to form one long strip. Strip should be about 2½ times as long as measurement along one side, around point, and along other side of triangle, plus about 10″ extra. (Base is not

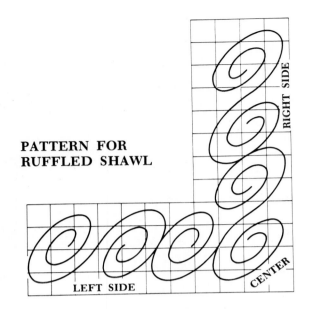

PATTERN FOR RUFFLED SHAWL

RIGHT SIDE

LEFT SIDE

CENTER

Diagram 1 (cutting)

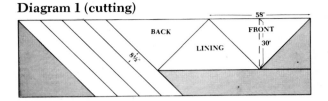

BACK

FRONT

LINING

58″

8½″

30″

Diagram 2

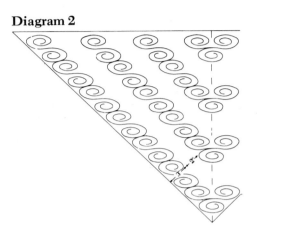

ruffled.) Fold strip in half lengthwise. Sew across one end of strip ⅝″ from raw edges; repeat at other end. Trim corners and turn strip to other side. Pull out corners. Following instructions that come with ruffler attachment, set ruffler on sewing machine to gather strip to required length. (**Note:** Test on scrap fabric first to determine setting. Mark 5″ length on scrap; pass through ruffler and measure length. Ruffled scrap should measure about 2″ when setting is correct.)

Ruffle entire length of strip, through both thicknesses, ¼″ from raw edges. Place ruffle on lining with all raw edges flush; make sure ruffle is eased enough at point of triangle to fit. Baste ruffle and edges of shawl together.

With ruffle between, pin, then baste remaining triangle for backing. Sew all around through all thicknesses ½″ from raw edges, leaving a 3″ opening at center of long straight edge. Remove basting threads. Clip corners and turn shawl to right side. Turn edges of opening in ½″ and slip-stitch closed. Press only on back of shawl.

POMEGRANATE TOTE AND MEXICAN SHAWL

The striking pomegranate motif is worked in fine wool for a handy, distinctive tote. A deep cross-stitch border and a sprinkling of motifs turn a soft wool wrap into a delicate, elegant shawl. Count the threads and work from a chart for this delightful Mexican shawl.

POMEGRANATE TOTE

SIZE: About 13″ deep.

EQUIPMENT: Paper for pattern. Pencil. Ruler. Scissors. Embroidery hoop. Crewel embroidery needle. Sewing needle. Straight pins. Sewing machine. Steam iron.

MATERIALS: Smooth-weave, medium-weight wool fabric, 36″ to 60″ wide, ½ yard, bright rose. Piece of organdy 17″ square. Persian yarn (3-ply), 10 yards each: bright pink (A), rose (B), fuchsia (C), magenta (D), wine (E), pale green (F), chartreuse (G), dark olive green (H),

tan (J), brown (K), charcoal brown (L). Light-weight buckram for interlining, 36″ wide, ½ yard. Fusible web, 18″ wide, ½ yard. Piece of cardboard 3″ x 12″. All-purpose glue. Bright rose polished cotton for lining, 36″ wide, ½ yard. Pink and white sewing thread. Two wooden bag handles 12″ wide.

DIRECTIONS: Read directions for embroidery on page 280. Cut a piece of rose wool fabric 17″ square. Enlarge pomegranate design by copying on paper ruled in 1″ squares. Place organdy over pattern and with pencil trace

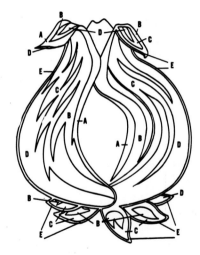

design onto organdy. Baste organdy, penciled side down, to wrong side of rose wool fabric. Using white thread, machine-stitch along all lines of design on organdy side to make design on right side of fabric.

To embroider, place fabric in hoop. Refer to stitch details on page 282. Use one ply of yarn in needle throughout. Work embroidery following color key on pattern and detail for pomegranate shading (letters refer to color letters in materials). Use satin stitch for leaves, which are divided into sections; work each section separately, changing directions of stitch for some sections. Use satin stitch for seeds in center; for each seed, make a second layer of satin stitch diagonally, crossing over first layer of satin stitch. Keep satin stitches firm, smooth, and parallel.

Work stems and pomegranate with rows of outline stitch to fill in area, conforming to the outline of the area being filled.

When embroidery is finished, pull out any visible machine stitches. To block, stretch and pin fabric right side down on ironing board and steam-press.

To assemble, trim embroidered fabric to 13" square. Cut another piece 13" square for back; cut a strip of same fabric 34" long, 4" wide for bottom and sides. Cut buckram and fusible web the same shape as each of these pieces, but ½" smaller on all edges. Using iron, fuse buckram to wrong side of each fabric piece, following directions that come with the fusible web. Fold each end of strip ½" to wrong side and stitch ⅛" from fold. With right sides facing, pin one long edge of the strip to bottom and sides of embroidered square, with crosswise center of strip at center bottom of embroidered square. Strip is 2" shorter than top edges of square. Sew pieces together making ½" seams. Sew other long edge of strip to second 13" square. Turn bag to right side. Fold sides and front, and sides and back together along seams. Machine-stitch through both thicknesses; continue stitching across front and back on bottom strip, with ½" seams folded flat on bottom. Turn

top edge of back and front of bag down ½" and tack. Spread glue over one surface of 3" x 12" cardboard; let glue get slightly tacky and press cardboard to inside bottom of bag; let dry.

For handle attachments, cut two pieces of rose wool each 3" wide, 12" long. For each, turn ½" to wrong side of each end; press. Center one long edge of one along top of bag front ¼" below edge, and other on back; pin. Insert other long edge of fabric through slit in each handle; place over pinned edge. By hand, stitch these edges to inside of bag ¼" below top edge.

To make lining, cut pink cotton fabric the same shape as the back, front, and bottom-side strip, making each ⅛" smaller on all edges. Press each end of strip ½" to wrong side. Seam the pieces together as for bag. Insert lining into bag. Turn top raw edges of lining in and slip-stitch to inside of bag all around top edge.

MEXICAN SHAWL

SIZE: 27" x 87" (including fringe).

EQUIPMENT: Ruler or tape measure. Straight pins. Embroidery needle. Embroidery hoop. Graph paper for planning placement of embroidery. Pencil. Iron.

MATERIALS: Finely woven wool shawl with 11" fringes. Six-strand embroidery floss in a contrasting color, 26 (7-yard) skeins.

DIRECTIONS: Note: If ready-made shawl in this size is unavailable, use finely woven wool fabric cut to 27½" x 65½". Make a tiny (1/16") rolled hem all around, using matching thread. Make a simple fringe along each short side with a fine yarn (such as baby yarn or fingering yarn) in a color to match fabric or embroidery floss. You will need about 35 yards of yarn, cut into 22" lengths. Using two strands together, fold in half, forming a loop. With right side up, insert small crochet hook in corner of shawl just above hem; draw loop through. Draw loose ends through loop and pull up tightly to form a knot. Repeat across to other corner, spacing strands about ½" apart. Single-knotted fringe will not resemble fringe in illustration.

Read directions for working cross-stitch, and refer specifically to section on counted-thread fabric. Place fabric in hoop. Cross-stitch embroidery is worked from chart; each X on the chart represents one cross-stitch. Use three strands of six-strand floss throughout, and work over two threads of fabric for each cross. Secure the ends on the wrong side by running them under the work.

It is desirable that cross-stitching be worked on an even-weave fabric—that is, fabric that has the same number of threads per inch when counted vertically or horizontally. However, in many fabrics the number of vertical and horizontal threads do not correspond. We used a hand-woven shawl from Mexico, and it has 26 threads running vertically, and 23 horizontally. Therefore the design is slightly elongated (each large border repeat measures 5¼" x 5¾"). To determine the width of each large border repeat when worked on your fabric, multiply the number of crosses horizontally (64) by two (the number of threads over which the crosses are worked); then divide the total by the thread count per inch. If weave of fabric is uneven, repeat the procedure to determine the height.

Plan the placement of four border motifs across each fringe end of shawl. The bottom of large repeat is 3½" from fringe; leaving about ¼" margin at left and right edges, place four motifs equally spaced across end. Work out the spacing on paper, and then transfer to shawl by marking the positions with pins. Work both ends the same. Work narrow border strip ½" from large border repeats. Begin at center of end, and work outward to right and left, repeating the chart to ¼" margin. Following the same procedure as for the large border motifs, work out

the spacing for the small individual motifs. There are three rows of six motifs, with the same space (about 4") between each vertically, horizontally, and from the edges and borders. When embroidery is completed, place shawl, face down, on a padded surface, and press lightly.

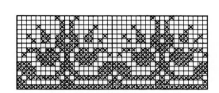

PERSIAN SLIPPERS
Leather-soled slippers are surprisingly easy to make. Embroidered patterns, sequins, and spangles give them an authentic Mideastern look!

EQUIPMENT: Paper for patterns. Pencil. Ruler. Scissors. Straight pins. Embroidery and sewing needles. Scraps of muslin.

MATERIALS (for one pair): Pair of felt or fabric-covered foam shoe soles in correct size. Small amount of sheet foam and cotton fabric to cover sole. Small pieces of felt in various colors as shown, or as desired. Sequins and spangles. Four small plastic rings. Two shoelaces. Fine embroidery yarn in colors matching and contrasting to felt. Sewing thread. Pieces of old leather. All-purpose glue.

DIRECTIONS: Read directions for embroidery on page 280. Refer to stitch details on page 282. Enlarge patterns for front and back slipper pieces by copying on paper ruled in 1" squares; complete half-patterns, indicated by long dash lines. Using patterns, cut one front (F) piece and two back (B) pieces of muslin. Stitch back pieces together along short dash line. Place the muslin pieces next to the sole and over your foot to be sure they fit correctly; make any adjustments necessary with another muslin piece. Using adjusted muslin pattern, cut one front and two back pieces of felt in color desired. For

trim, cut circles, triangles, strips, and flower shapes from contrasting colors of felt, following patterns and referring to illustration. Sew sequins and spangles to the trimming pieces; embroider around the sequins in buttonhole or straight stitch, and along edges of some pieces in chain stitch. Baste decorated felt trims in place on front and back slipper pieces. Attach trim by embroidering with contrasting colors of yarn in various stitches, such as buttonhole stitch, chain stitch, lazy daisy stitch.

To cover the soles, place a thin layer of foam on top of each sole; cut to shape; glue on. Trace sole shape on cotton fabric for each; cut out, adding ½" all around. Place fabric piece over foam side of sole; slash into ½" allowance around curves. Turn in allowance and pin edges to sole. Using sewing thread, slip-stitch fabric cover to sole.

Pin edges of heel and front pieces around soles. Using contrasting yarn and buttonhole stitch, sew pieces to sole; continue buttonhole stitch around edges of sole between felt front and back.

With contrasting yarn, work buttonhole stitch all around free edges of front and back pieces. For firmer edge, use matching or contrasting color yarn to work chain stitch along edges of buttonhole stitches. Sew a small ring to each front top corner of back piece. Sew center portion of each shoelace across wrong side of tab on front piece. Run ends of laces through rings. Cut two pieces of leather same size as sole. Glue to bottom of soles.

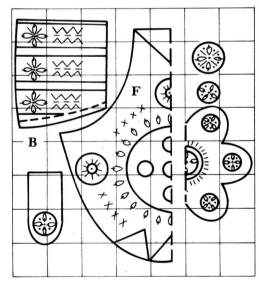

PERSIAN SLIPPERS

Bags

TILE TOTE BAG

This exciting red burlap tote bag is quickly embroidered in big, bold running stitches to make squares of orange, yellow, and pink. There's even an inside pocket for keeping glasses, a tape measure, and sundry small items within easy reach.

SIZE: Approximately 10" x 16".

EQUIPMENT: Scissors. Ruler. Pencil. Paper for pattern. Tape measure. Sewing and embroidery needles. Straight pins. Single-edged razor blade. Iron.

MATERIALS: Red burlap, 36" wide, ½ yard. Red cotton lining material to match burlap, 36" wide, ½ yard. Buckram, ½ yard. Sewing thread to match fabric. Knitting worsted: one 4-oz. skein variegated in orange, yellow, rose, pink, or 1 oz. of each color. About 140 green beads about ⅛" diameter. Heavy cardboard, ⅛" or ¼" thick, 5" x 15". Heavy thread.

DIRECTIONS: Enlarge pattern for bottom by copying on paper ruled in 1" squares; complete half-pattern, indicated by long dash line. From burlap and lining fabric, cut piece 11½" x 36" for bag; piece 5" x 19" for handle; and bottom piece, using pattern and adding ½" all around for seams. From buckram, cut bag piece 10½" x 35" and handle 3½" x 17". Trace bottom pattern on cardboard and cut out with razor blade.

With pins or basting thread, mark rows of 1¾" squares across burlap bag piece, starting ½" from edges. Rows will be 6 squares deep, 20 squares wide. Embroider first row of squares across burlap, starting with a yellow-to-orange shaded square and ending with a pink-to-rose shaded square. Using long running stitches, follow actual-size stitch diagram and catch a thread of burlap at corners. Each square has three outer lines of darker colors, inner lines of lighter colors. Complete embroidery, alternating colors in each row. Sew a green bead in center of squares.

On burlap handle piece, embroider two rows of squares, 10 squares deep, starting ¾" in from edges. Plan colors so that, when handle is sewn to bag, squares at handle ends are alternate colors to squares at the bag edge.

Fold embroidered bag piece in half crosswise with embroidered sides facing. Stitch 11½" sides together ½" from edges, being careful not to catch in yarn. Press seam open. Stitch bottom burlap piece to bottom of bag, right sides together, making ½" seam; turn bag to right side. Place cardboard bottom in bag. Using heavy thread, tack cardboard bottom in bag by running long threads across bottom from seam to seam.

Turn in ¾" on sides of embroidered burlap and lining handle pieces; press. Place buckram handle piece on wrong side of lining piece, under folded edges. With wrong side of burlap and buckram facing, stitch lining to burlap around edges. Turn in ½" around top of burlap bag and tack in place. Sew ends of handle inside bag, having

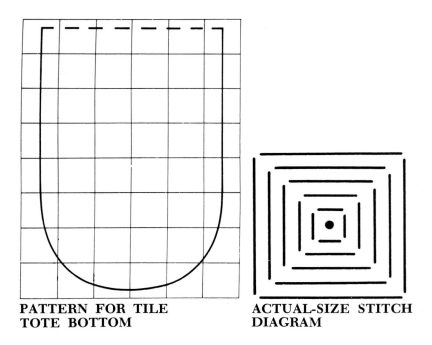

PATTERN FOR TILE TOTE BOTTOM

ACTUAL-SIZE STITCH DIAGRAM

squares at ends of handle abutting two center squares at front and back of bag.

Cut a 5″ x 10″ piece of lining fabric for pocket. Make a 1″ hem on one 10″ edge for top. Fold bag lining piece in half crosswise and mark center point on one half. Fold in edges of pocket ½″ on sides and bottom. Stitch pocket to right side of bag lining, centering pocket at marked point and 1¼″ from a long edge (top). Place buckram piece on wrong side of lining; fold ½″ of lining top edge over buckram; stitch together ¼″ from fold. Refold lining with buckram, in half crosswise; with right sides facing, stitch along 11½″ edge, making ½″ seam. With right sides facing, stitch bottom lining piece to bottom of bag lining, making ½″ seam. Clip around curved edges. Place lining in bag and slip-stitch to bag at top.

THREE BURLAP TOTES

Fabulous fun and very easy to make—large burlap totes splashed with brilliant embroidered felt motifs. Spark your summer wardrobe with these frankly frivolous, yet marvelously practical, carry-everything bags. Use the variety of stitches illustrated or ad lib your own on these versatile 12-3/4″ by 21″ totes.

EQUIPMENT: Scissors. Pinking shears. Ruler. Compass. Pencil. Paper for patterns. Large-eyed needle.

MATERIALS: For each bag: Burlap, ½ yard, 47″ wide, in colors shown, or as desired. Cotton fabric, ¾ yard, 36″ wide, in contrasting or matching color for lining. Sewing thread to match burlap, cotton fabric, and felt. Nonwoven interlining, ¾ yard, 36″ wide. Absorbent cotton. Small amounts of felt and knitting worsted as follows: **For Fruit Tote:** Felt in brown, bright and pale orange, bright yellow, gold, and rust. Knitting worsted in light gold, dark gold, brown, and rust. **For Flower Tote:** Felt in chartreuse, dark green, orange, brown, white, yellow, turquoise, and royal blue. Knitting worsted in olive green, royal blue, medium blue, and brown. **For Fish Tote:** Felt in dark green, royal blue, medium blue, chartreuse, and pink. Knitting worsted in olive green, royal blue, and cerise.

DIRECTIONS: Enlarge patterns for designs by copying on paper ruled in 1″ squares; enlarge tote pattern on 2″ squares. Complete the half-patterns, as indicated by the long dash lines.

Using tote pattern, cut two pieces of burlap, two pieces of interlining, and two pieces of cotton fabric for lining. Place burlap pieces together, right sides facing, then

TOTE PATTERN

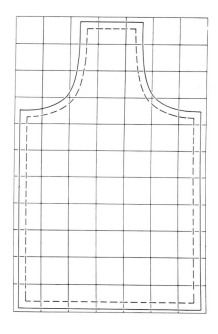

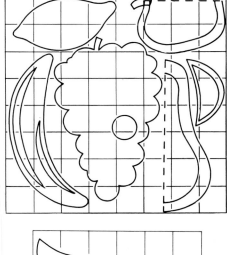

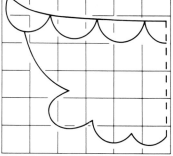

place a piece of interlining on each side of burlap and sew the four pieces together ¼″ from edges on bottom, sides (only up to curves of handles), and across top. Trim seams. Clip along curved raw edges; turn raw edges ½″ to wrong side and press. Make lining of cotton fabric as for tote, omitting interlining. Turn burlap tote right side out; insert lining (with wrong side toward interlining) inside burlap. Slip-stitch curved edges of lining to curved edges of burlap, then topstitch lining and burlap together around curved edges, ½″ in from edges. Using illustrations as color guides, cut the designs and appliqués of felt and embroider them with yarn before sewing fruit, flower and fish pieces together as indicated in individual directions. See stitch details on page 282.

FRUIT TOTE

Use natural-color burlap for tote and orange cotton fabric for lining. Cut two pieces for each fruit and each stem (use apple stem pattern for pear). Cut only one piece for each appliqué on the fruit. Cut two 3¾″-diameter circles for orange and one 2¾″ circle for appliqué.

Make a line of backstitches down center of pear appliqué, then make three pairs of graduating lazy daisy stitches. With tiny running stitches, sew appliqué to one pear piece, then sew both pear pieces together with light cotton stuffing between. Sew two stem pieces together at one end; place pear between unsewn ends of stem and tack.

Make seven long straight horizontal stitches across apple appliqué about ¼″ apart. Then make eight diagonal stitches about ¼″ apart, weaving under and over horizontal stitches. Make eight diagonal stitches in opposite direction, weaving under and over all other stitches. Finish apple as for pear.

Make seven large lazy daisy stitches in a circle on orange appliqué; complete orange as for pear, omitting stem.

Make several French knots at both ends on one lemon piece. Sew lemon together as for other fruit. Make several radiating straight stitches on lemon-slice appliqué. Stitch lemon slice and appliqué pieces to top part of lemon as shown.

Cut 16 grapes using three colors of felt. Sew each grape piece onto one large grape-bunch piece, with a little cotton between for padding. Cut and sew two pairs of grape pieces together, with cotton padding, separate from the bunch. Sew the grape-bunch pieces together, padding between.

Sew banana appliqué strips onto one piece of banana, then work coral stitch along appliqué as shown. Sew banana together as for other fruit.

Cut bowl and top scalloped trim. To embroider bowl, work outline stitch across bowl near bottom as shown. Make about three rows of large cross-stitches. Lay yarn along curved edges of scallops; whip laid yarn along scal-

loped edge. Sew scalloped trim to top of bowl. Sew bowl to bag front as shown along sides and at outline stitch, padding bowl slightly with cotton; leave bottom scallops and top edge free. Tack fruit in place as shown. Tack top of bowl under and over edges of fruit as shown.

FLOWER TOTE

Use light green burlap for tote and darker green cotton fabric for lining. Cut each flower of felt as shown, cutting orange poppy petals double. Cut blue and turquoise flowers 2¼″-diameter with pinking shears.

Cut six dark green leaves and embroider along centers with open leaf stitch; embroider blue flowers with radiating straight stitches and French knots in centers.

Stitch poppy-center appliqué to one poppy petal, then make several radiating straight stitches as shown; fill center with French knots. Tack two poppy-petal pieces together ¾″ from edges.

To make daisy, sew white appliqué to yellow background piece all around edges with cotton between for padding; then stitch on center appliqué with a little padding of cotton. Make another daisy the same.

With illustration as guide, embroider vase as follows: Starting 1¼″ from top of vase, make a row of chain stitch across, with a row of backstitch directly under chain, buttonhole stitch under this, chain stitch directly under buttonhole stitch. Leave ¼″ space and chain-stitch another row, then backstitch a row directly under chain, and buttonhole-stitch under this. Make a row of lazy daisy stitches across center of vase, tacking top of stitches on both sides; add second row of lazy daisies as shown. Chain-stitch another row; then make two rows of chevron stitch, with French knots in center openings. Then work lazy daisy stitches in groups of various lengths, and finish with two rows of chain stitches. Sew vase onto burlap tote with cotton for padding. Outline entire vase with yarn, tacking it in place. Sew flowers and leaves on as shown, leaving outer portions free.

FISH TOTE

Use aqua burlap and green cotton fabric for lining. Before sewing bag together, make the fishnet design on one piece of burlap as follows: 4½″ below curved side edges, work two rows of coral stitch, ½″ apart, across burlap, with cross-stitch between. Tack 13 diagonal strands of yarn on burlap as shown; then make 13 diagonal strands going in opposite direction and knotting around other diagonals where they intersect. Then finish bag according to directions.

Appliqués decorate both sides of fish. Cut two felt eyes, two bodies, and two appliqués for each fish. Make two small and three large fish. Both small fish are embroidered identically: make featherstitches along centers of each appliqué piece. Make about three straight stitches on each eye piece as shown. Make straight stitches on tail

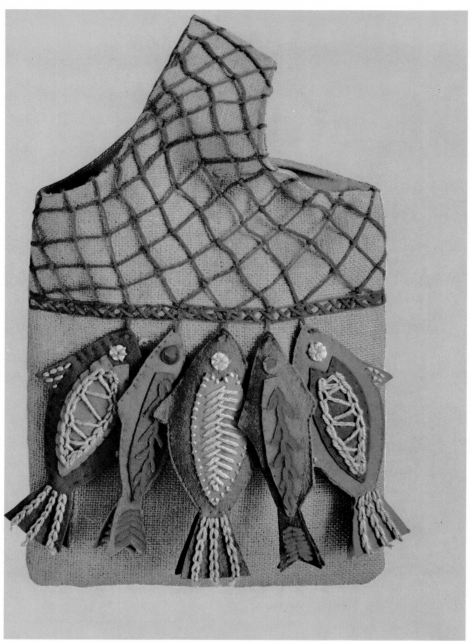

as shown. Stitch appliques and eyes in place on bodies; stitch two body pieces for each together, padding with cotton; leave tails free.

The two large blue fish are made in the same manner. Embroider the appliqués with chain stitches as shown, then work yarn in zigzag fashion through inner chain loop. Make three rows of chain stitches on each tail. Stitch appliqués and eyes to bodies, stitch both body pieces together padding slightly with cotton. Make a few radiating straight stitches on each eye and backstitches on fins. For center green fish, make open leaf stitch along each appliqué, then whipstitch appliqués to each side of body with yarn. Omit stitches on fins and continue as for other large fish. Tie each fish to bag with yarn as shown.

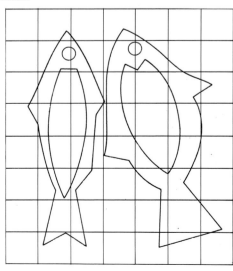

MIRRORED TOTE

Upholstery-fabric bag is decorated with mirrors and easy-stitch yarn embroidery for a truly special tote.

EQUIPMENT: Paper for pattern. Tracing paper. Pencil. Dry ball-point pen. Ruler. Scissors. Straight pins. Embroidery and sewing needles.

MATERIALS: Deep blue upholstery fabric, heavy buckram, and blue cotton fabric for lining, one 34″ x 19½″ piece of each. Sewing thread to match lining and upholstery fabric. For embroidery: small amounts of about five yarns of different weights and textures in white and various shades of blue. Mirrors: 1″ diameter, 6; 1½″ diameter, 1.

DIRECTIONS: Referring to cutting layout, cut main tote piece and sides out of upholstery fabric, lining fabric, and buckram; cut shoulder strap out of upholstery fabric only. Cut along heavy lines; dash lines indicate folds.

Enlarge embroidery pattern by copying on tracing paper ruled in 1″ squares. Baste tracing paper to right side of upholstery fabric, on rounded section of tote (flap). To transfer design, use contrasting thread to outline all parts of the design with small running stitches. Pull away the paper, leaving the running-stitch outline.

To secure mirror to fabric (see detail): Hold mirror in place on right side of fabric between thumb and index finger of one hand. Bring needle threaded with yarn up at A, very close to edge of mirror. Insert needle at B, very

close to edge; pull yarn taut. Bring needle out at C, insert at D, pulling yarn taut. Pass needle under mirror and bring out at E. Pass over and under AB and then DC; insert at F. Bring out at G, pass over and under DC and then AB; insert at H. Bring out at I; pull yarn taut, and be sure it remains taut. Working from left to right, * work buttonhole stitch over ties as follows: with working thread down and to right, bring needle over intersection

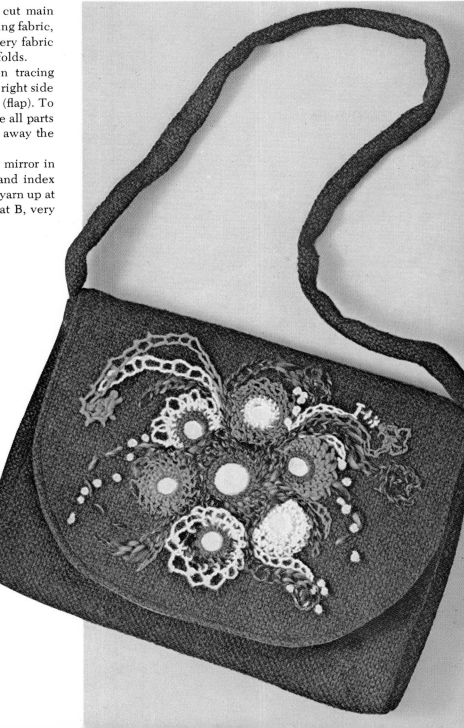

MIRRORED TOTE

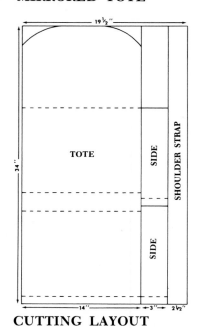

CUTTING LAYOUT

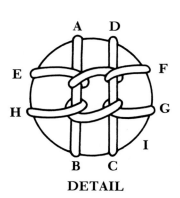

DETAIL

EMBROIDERY PATTERN

CG and then down toward edge of mirror; insert close to I. Bring up directly under I and work one chain stitch on outside edge of buttonhole stitch (only chain stitch goes through fabric). Repeat from * all around inner square until round frame is formed and chain stitches form a concentric circle next to mirror frame. Secure all seven mirrors to fabric in same manner, with large mirror at center. Refer to stitch details on page 282, and embroider remainder of design, using desired colors or following illustration. 1 indicates Mirror Frame; 2 is Buttonhole Stitch; 3 is Chain Stitch; 4 is Roman Chain Stitch; 5 is Running Stitch; dots indicate French Knots. Remainder of Buttonhole Stitch is worked on loops of previous row of stitching (as when working frame to secure mirror). Loops of last row of buttonhole stitch are couched down. When embroidery is completed, block, following directions on page 280.

Assemble tote as follows: To make outer tote, baste buckram pieces to wrong side of corresponding upholstery fabric pieces. With right sides facing, place one side piece on each side of main tote piece, with short edge of side piece matching straight edge of main piece. Stitch long edge of main piece with ½″ seams along both long edges of side piece, and short end of side piece (rounding corners); leave long edge of piece unstitched for last 1″ on flap side. Turn to right side. Turn unstitched straight edges of main piece and sides in 1″; press and baste. Prepare lining pieces in same manner; do not turn; turn unstitched straight edges out 1″.

With right sides facing, stitch lining to outer tote along curved edge of flap with ½″ seam. Trim seam, clip into curve, and turn to right side. Press and topstitch along curve, ¼″ from edge. With right sides facing, fold strap piece in half lengthwise; stitch along long edge, making ¼″ seam; turn. Stitch one end of strap ½″ above raw edge to outer tote ½″ below folded edge at inside of side piece. After adjusting to desired length, stitch remaining end of strap to remaining side piece in same manner. Topstitch around side and front of tote edges ¼″ from fold. Insert lining into outer tote and slip-stitch along folded edges. Topstitch across flap along fold line.

Hprons and Hpron Sets

FOUR SEASONS APRON AND POTHOLDER SET

Cross-stitched aprons of pink, green, yellow, and blue celebrate the four seasons of the year. The special cross-stitch scene on each of the aprons is repeated on the matching potholder for practical, all-year use.

EQUIPMENT: Tape measure. Ruler. Straight pins. Scissors. Pencil. Sewing needle. Embroidery needle. Embroidery hoop.

MATERIALS: Gingham, 7 checks to the inch, ¾ yard, 45″ wide, in each color: pink for summer; yellow for autumn; blue for winter; light green for spring. Coordinating broadcloth, two 7″ squares in each color. Matching sewing threads. Rickrack, 24″ long, in red, green, white, or yellow. Plastic ring, 1″ in diameter, one for each potholder. Small amount of polyester batting for each potholder. One skein each of six-strand embroidery floss in colors indicated below (less will be needed if making all seasons):

Summer: Medium green, dark green, red, white, medium brown, dark brown, dark gray, light gray, bright yellow, medium-light blue, dark gold, light brown, black.

Autumn: Red, medium green, dark green, chartreuse, pale blue-green, dark brown, medium brown, bright yellow, orange-gold, bright orange, white, black, dark gray, light-gray, medium-light blue, pale peach.

COLOR KEY

- ☒ Red
- ◼ Black
- ⊡ White
- ▼ Dark brown
- ⊟ Medium brown
- ⊞ Light brown
- ◪ Dark green
- ◿ Medium green
- ☑ Bright yellow
- ⦀ Pale yellow
- ⬒ Dark gold
- ⊙ Dark gray
- ⊓ Light gray
- ⬤ Medium-light blue
- ⊖ Chartreuse
- ◤ Lavender
- ◩ Pale peach
- ⊡ Orange-gold
- ⬕ Bright orange
- ⊞ Blue-green

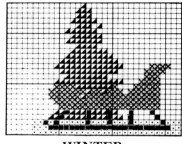

WINTER

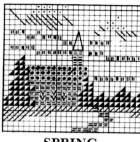

SPRING

SUMMER

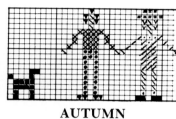

AUTUMN

WINTER

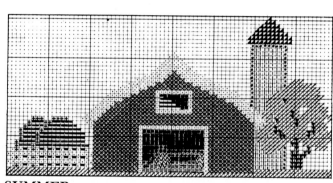

SUMMER

SPRING

AUTUMN

Winter: Red, black, white, dark gray, light gray, medium green, dark green, medium-light blue, medium brown.

Spring: Chartreuse, medium green, dark green, black, dark brown, light brown, white, dark gray, light gray, bright yellow, pale peach, lavender, bright orange, medium-light blue, pale yellow.

DIRECTIONS: For apron skirt, cut one piece 32½″ wide, 20½″ long. Cut waistband 18″ long, 3½″ wide. Cut

two ties each 17″ long, 3¾″ wide. Mark piece for potholder 5¼″ square in center of excess material; do not cut, as this allows for fabric to catch in embroidery hoop.

Follow directions for working cross-stitch on gingham, page 284. Thread needle with three strands of six-strand floss. Following charts and Color Key, embroider cross-stitch design on apron skirt, placing bottom row of design 5″ up from lower edge of apron fabric. Embroider potholder front in center of marked square.

268

Satin-stitch steeple in blue floss on Spring potholder and bells in black on Spring and Autumn aprons.

To make birch markings on tree at right side of Spring apron, work straight stitches with black floss on white cross-stitches, using wiggly lines on chart as a guide for placement.

To Assemble Apron: Stitch ¼″ hems along sides of apron skirt. Stitch 2¼″ hem across bottom edge. Gather waist of apron skirt to 17½″ to fit waistband, leaving ¼″ seam allowance at each side. Place right sides of apron and waistband together with raw edges even. Stitch band onto apron, easing in gathers. Turn waistband right side up; do not fold.

Stitch ⅛″ hem along lower edge of both ties. To make diagonal ends of ties, fold hemmed edge of each diagonally to upper edge. Stitch ⅛″ hem along upper edge, being sure to catch folded end. At unhemmed ends, pleat ties to fit half of waistband width. With right sides facing and raw edges even, lay pleated ends on lower half of band. Fold upper half of band down over lower half, right sides in. Stitch across ends ¼″ from edges through all thicknesses. Turn waistband, bringing ties out to sides; press along fold. Turn raw edges of band under; slip-stitch to back.

POTHOLDER

When embroidery is complete, cut away excess material, leaving 5¼″ square. Turn gingham edges under ¼″, center and topstitch onto one square of broadcloth. Carefully cut away broadcloth that is under gingham to within ½″ of stitching; this allows batting to puff out embroidery. Place second square of broadcloth over gingham, right sides together. Stitch around three sides, making ¼″ seams; turn right side out. Insert two layers of batting out to all edges, and one more under gingham area only. Turn under raw edges and slip-stitch fourth side closed. Topstitch rickrack over edges of gingham square, stitching through all thicknesses. Tack ring on top right corner.

RED GINGHAM SET

Cheery red apron and matching potholder will brighten any kitchen. The crisp gingham bands on the apron are embroidered with cross-stitch, and rickrack rows of red and white accent the embroidery. The gingham potholder boasts the same motif as the apron.

EQUIPMENT: Scissors. Embroidery needle. Sewing needle. Tape measure.

MATERIALS: Cotton fabric, 36″ wide, plain red, ½ yard; red-and-white-checked gingham, ¼ yard. Red and white sewing thread. Six-strand embroidery floss, two skeins each black and white. Regular rickrack, one package each red and white. Flannel or batting for padding, three pieces, each 6¼″ square.

DIRECTIONS: From plain red fabric, cut apron skirt 14″ x 29½″, pocket 5½″ x 7″, and two ties each 2½″ x 28½″. From checked gingham, cut skirt band 7″ x 29½″; waistband 4″ x 18″; pocket band 2½″ x 5½″; two potholder pieces 7″ square.

EMBROIDERY: Read directions for working cross-stitch on gingham, page 284. Use three strands of six-strand floss in needle. Make all crosses in the shaded checks of gingham. Follow charts for wide and narrow bands: X's are black, O's are white crosses. Sew on rickrack, stitching at each point and between.

On skirt band, embroider wide band across 29½″ width from left to right, starting at top ½″ down from edge of gingham. Fold waistband in half lengthwise and embroider straight narrow band across, starting one row of checks below fold on front half. On pocket band, embroider straight narrow band across 5½″ width, starting three rows of checks below top edge. Sew red rickrack across waistband and pocket below embroidery.

For potholder, embroider narrow bands along each side of gingham piece for front, starting each end ¼″ in from edge of fabric. Following chart from right to left and bottom to top, cross bands for each corner.

To Assemble Apron: With right sides together, stitch skirt band to bottom of apron skirt, making ¼″ seam. Make a 1½″ hem across bottom of band and stitch ¼″ hems at sides of skirt. Sew white rickrack across front over seam line and red rickrack over hemline. Gather top of skirt in to 17″.

On each tie, fold one end over diagonally and stitch sides together to make point. Stitch narrow hems along both long edges of each tie. Fold waistband in half lengthwise, right sides together. Place ties between folded waistband, with raw ends of ties even with ends of waistband. Stitch across each end of waistband, catching in tie ends. Turn waistband right side out. Place front of waistband and gathered edge of skirt, right sides together, and stitch across with ¼″ seam. Fold waistband in half to back. Turn in raw edge and slip-stitch in place.

With right side of pocket band facing wrong side of

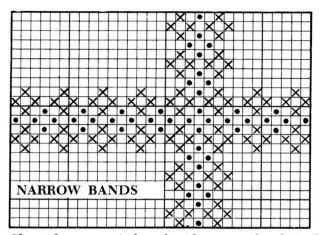

NARROW BANDS

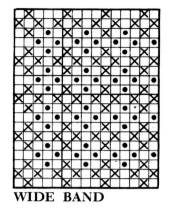

WIDE BAND

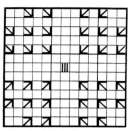

Teneriffe chart for
Black Gingham Apron.

Charts for cross-stitch embroidery on red and gingham-check apron.

Teneriffe

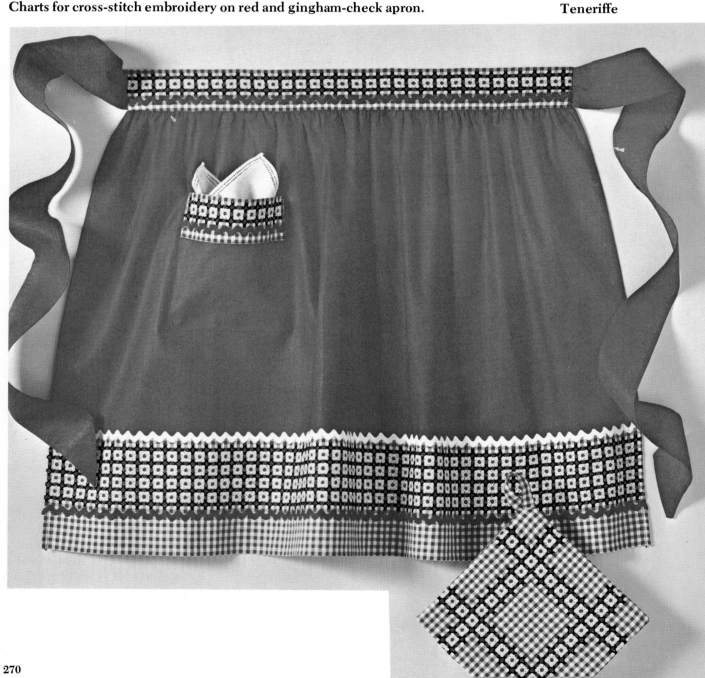

pocket, stitch together across 5½″ edge. Fold band over to right side. Turn in lower edge of band and topstitch to pocket. Turn in ¼″ around sides and bottom of pocket and stitch to apron 5″ in from left side and 3½″ below waistband.

POTHOLDER

Baste padding pieces together. Cut strip of gingham for hanging loop 1½″ x 4″. Fold in half lengthwise; turn in long edges and stitch together close to edge; stitch along other long edge also. Fold in half crosswise. Place front and back gingham pieces together, right sides facing, with loop between (ends outward). Stitch pieces together around three sides, making ¼″ seams, catching in loop ends. Turn right side out. Insert padding. Turn in raw edges of potholder and slip-stitch remaining side closed. Stitch through all thicknesses around four sides inside the cross-stitch embroidery.

BLACK GINGHAM APRON

This elegant black-and-white-checked gingham apron is spiced with handwork in a lively red. Cross-stitch, teneriffe embroidery, hemstitching, and rickrack decorate the apron skirt and are easy to work using the checks as a guide.

EQUIPMENT: Scissors. Tape measure. Embroidery and sewing needles.

MATERIALS: Black-and-white-checked gingham, 4 checks to the inch, ¾ yard, 36″ wide. One package red rickrack. Two skeins red six-strand embroidery floss. White and red sewing thread to match.

DIRECTIONS: Cut gingham for apron skirt 29″ across fabric and 20″ long. Cut two ties 30″ long across fabric and 3″ wide. Cut waistband 16″ long and 4½″ wide. Cut pocket 7″ deep and 6″ wide, from gingham.

Hemstitching: Measure up about 8¾″ from one long edge (bottom) of apron skirt, adjusting measurement to come at line of white checks. Carefully pull out white threads across fabric at this measurement; pull all threads across skirt that make one row of checks. Leave one row of checks above drawn row and pull out threads of row of checks above.

With fabric wrong side up and starting at left side, work plain hemstitching across top (see Figs. 1 and 2 on page 53); use white thread and, for each stitch, pull together all

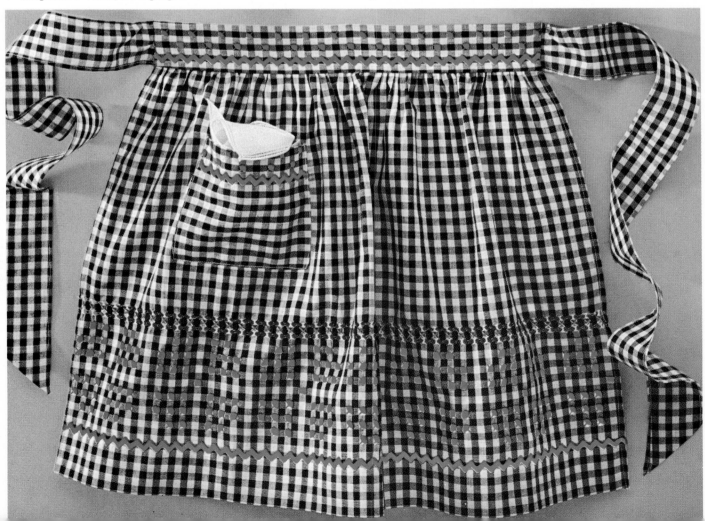

threads that make one check. Turn work around and repeat hemstitching on other edge of same drawn row. Work hemstitching along top and bottom edge of lower drawn row, in same way.

Read directions for working cross-stitch on gingham, page 284. With three strands of six-strand floss in needle, embroider a cross-stitch in every other check (lighter shade checks) across skirt, between hemstitching.

Teneriffe: Skip one row of checks below hemstitching and work teneriffe design, using three strands of six-strand embroidery floss in needle. Follow chart (page 270) for teneriffe design; each square of chart represents one check of gingham. To do teneriffe, make the three spokes first, as shown; then starting at tip where spokes converge, weave back and forth, over and under spokes (see diagram) to fill, pushing weaving gently toward tip. To make the square boxes at center of each design, make three vertical spokes and weave back and forth, over and under spokes. On third row of checks below teneriffe, sew rickrack across skirt.

Fold waistband in half lengthwise. On front half, embroider two rows of single teneriffe motifs, one row of

checks from fold, skipping three checks between each and one row of checks between rows; alternate spacing of motifs in the two rows. Sew rickrack across waistband on second row of checks below teneriffe.

On sixth row of checks from top end of pocket (6″-long edge) embroider two rows of teneriffe motifs as for waistband, and sew rickrack across below.

To Assemble: Make ¼″ hems at sides of apron skirt. Make 2″ hem at bottom. Gather top of apron skirt to 15½″. With right sides of gathered edge of skirt and front half of waistband together, stitch across with ¼″ seam. Fold waistband in half to back; turn in ¼″ on long edge and whip in place.

For ties, stitch narrow hems on each long edge. To make the diagonal end on ties, fold end over to side, with right sides together, and stitch at side edge; turn right side out. Turn in raw edges at ends of waistband, insert unfinished ends of ties, and stitch together.

Make a 1¼″ hem at top of pocket. Turn in ¼″ on other three sides and stitch pocket to apron skirt 4½″ from side and 3″ from waistband.

BIAS-TRIM APRON AND POLKA-DOT POSY SET

A perennial favorite, the bias-trim apron is decorated with bias tape, rickrack, and embroidery. The polka-dot posy set uses the polka dots as centers for these piquant embroidered flowers!

BIAS-TRIM APRON

EQUIPMENT: Scissors. Tape measure. Embroidery and sewing needles.

MATERIALS: White cotton piqué, 36″ wide, 1 yard. Cotton bias binding, ½″ wide: orange, 3⅓ yards; green, 2 yards. Yellow rickrack, 2 yards. Pearl cotton No. 3: one skein each dark olive, bright golden yellow, rose, rust, light olive green, orange, bright green. Sewing thread in colors to match fabric and trims.

DIRECTIONS: From white piqué, cut skirt 20¾″ x 36″, waistband 4″ x 18½″, and two ties, each 4″ x 36″. All

seam allowances are ¼″ unless otherwise indicated in directions.

To trim skirt, baste a strip of yellow rickrack across width of skirt, 7″ up from one long edge. Baste a strip of orange bias binding overlapping top edge of rickrack. Slip-stitch folded bottom edge of binding to skirt fabric, catching in rickrack. Slip-stitch top edge of binding to apron skirt.

Using matching sewing thread, couch one strand of light olive green pearl cotton along top edge of orange binding (see stitch details, page 282). Baste a second strip

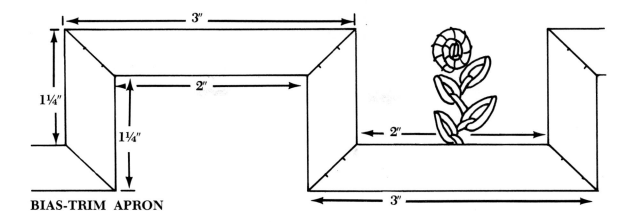

BIAS-TRIM APRON

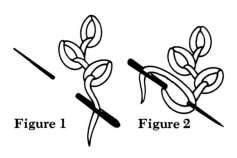

Figure 1   **Figure 2**

of rickrack 2″ above first. Following directions for first trim, baste green bias binding at bottom of rickrack. Work couching in rust. Using rust pearl cotton, embroider a row of zigzag lazy daisy stitches (see stitch details) across apron between the two bands.

Following diagram, mark outline for top border ¾″ above top edge of green binding. Baste orange bias binding across apron following marked outline. To form mitered corners, fold binding diagonally across itself; tack corners down. Slip-stitch top and bottom edges of binding to apron. Using matching sewing thread, couch one strand of dark olive pearl cotton along lower edge of orange binding. Referring to Figs. 1 and 2 on diagram, embroider flowers in border as indicated: For centers, work French knots in bright golden yellow pearl cotton; for leaves, work lazy daisy stitches in bright green; for flower, couch rose pearl cotton with matching sewing thread.

Gather unfinished top edge of apron to 17½″. Make ¼″ hems at sides of skirt. Make 2″ bottom hem.

For waistband: Press seam allowance to wrong side on both long edges. With folded edges flush, baste green binding to right side of one long edge of waistband (this will be bottom edge). Slip-stitch top edge of binding to waistband. Couch one strand of rust pearl cotton across band along top edge of green binding. Baste a strip of orange binding along top edge of waistband; slip-stitch top and bottom of binding to waistband. Couch one strand of pale green pearl cotton across lower edge of orange

binding. Using rust pearl cotton, embroider a row of zigzag lazy daisy stitches across center of waistband in space between trims.

For ties: Make narrow hems on lengthwise edges. For pointed ends, fold one end of each tie in half lengthwise, with right sides facing; sew along straight end; trim seam allowance to a point near fold; turn right side out; press to a point. Make two pleats on raw end of each tie. With right sides facing and raw edges flush, baste a pleated tie to each end of trimmed side of waistband. Fold waistband in half lengthwise, with right sides facing and tie ends between; stitch across ends. Turn right side out. Fit gathered top edge of apron into open long sides of waistband; allowing ½″ seam allowance, baste. Using green thread on top, white thread in bobbin, topstitch across, close to bottom edge of green bias binding.

POLKA-DOT POSY SET

EQUIPMENT: Scissors. Tape measure. Embroidery and sewing needles.

MATERIALS: Red cotton fabric, 36″ wide, 1 yard. Red-on-white polka-dot cotton fabric (dots about 1″ apart), 36″ wide, ½ yard. One package each of narrow white and red rickrack: Pearl cotton, No. 5, one 55-yard spool each of white and red. Sewing thread to match fabrics. **For Potholder:** Cotton flannel for padding, 36″ wide, ¼ yard.

APRON

From red fabric, cut skirt 9¾″ x 36″; bottom band 5″ x 36″; two ties 3″ x 32″; pocket 7″ square. From red-and-white polka-dot fabric, cut waistband 5″ x 18½″; bottom inset 4¾″ x 36″; pocket trim 3″ x 7″.

All seam allowances are ½″ unless otherwise indicated. With right sides facing and raw edges even, sew bottom red band to polka-dot inset along one long edge. Press seam to red side. Fold and press seam allowance on other lengthwise edge of band. Fold band in half lengthwise to wrong side; bring folded hem edge of band to stitched line of polka-dot inset; hem. With right sides facing and raw edges even, sew polka-dot inset to red apron skirt

SKIRT INSET DIAGRAM

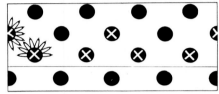

POCKET BAND DIAGRAM

along lengthwise edge. Press seam to red side. Sew white rickrack across top and bottom edges of polka-dot inset.

Read directions for embroidery on page 280 and refer to stitch details on page 282. Follow Skirt Inset Diagram to embroider polka-dot inset. Using one strand of white pearl cotton in needle, work crosses in centers of indicated red dots; using red cotton, work lazy daisy stitch around each dot with a cross. Repeat embroidery across inset band. Hem side edges of skirt.

For pocket, fold and press seam allowance on bottom lengthwise edge of polka-dot trim, making sure to leave a row of polka dots parallel to bottom edge. Follow Pocket Band Diagram to embroider trim. Having raw edges even, place right side of embroidery on wrong side of pocket piece. Sew one edge of pocket piece to unfinished top edge of polka-dot trim. Turn trim to front side of pocket, embroidered side up. Topstitch trim to pocket below the bottom row of polka dots and close to bottom edge of trim. Sew a 7″ strip of red rickrack across bottom of trim where indicated by fine line on diagram. Press seam allowances along bottom and sides of pocket. Place pocket on skirt 3½″ from top edge and 5″ from right side edge of skirt. Topstitch pocket to skirt close to pocket edges on three sides, leaving top open.

Gather top edge of apron skirt in to 17½″. For waistband, press seam allowances on all sides, leaving a row of polka dots parallel to bottom edge. To embroider waistband, follow Pocket Band Diagram, repeating embroidery across band. Sew 18½″ length of red rickrack across bottom of waistband as for pocket trim. With right sides facing and raw edges even, sew bottom edge of waistband to gathered edge of skirt. Leave waistband side seam allowances extending.

For apron ties, make narrow hems along long edges of each tie. To make pointed ends, fold one end of each tie diagonally, bringing right sides together; stitch together on straight side. Turn point right side out. With right sides facing and raw edges even, baste one unfinished tie end to extended seam allowance at each side of waistband. If necessary, gather tie end slightly to fit. Fold waistband in half lengthwise so that right sides are facing and tie ends lie between. Sew each tie end and side edges of waistband together along seam lines. Turn to right side; slip-stitch folded edge of back waistband to apron skirt on stitching line.

POTHOLDER

From red fabric, cut 6½″ square. From polka-dot fabric, cut one 6½″ square and one 4¾″ square (making sure to leave a row of polka dots parallel to each side edge) for front patch.

On front patch, embroider three center rows of three polka dots each in same manner as for apron. Press ¼″ seam allowances on all sides. Center patch, right side up, on right side of red square; baste in place. Baste 20″ strip of white rickrack on red square around patch with points of rickrack overlapping edges. Carefully slip-stitch in place through points of rickrack and edges of patch. Cut five 6″ squares of cotton flannel. Layer squares to form a pad. Center on wrong side of polka-dot square; stitch padding to square 1¼″ in from edge on all four sides. For hanging loop, from red fabric, cut strip 1″ x 4½″. Fold in half lengthwise bringing right sides together; turn long raw edges to inside. Stitch through all thicknesses along each long edge of strip. Turn in short ends and fold strip in half crosswise. Sew ends to wrong side of polka-dot square at one corner with ends facing out. With right sides of pot holder back and front together and hanging loop between, stitch through all thicknesses, making ¼″ seams on three sides. Leave fourth side open. Turn right side out. Fold in ¼″ seam allowance; slip-stitch closed.

For Baby

FELT BOOTIES

Soft baby shoes, sprinkled with embroidery, are quick and easy to make out of felt. A herringbone stitch laces the shoe tops to the sole.

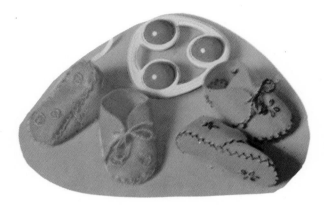

EQUIPMENT: Paper for patterns. Ruler. Pencil. Scissors. Straight pins. Large-eyed needle. Awl.

MATERIALS: Felt, one 8″ x 10″ piece in desired color for each pair. Pearl cotton, one small skein in desired color for each pair (one skein will do for two pairs).

DIRECTIONS: Enlarge patterns by copying on paper ruled in 1″ squares; complete half-patterns, indicated by long dash lines. Cut left sole from felt; reverse pattern and cut right sole. Cut two each of front and back pieces from felt.

Placement for the embroidery motifs for the pink booties are indicated by circles on patterns. With pencil, lightly mark locations on bootie pieces. For gold booties, embroidery motifs are centered on the shoe front, on each side of the side-back piece, and on the toe of the sole. Use short single strand of pearl cotton and follow stitch details

on page 282. Knot ends of cotton to secure stitches. For pink bootie motifs, work buttonhole stitch in a circle, with ends of stitches meeting in center. For gold bootie motifs, work five lazy daisy stitches in a circle to form each flower. Using awl, make holes indicated by dots on side-back pieces.

With wrong sides facing, match arrow on sole with center of shoe front. Hold pieces so that felt edges meet but do not overlap. Using herringbone stitch, begin stitching top to sole from X at one side, around toe, to X at other side. Hold side-back piece in place above sole matching center backs. Using herringbone stitch, stitch back to sole from X, around heel, along side to other X. Overlap sides of back piece onto tongue of shoe front; stitch together from X to Z, using herringbone stitch. Assemble other shoe in same manner.

For each shoelace, cut two strands of pearl cotton each 30″ long. Make two twisted cords (see page 287), using two strands for each. Insert cord through hole in each side of shoe and knot cord ends, using overhand knot.

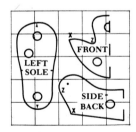

FELT BOOTIES

STITCHED-UP T-SHIRTS

A few embroidery stitches transform ordinary T-shirts into gala outfits for baby.

EQUIPMENT: Scissors. Pencil. Embroidery needle.
MATERIALS: Baby knit undershirt to size. Six-strand embroidery floss, one skein in each of three or four light colors.

DIRECTIONS: Thread needle with about 18″ length of three strands of floss. Work embroidery carefully to avoid stretching or puckering the knit fabric. Knot ends of floss on wrong side to secure.

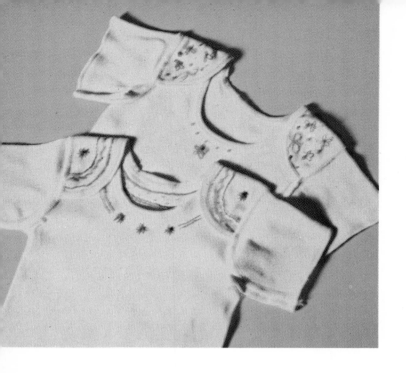

Plan scattered flower design or striped motifs as shown in illustration to fit the two side shoulder flaps of shirt. Use any variety of simple embroidery stitches (see stitch details on page 282) except satin stitch. Flowers may be worked in radiating lazy daisy stitches or straight stitches with French knot centers; bow motif may be worked in backstitch or outline stitch; borders can be outline, herringbone, featherstitch, or backstitch. Work borders and motifs around neckline, around back, and on flaps.

CROSS-STITCH BIBS

A frisky kitten with his red ball and a white bunny are easy to cross-stitch on these checked gingham bibs. The bibs, in three thicknesses, are bound with bias tape.

EQUIPMENT: Paper for pattern. Pencil. Ruler. Scissors. Embroidery and sewing needles.

MATERIALS: Checked gingham with 8 checks to the inch, ¼ yard. Matching double-fold bias binding tape. Matching sewing thread. Six-strand embroidery floss. Cotton flannel, 9″ x 10″.

DIRECTIONS: Enlarge pattern for bib by copying on paper ruled in 1″ squares; complete half-pattern, indi-

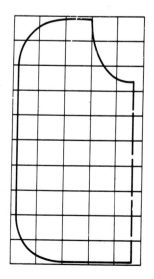

**Cross-Stitch Bibs:
Enlarge half-pattern by
copying on 1″ squares.**

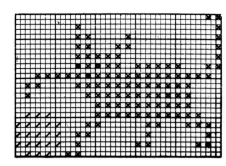

Chart for working Kitten and his toy on checks.

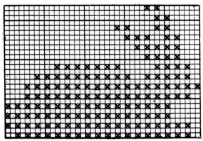

Chart for embroidering Bunny on the dark checks.

cated by long dash line. Using pattern, cut two bib pieces of gingham; cut one bib piece of flannel.

Read directions for working cross-stitch on gingham, page 284. On one gingham piece for front, work design in cross-stitch, following charts; start embroidery 1″ above bottom of bib. Using four strands of floss in needle, embroider cat in black with red ball and blue eyes, working in light checks of gingham; embroider rabbit with white floss, working in dark checks, or as desired.

Place flannel piece between gingham pieces, with embroidered piece up; baste together. Bind sides and bottom with bias tape. Bind neck edge with tape, leaving 9″ ends for ties. Stitch long edges of ties together. Turn ends in and slip-stitch closed.

IV General Directions

EQUIPMENT AND MATERIALS

The appearance of your work is greatly influenced by the material that you choose. You can make a delicate piece of work with fragile fabric and a fine thread, or translate the identical design onto coarser fabric, using a heavier thread. The needle to use with each yarn or floss should have an eye large enough to accommodate the yarn, but not larger than needed. Embroidery needles are rather short and have a long, slender eye. They are readily available in sizes 1 to 10; the higher numbers are finest. Some types of embroidery traditionally use a certain yarn or floss, while others technically require a specific kind. Crewel wool, for example, is a fine, twisted two-ply wool yarn used in crewel embroidery. Chart below relates threads and needles to type of work.

Keep a good selection of needles on hand and protect them by storing them in a needle case. It is also advisable to run your needles through an emery strawberry occasionally to clean and sharpen them.

You will need proper scissors. Embroidery scissors should be small, with narrow, pointed blades, and must be sharp. Protect the blade points by keeping them in a sheath.

Embroidery is usually worked in a frame. With the material held taut and even, your stitches are more likely to be neat and accurate than if the fabric were held in the hand while working. Many embroidery hoops and frames are equipped with stands or clamps to hold the embroidery piece and leave both hands free.

Before you begin work on a piece of embroidery, arrange a system for keeping your threads handy and colors neatly separated. Cut skeins into convenient sewing lengths—18″ or 20″ is usually best, as longer threads may become frayed. Place each strand between the pages of a book. Allow one end to extend beyond the edge of the page. Fold the other end back and forth on the page. Or loosely braid all colors to be used together, then pull the end from the braid as each color is used.

Six-strand embroidery floss can be separated into one,

MATERIALS OR TYPE OF WORK	THREAD	NEEDLE
Fine Fabrics or thin material	Six-strand embroidery thread (split for very fine work) Twisted cotton or fine mercerized thread Rayon, silk, or linen embroidery floss	Embroidery or crewel needle No. 1 to 10
Medium Textures such as linen, piqué, or other cottons; or lightweight sweaters of wool, nylon, or angora	Pearl cotton No. 3, 5, and 8 Six-strand embroidery thread combining number of strands Rayon or linen embroidery floss Fine wool yarns or crewel yarn	Crewel No. 1 to 10 Tapestry No. 14 to 24 Darning No. 14 to 18
Heavyweight or Coarse Fabrics such as monk's cloth, burlap, felt, wool suitings, or heavy sweaters	Double-strand pearl cotton Metallic cord and thread Tapestry yarn or Persian yarn Sock and sweater yarn, nylon, angora, chenille, Germantown Rug yarn	Crewel No. 1 to 10 Tapestry No. 14 to 24 Chenille No. 18 to 22 Darning No. 14 to 18 Needles for rug yarn

two, or more strands for working in fine stitches. To separate strands after cutting thread length, count the desired number of strands and carefully pull them out, holding the remainder apart to prevent tangling and knotting. Plies of wool yarn can also be separated in the same manner for a finer thread.

BASIC EMBROIDERY TIPS

To thread yarn or floss through the needle eye, double it over the end of the needle and slip it off, holding it tightly as close as possible to the fold. Push the eye of the needle down over the folded end and pull the yarn through.

To begin a stitch, start with two or three tiny running stitches toward the starting point, then take a tiny backstitch and begin. Knots are not advisable for beginning or ending stitches. Where there is a hem, insert the needle under the edge of the fold, taking up two or three threads of the material and bringing the needle out again so the stitch does not show, making a blind stitch. As you work, watch the tension of your yarn—if worked too tight, the background material will be pulled out of shape. Fasten off the thread when ending each motif, rather than carrying it to another motif. Pass the end of the thread through the last few stitches on the wrong side or take a few tiny backstitches.

To remove embroidery when a mistake has been made, run a needle, eye first, under the stitches. Pull the embroidery away from the fabric; cut carefully with scissors pressed hard against the needle. Pick out the cut portion of the embroidery. Catch loose ends of the remaining stitches on back by pulling the ends under the stitches with a crochet hook.

When your needlework is completed, it often needs to be pressed or blocked into shape. Sometimes it is soiled from working and must be laundered. This should always be done with care to preserve as much of the freshness of the fabric and thread as possible. Treat embroidery gently.

To help keep your work neat and clean, keep it in a plastic bag when not embroidering. When your embroidered piece is completed, finish off the back neatly by running ends into the back of the work and clipping off any excess strands. If wool embroidery is not really soiled but needs just a little freshening, simply brushing over the surface with a clean cloth dipped in carbon tetrachloride or other good cleaning fluid may be satisfactory. This will brighten and return colors to their original look.

FINISHING TECHNIQUES

Fabric Embroidery: Better results will be obtained by blocking (directions at right) rather than pressing an embroidered piece for a picture or hanging. However, articles that are hemmed, such as tablecloths or runners, should be pressed, as blocking would damage the edge of the fabric. To press your embroidered piece, use a well-padded surface and steam iron, or regular iron and damp cloth. Embroideries that have been worked in a frame will need very little pressing. If the embroidery was done in the hand, it will no doubt be quite wrinkled and may need dampening. Sprinkle it to dampen, and roll loosely in a clean towel, Embroidery should always be pressed lightly so that the stitching will not be flattened into the fabric. Place the embroidered piece face down on the padded surface and press from the center outward. For embroidery that is raised from the surface of the background, use extra thick, soft padding, such as a thick blanket.

If beads or sequins are added to embroidery, take care not to use too hot an iron, as some of these may melt. These should also be pressed wrong side down. The padding below protects them from breaking.

Embroideries made of colorfast threads and washable fabrics can be laundered without fear of harming them. Wash with mild soap or detergent and warm water, swishing the piece through the water gently—do not rub. Rinse in clear water without wringing or squeezing. When completely rinsed, lift from the water and lay on a clean towel; lay another towel on top and roll up loosely. When the embroidery is sufficiently dry, press as described above.

After blocking or pressing, an embroidered picture should be mounted right away to prevent creasing. To store other embroidery, place blue tissue paper on front and roll smoothly, face in, onto a cardboard tube. Then wrap outside in tissue.

To Block an Embroidered Picture: With needle and colorfast thread, following the thread of the linen and taking ¼″ stitches, mark guidelines around the entire picture to designate the exact area where the picture will fit into the rabbet of the frame. The border of plain linen extending beyond the embroidery in a framed picture is approximately 1¼″ at sides and top and 1½″ at bottom. In order to have sufficient linen around the embroidered design for blocking and mounting, 3″ or 4″ of linen should be left around the embroidered section. Now, matching corners, obtain the exact centers of the four sides and mark these centers with a few stitches.

If the picture is soiled, it should be washed, but it should be blocked immediately after washing. In preparation, cover a drawing board or soft-wood breadboard with a piece of brown paper held in place with rustproof thumbtacks, and draw the exact original size of the linen on the brown paper. Be sure linen is not pulled beyond its original size when the measurements are taken. (Embroidery sometimes pulls linen slightly out of shape.) Check drawn rectangle to make sure corners are square.

Wash embroidery; let drip a minute. Place embroidery right side up on the brown paper inside the guidelines and tack down the four corners. Tack centers of four sides. Continue to stretch the linen to its original size by tacking all around the sides, dividing and subdividing the spaces between the tacks already placed. This procedure is followed until there is a solid border of thumbtacks around the entire edge. In cross-stitch pictures, if stitches were not stamped exactly even on the thread of the linen, it may be necessary to remove some of the tacks and pull part of embroidery into a straight line. Use a ruler as a guide for straightening the lines of stitches. Hammer in the tacks or they will pop out as the linen dries. Allow embroidery to dry thoroughly.

To Mount An Embroidered Picture: Cut a piece of heavy white cardboard about ⅛" smaller all around than the rabbet size of the frame to be used. Stretch the embroidery over the cardboard, using the same general procedure as for blocking the piece. Following the thread guidelines, use pins to attach the four corners of the embroidery to the mounting board. Pins are placed at the centers of sides, and embroidery is then gradually stretched into position until there is a border of pins completely around picture, about ¼" apart. When satisfied that the design is even, drive pins into the cardboard edge with a hammer. If a pin does not go in straight, it should be removed and reinserted. The edges of the linen may be pasted or taped down on the wrong side of the cardboard or the edges may be caught with long zigzag stitches. Embroidered pictures can be framed with glass over them, if desired.

TO ENLARGE OR REDUCE DESIGNS

There are various ways of enlarging or reducing designs so that all parts remain in proportion. The most commonly used are the "square" method, No. 1, and the diagonal method, No. 2. (Designs can also be enlarged or reduced by photostat, wherever such services are available.)

Method 1: If design is not already marked off in squares, make a tracing or original design. Mark off tracing with squares, ⅛" for small designs and ¼", ½", or 1" for proportionately larger designs. On paper, mark the same number of squares, similarly placed, in the space to be occupied by the enlarged design. For instance, if you want to make the original design twice as high and twice as wide, make the squares twice as large. Copy design from smaller squares. Reverse procedure for reducing design to size needed.

Method 2: Make a tracing of original design. Draw a rectangle to fit around it. Draw a second rectangle of same proportions to fit desired size of design. Draw diagonals from corner to corner of each rectangle, as illustrated. In each rectangle, the point where diagonals meet is the center. Draw horizontal and vertical lines to divide each rectangle equally. Copy design from smaller divisions in corresponding larger divisions.

Method 3: To enlarge or reduce a magazine illustration easily and quickly, halve and quarter the original picture as indicated in figure. Mark the dimensions for actual-size design on plain paper. On illustration to be copied, draw vertical and horizontal lines 1-1 to halve and quarter picture. Draw lines 2-2 to divide picture into 16 equal parts. Draw lines 3-3 vertically and horizontally to divide picture into 64 equal sections. Continue dividing the sections down to the size needed to accurately copy details of the original illustration. Divide actual-size area into the same number of sections. Copy design from each section of original in corresponding section on actual-size pattern. Same method may be used for reducing pictures.

METHOD 1 **METHOD 2**

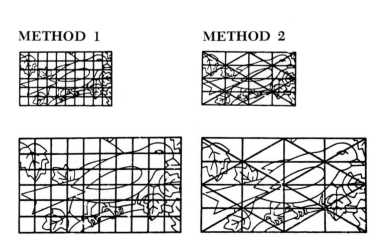

METHOD 3

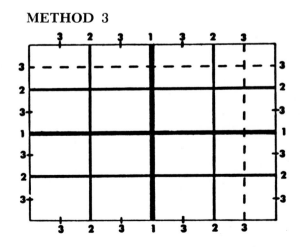

EMBROIDERY STITCH DETAILS

SPLIT STITCH

FLY STITCH

RUNNING STITCH

WHIPPED RUNNING STITCH

THREADED RUNNING STITCH

LONG AND SHORT STITCH

OUTLINE STITCH

BUTTONHOLE STITCH

CLOSED BUTTONHOLE STITCH

TURKEY WORK STITCH

STRAIGHT STITCH

FRENCH KNOTS

CROSS-STITCH

CHAIN STITCH

ROMAN CHAIN STITCH

DOUBLE CHAIN STITCH

HEAVY CHAIN STITCH

BACKSTITCH

STEM STITCH

COUCHING STITCH

LAZY DAISY STITCH

SATIN STITCH

HERRINGBONE STITCH

DOUBLE HERRINGBONE STITCH

COUCHED HERRINGBONE STITCH

THREADED HERRINGBONE STITCH

VAN DYKE STITCH

CLOSE FLY STITCH

DOUBLE CROSS-STITCH

STAR FILLING STITCH

CLOSE HERRINGBONE STITCH

BLANKET STITCH

CLOSED BLANKET STITCH

CROSSED BLANKET STITCH

INTERLACING WITH BACKSTITCH

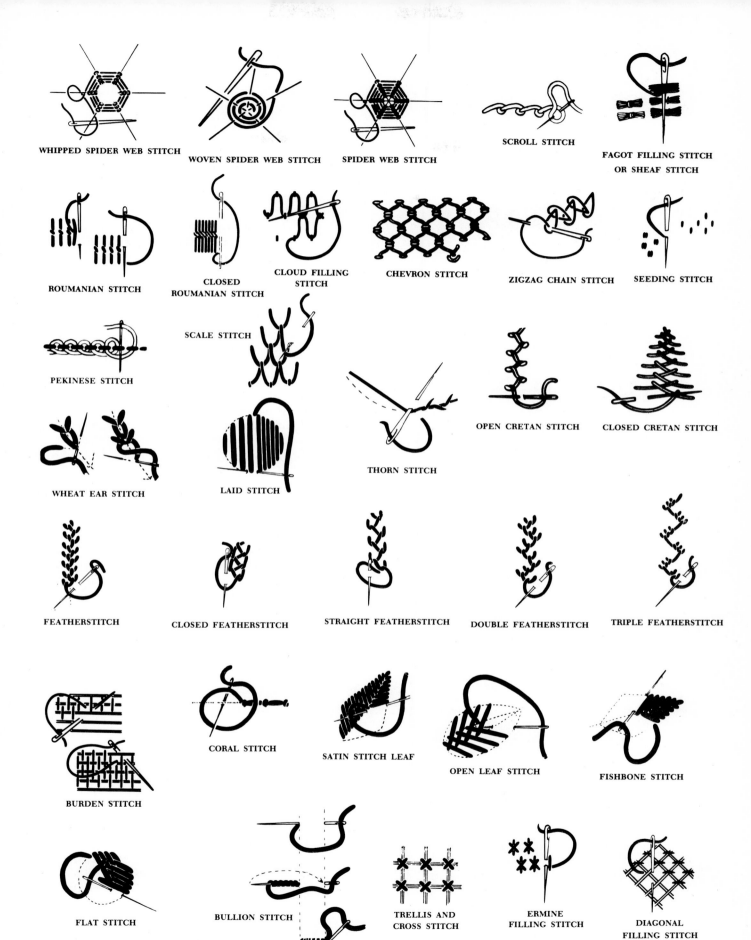

WHIPPED SPIDER WEB STITCH

WOVEN SPIDER WEB STITCH

SPIDER WEB STITCH

SCROLL STITCH

FAGOT FILLING STITCH
OR SHEAF STITCH

ROUMANIAN STITCH

CLOSED
ROUMANIAN STITCH

CLOUD FILLING
STITCH

CHEVRON STITCH

ZIGZAG CHAIN STITCH

SEEDING STITCH

PEKINESE STITCH

SCALE STITCH

THORN STITCH

OPEN CRETAN STITCH

CLOSED CRETAN STITCH

WHEAT EAR STITCH

LAID STITCH

FEATHERSTITCH

CLOSED FEATHERSTITCH

STRAIGHT FEATHERSTITCH

DOUBLE FEATHERSTITCH

TRIPLE FEATHERSTITCH

BURDEN STITCH

CORAL STITCH

SATIN STITCH LEAF

OPEN LEAF STITCH

FISHBONE STITCH

FLAT STITCH

BULLION STITCH

TRELLIS AND
CROSS STITCH

ERMINE
FILLING STITCH

DIAGONAL
FILLING STITCH

1   2

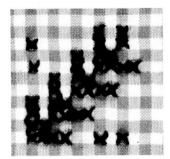

ON MONK'S CLOTH

ON GINGHAM

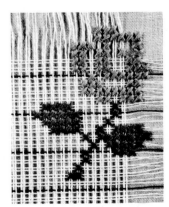

ON EVEN-WEAVE FABRIC

OVER PENELOPE CANVAS

FOUR WAYS TO WORK CROSS-STITCH

Several different ways to do cross-stitch are described below and illustrated. All yield equally good results if care is taken to make sure that the strands of thread or yarn lie smooth and flat. Begin by leaving an end of floss on back and working over it to secure; run end of strand in on back to finish off. Try not to make any knots.

It is important when working cross-stitch to have the crosses of the entire piece worked in the same direction. Work all underneath threads in one direction and all the top threads in the opposite direction. Keep the stitches as even as possible. Be sure to make all crosses touch; do this by putting your needle in the same hole as used for the adjacent stitch.

On Monk's Cloth: The design can follow the mesh of a coarse, flat-weave fabric, such as monk's cloth. Here the design may be worked from a chart simply by counting each square of fabric for one stitch.

On Gingham: A checked material, such as gingham, can be used as a guide for cross-stitch. Crosses are made over checks, following a chart.

On Even-Weave Fabric: The threads of an even-weave fabric, such as sampler linen, may be counted and each cross-stitch made the same size. For example, in the detail, a three-thread square is counted for each stitch.

Over Penelope Canvas: Penelope (or cross-stitch) canvas is basted to the fabric on which the design is to be embroidered. First, center canvas over fabric, making sure that horizontal and vertical threads of canvas and fabric match, then make lines of basting diagonally in both directions and around sides of canvas. The design is then worked by making crosses as shown, taking each stitch diagonally over the double mesh of canvas and through the fabric, being careful not to catch the canvas.

When design is completed, the basting is removed and the horizontal threads of the canvas are carefully drawn out, one strand at a time, then the vertical threads, leaving the finished cross-stitch design on the fabric.

Penelope canvas is available in several size meshes. Choose finer sizes for smaller designs; larger sizes are suitable for coarse work in wool.

TO APPLIQUÉ

Appliqué is worked by laying pieces of fabric on a background fabric and stitching them in place with sewing thread. First mark complete design on background fabric. Then make pattern piece for each part of design. Taking each pattern piece in turn, mark the outline on the fabric to be appliquéd, and mark a seam allowance of ¼″ all around. Machine- or hand-stitch on design outline for a neat turning edge (Fig. 1). Cut piece out on outer seam

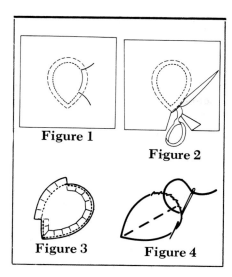

Figure 1

Figure 2

Figure 3

Figure 4

allowance line (Fig. 2). Clip curved edges and corners; turn in seam allowance just inside stitching (Fig. 3); steam-press. Pin appliqué piece in place; slip-stitch with tiny stitches (Fig. 4).

TO TRANSFER DESIGNS

If you are spending your own precious time to create an heirloom for tomorrow, you will want to be sure the design is as attractive as possible.

If you have a fine museum in your neighborhood, study the lovely embroidery designs it shows. Sometimes you can choose an embroidery motif from a bed hanging and apply it around the border of a luncheon cloth. Sometimes you may choose to translate a painting into embroidery.

If you have a research library available, with fine books on art or design, on rare old china or beautiful linens, then you can use these sources.

If you plan to copy a museum design or a print from some other source, place tracing paper over the photograph of the design and carefully copy the complete design; to protect the print, place a piece of glassine between the design and the tracing paper. Mark the correct colors and shades, using colored crayons or pencils. The design, if it is to be used in the same size, is now ready to be used on your fabric; there are a number of ways of transferring a design.

Carbon Paper: Typewriter carbon may be used between your fabric and the tracing. However, this is apt to be smudgy and can soil the fabric. Dressmaker's carbon is better to use for this purpose and comes in light and dark colors. Anchor the fabric to a smooth surface with masking tape; place carbon face down on fabric, with tracing on top in correct position; tape in place. With an instrument, such as a dry ball-point pen, a hard-lead pencil,

or a tracing wheel, carefully mark all lines of design, using enough pressure to transfer clearly.

Back Tracing: A design may also be transferred to a smooth fabric by going over all lines on back of tracing with a soft pencil. Then tape tracing onto your fabric, right side up, and trace all lines again, using a hard pencil.

Direct Tracing: If the fabric and tracing are not too large and unwieldy, the design can be transferred by means of a light box, or ordinary glass window. With this method, the fabric must be of a light color and not very heavy. Place tracing (which must be marked with heavy, dark lines) right side up on a light box, or tape to window in bright daylight. Tape fabric on top of tracing. With the light coming from the back, the traced design will show clearly through the fabric and can be traced directly on the fabric with a sharp pencil.

Perforated Pattern: There is another method, which makes a good permanent pattern, called perforating. In many large cities it is possible to have a perforated pattern made professionally from your tracing. Look for such a company under "Perforated Patterns" in the classified directory. To make your own perforated pattern, mark design accurately on heavy quality tracing paper. Then the traced design is perforated on all outlines. With tracing placed on a lightly padded surface, use a pin or unthreaded sewing machine to make the holes in the tracing paper, about 1/16" apart. Hold the pin straight up and push through paper enough to make clear holes. When the perforating is finished, place it over your fabric, smooth side up, and weight it down around the edges to hold it in place while transferring. The design may be transferred by means of a perforating powder called pounce, and a pouncer. To make a pouncer, roll up a strip of flannel or felt tightly, sewing it so it remains rolled. Dip the end of the pouncer in powder, tap off excess; then dab and rub it over the perforated outlines. Carefully lift up corner of perforated pattern to see if design has been transferred clearly. If not, go over it again with pounce. When the transferring is completed, carefully lift off pattern. Perforating paste may be used instead of powder. Directions for its use will come with the paste.

Transfer Pattern: If you do not wish to create your own design, you can transfer a printed pattern to fabric with a hot iron. These transfers are available at pattern departments. Printed transfers can be cut up and rearranged in a variety of ways to suit your own design needs, such as combining small motifs to make a large unit.

To use the transfer pattern, always cut away the pattern name or number or any other parts that you do not wish to use. Shake the paper to remove any loose particles. Lay the fabric on an ironing board or lightly padded surface and pin in position so it will not slide. Pin transfer design in place, design side down on fabric.

Experiment first with a small piece of transfer on a

sample of material. Before stamping, test heat of the iron with the number or trial sample on a sample of the material, *selecting a low heat or rayon heat for all materials.* Transfer design with a downward stamp of the iron (never press slowly and heavily as in ironing). If your test sample is not clear, the heat of iron is not correct.

When the iron is the correct temperature, stamp the design. Before removing the transfer lift a corner to see if the design has been transferred satisfactorily. When completely stamped, remove the transfer by running the warm iron lightly over it. This prevents the transfer ink from sticking to the paper as it is pulled away from the material.

Marking with Running Stitch: For very heavy or nubby fabrics, first trace the design on tissue paper. Then baste the tissue paper on the fabric, around the perimeter and in several other places, to hold the tissue securely. Using sewing thread in a contrasting color, outline all parts of the design with small running stitch. Carefully pull away the tissue, leaving the running-stitch outline on the fabric. For a fabric that easily stretches out of shape, such as jersey, sew a piece of fine material to the back of the embroidery area. Make sure that the grain of the backing material is straight in relation to the fabric to be embroidered. Then proceed as above.

Chinese Method: For very fine fabrics, such as silk, use a tissue pattern that is thin but strong. Baste the tissue to the fabric as for "Marking with Running Stitch." Then embroider the entire design, working through both tissue and fabric. When the embroidery is finished, carefully tear away the excess tissue, leaving the tissue under embroidery.

Transfer Pencil: Trace the design on tracing paper. Turn the tracing over and go over the lines with a hot-iron transfer pencil (available in light and dark shades). Place the transfer, pencil side down, on the fabric and stamp the design with an iron, following the directions for the "Transfer Pattern" method.

TO DRAW AN OVAL

Fig. 1: Draw a straight line longer than desired length of oval. At center of line, establish point A. With compass, swing arcs to points B and C, oval length.

Fig. 2: From B and C, swing arcs above and below line BC. Connect their intersections with line DE. On this line, mark points F and G equal distances from A to establish width of oval.

Fig. 3: Mark points 1 and 2 to match A and C on a straight, firm strip of paper.

Fig. 4: Turn this measuring paper vertically along line FG so that point 1 is at F. Mark point 3 at A.

Fig. 5: Rotate the measuring paper clockwise, moving point 3 along line AC and point 2 along AG. Make dots opposite point 1. Connect these dots with a line which completes first quarter of oval. Repeat procedure in other three parts to complete oval (or make tracing and transfer curve).

To Frame an Oval: Cut out of thick cardboard an oval ⅛" smaller than the rabbet of your frame. Copy the oval on tracing paper; fold the tracing in half lengthwise and crosswise to find the top, bottom, and side center points of the traced oval. Replace the cardboard oval on the tracing; lay a ruler over the cardboard along the fold lines of the tracing paper and mark four center points at the edge of the cardboard oval with lines about ¼" long. Find the four center points of the embroidered design and mark on edges of fabric in the same way. Place the embroidered fabric on the cardboard oval. Position the embroidery pleasingly. The markings on the cardboard should be visible through the fabric; if not, lift the fabric to check. The center-point markings on the fabric and the oval need not match but must be parallel, so that the fabric threads will be parallel with the axes of the oval. Push pins through the fabric into the edge of the cardboard at center of top, bottom, and sides. Continue pushing in pins on opposite sides as described above. Trim the edges of the fabric to

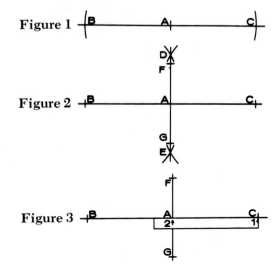

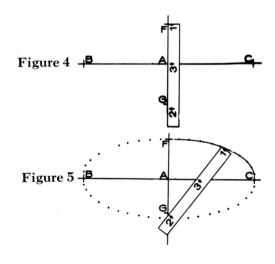

an oval and tape to the back of the cardboard. Place the oval in the frame. To hold the picture, hammer brads about ⅛″ into the rabbet, bracing the frame against a heavy object to prevent its coming apart. Cover the back with heavy brown wrapping paper.

TO MAKE A TWISTED CORD

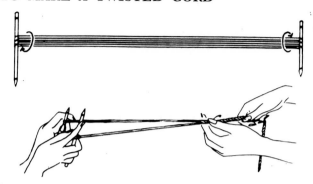

Method requires two people. Tie one end of yarn around pencil. Loop yarn over center of second pencil, back to and around first, and back to second, making as many strands between pencils as needed for thickness of cord; knot end to pencil. Length of yarn between pencils should be three times length of cord desired. Each person holds yarn just below pencil with one hand and twists pencil with other hand, keeping yarn taut. When yarn begins to kink, catch center over doorknob or hook. Bring pencils together for one person to hold, while other grasps center of yarn, sliding hand down at short intervals and letting yarn twist.

Seams may be covered with a twisted cord made of same yarn as embroidered piece. Leave about ½″ of cord free at one corner of a square pillow or least conspicuous place on a round pillow; sew cord over seam with matching thread, taking small blind stitches close together through cord and edges of embroidered piece; pin cord in place for a few inches ahead of sewing, being careful not to pull cord. At center where cords meet, trim off other end to ½″. Open seam of embroidered piece about ½″; overlap cord ends and insert into open seam. Sew seam closed over cord ends.

TO MAKE A TASSEL

Wind yarn around cardboard cut to size of tassel desired, winding it 20 or more times around, depending on plumpness of tassel required. Tie strands tightly together around top as shown, leaving at least 3″ ends on ties; clip other end of strands. Wrap piece of yarn tightly around strands a few times, about ½″ or 1″ below tie, and knot. Trim ends of tassel evenly.

TO MAKE A POMPON

Cut two cardboard disks desired size of pompon; cut out hole in center of both. Thread needle with two strands of yarn. Place disks together; cover with yarn, working through holes. Slip scissors between disks. Cut all strands at outside edge. Draw strand of yarn between disks and wind several times very tightly around yarn; knot, leaving ends for attaching pompon. Remove disks; fluff out yarn into a pompon.

TO MAKE AN INNER PILLOW

Cut two pieces of muslin each 1½″ larger than the finished outer pillow (this includes ¼″ seam allowance). Sew the two pieces together with ¼″ seam, leaving one side open. Turn to right side. Stuff pillow with batting or other stuffing material. Turn edges of opening in ¼″ and slip-stitch opening closed. Insert inner pillow into outer pillow; if necessary, fill out corners with additional stuffing. Turn edges of outer pillow in and slip-stitch closed.